X-FACTOR

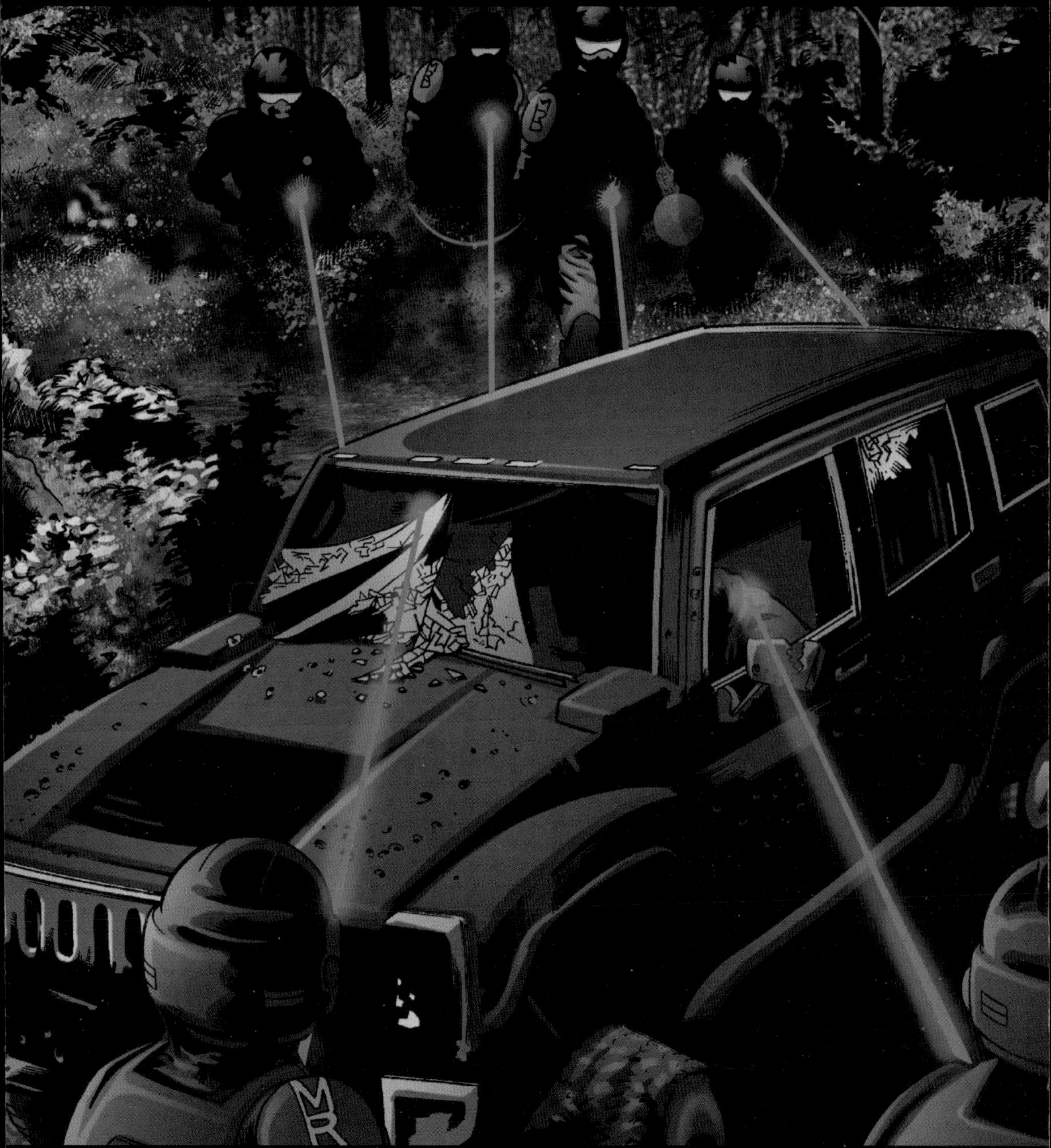

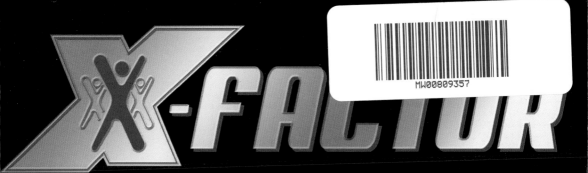

SECOND COMING

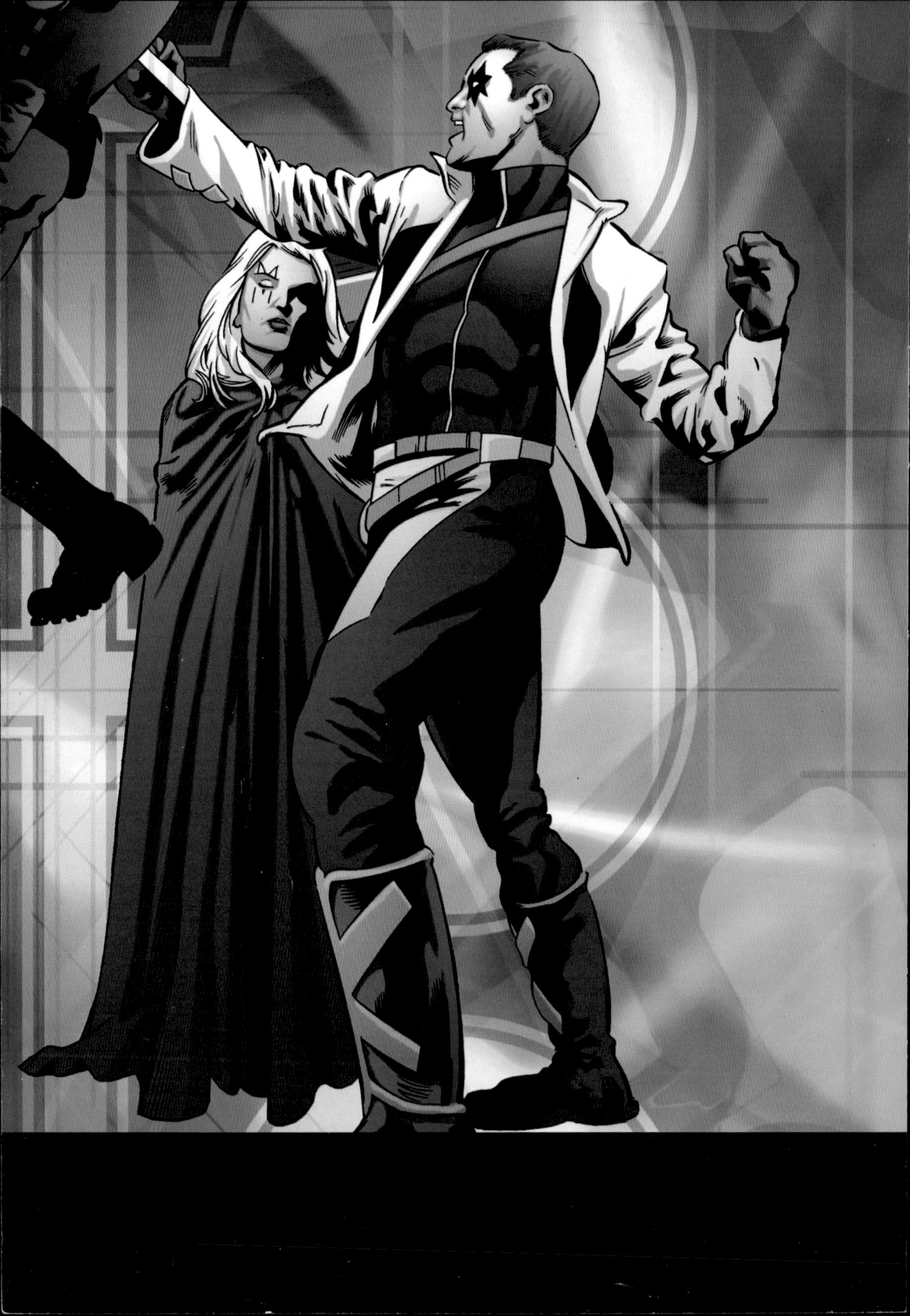

X-FACTOR

SECOND COMING

Writer: PETER DAVID

Pencils: VALENTINE DE LANDRO
Inks: PAT DAVIDSON
Colors: JEROMY COX
Letterer: VIRTUAL CALLIGRAPHY'S CORY PETIT
Cover Art: DAVID YARDIN & NATHAN FAIRBAIRN
AND CHRISTIAN MACNEVIN *(NATION X)*
Editor: JODY LEHEUP

Collection Editor: JENNIFER GRÜNWALD
Editorial Assistants: JAMES EMMETT & JOE HOCHSTEIN
Assistant Editors: ALEX STARBUCK & NELSON RIBEIRO
Editor, Special Projects: MARK D. BEAZLEY
Senior Editor, Special Projects: JEFF YOUNGQUIST
Senior Vice President of Sales: DAVID GABRIEL

Editor in Chief: JOE QUESADA
Publisher: DAN BUCKLEY
Executive Producer: ALAN FINE

PREVIOUSLY:

With the members of their race slowly dying out and no new mutants being born, mutantkind was on the brink of extinction. In need of a miracle, the X-Men were elated when one came in the form of Hope—a newborn mutant who held the promise of repopulation. Under attack by those who would see mutantkind extinguished, the X-Men sent the infant into the future with one of their own, Cable, to be raised under his protection and one day return to the present.

Now Cable and Hope have returned to the present. But the X-Men were not the only ones awaiting their return: Bastion, a super-Sentinel from the future hellbent on exterminating all mutants, has used an alien virus to revive many of the X-Men's enemies, including the creator of Sentinel technology Bolivar Trask. The virus allows Bastion to control those he reanimates but the minds of the undead remain intact, leading them in some cases to fight back against his control. But Bastion's hold is too strong and the members of his cabal are seemingly unable to free themselves from his influence. Now Bastion and his undead cabal are in pursuit of Cable and Hope in an effort to seal mutantkind's fate once and for all.

Meanwhile, Monet has gone deep into South America to retrieve her kidnapped father, only to herself be taken prisoner by her father's captor, Baron Mordo, who has his own plans for Monet. But Guido, a.k.a. Strong Guy, has tracked her to Mordo's lair and is now calling Mordo out...which could prove to be a disastrous mistake.

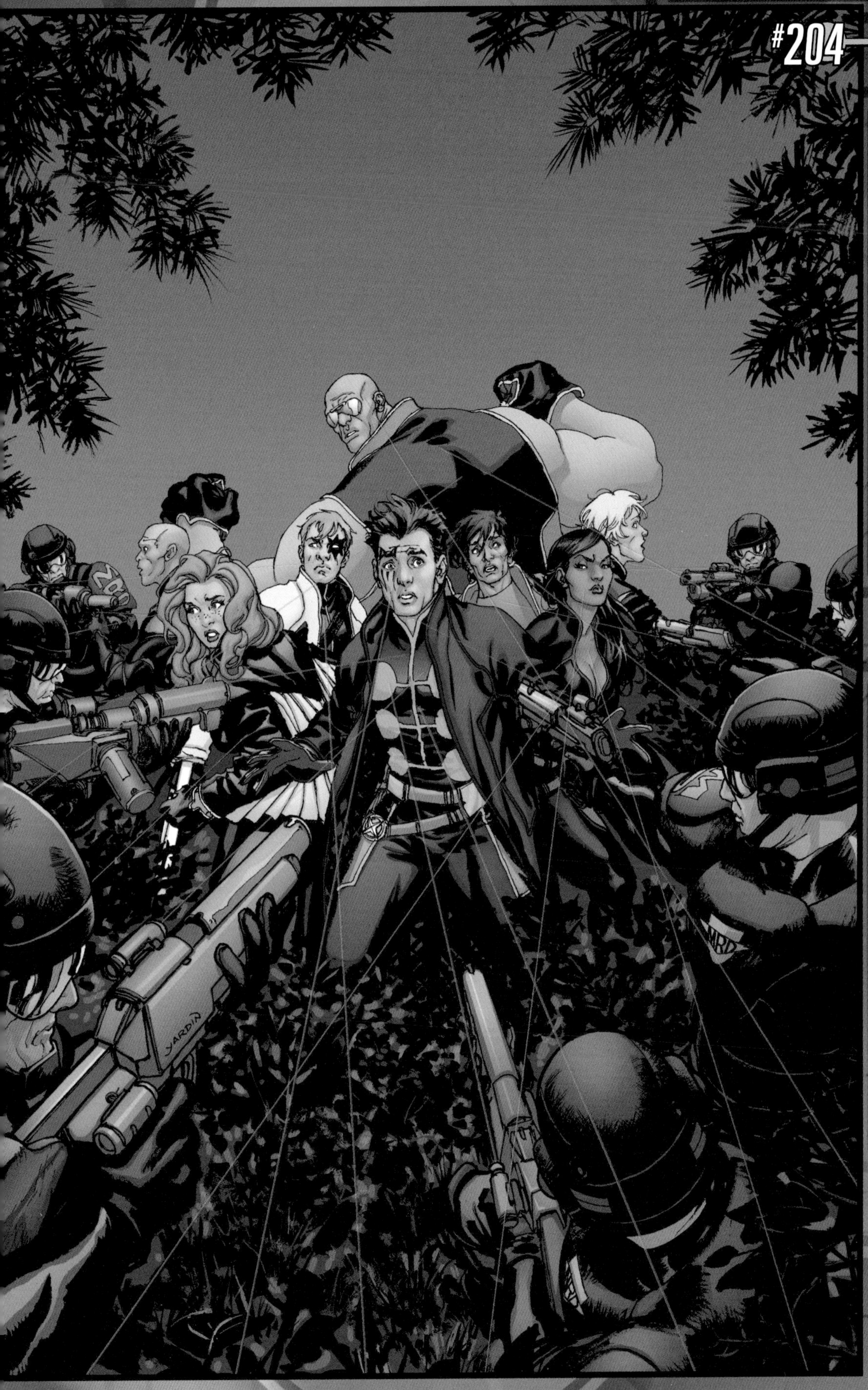
#204
MRD

ARRRHHH!
"WE HAVE GAINED ENTRANCE TO X-FACTOR HEADQUARTERS.
"TARGET 'RICTOR' IS READILY DISPATCHED."

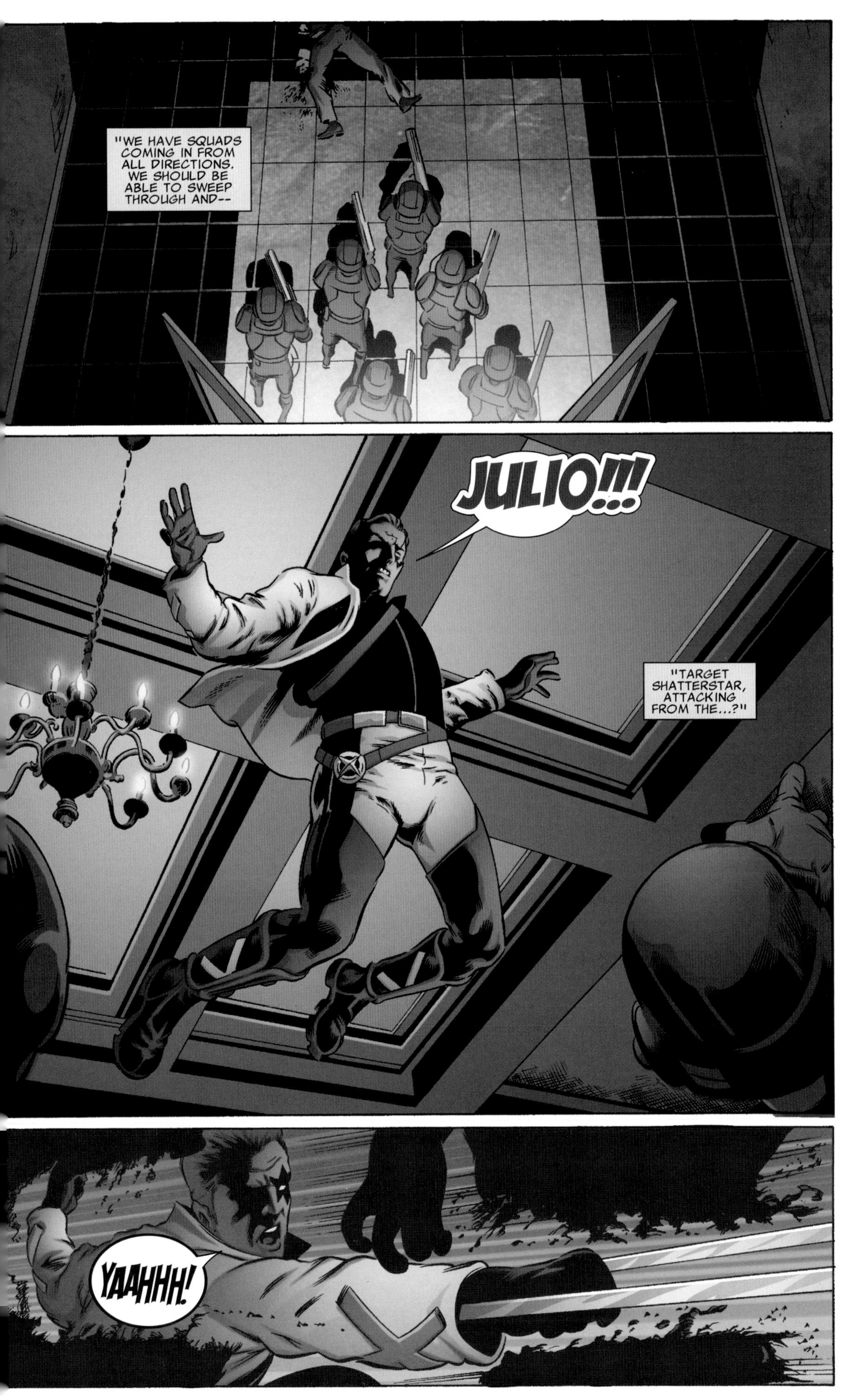
"WE HAVE SQUADS COMING IN FROM ALL DIRECTIONS. WE SHOULD BE ABLE TO SWEEP THROUGH AND--
JULIO!!!
"TARGET SHATTERSTAR, ATTACKING FROM THE...?"
YAAHHH!

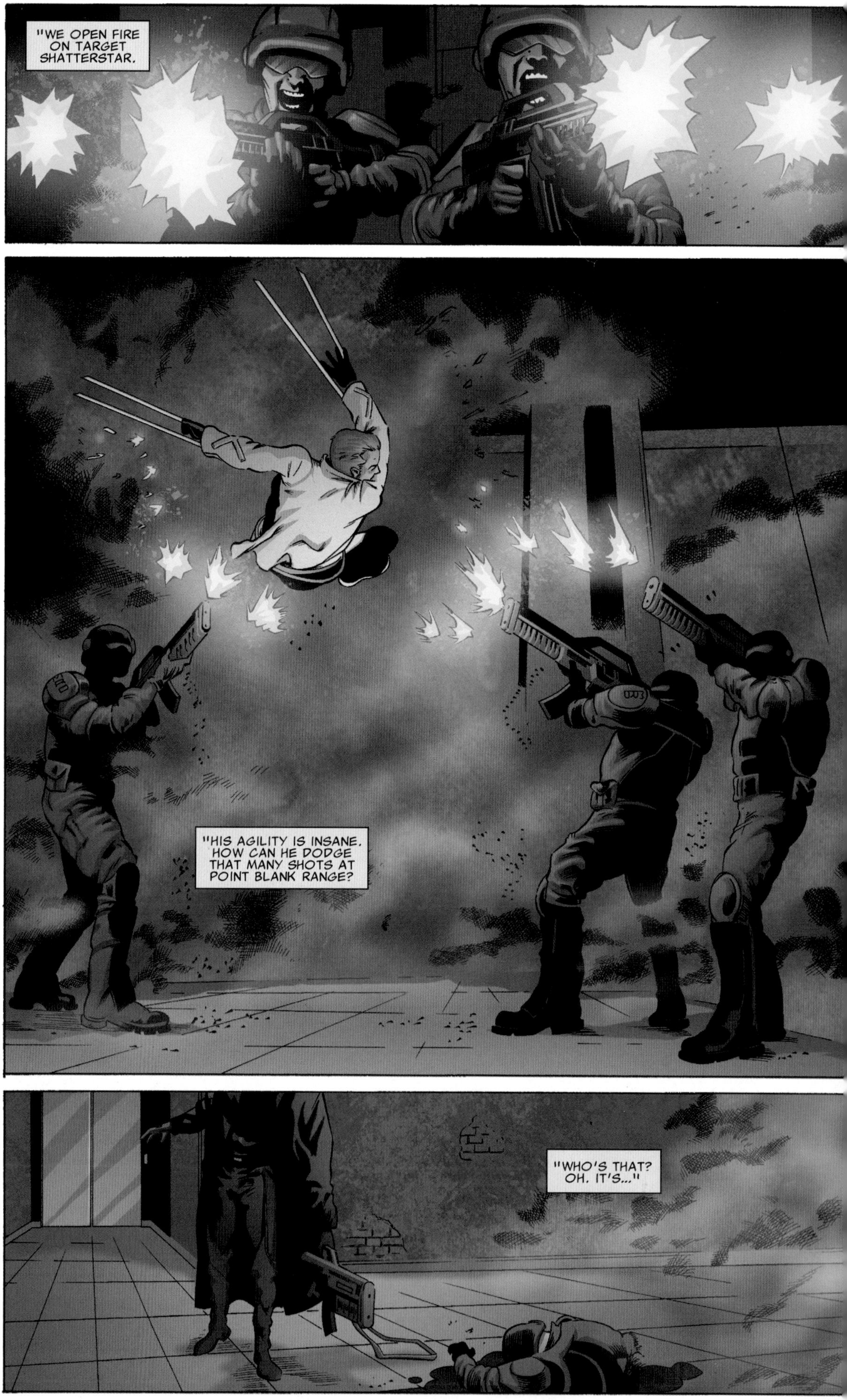
"WE OPEN FIRE ON TARGET SHATTERSTAR.
"HIS AGILITY IS INSANE. HOW CAN HE DODGE THAT MANY SHOTS AT POINT BLANK RANGE?
"WHO'S THAT? OH. IT'S..."

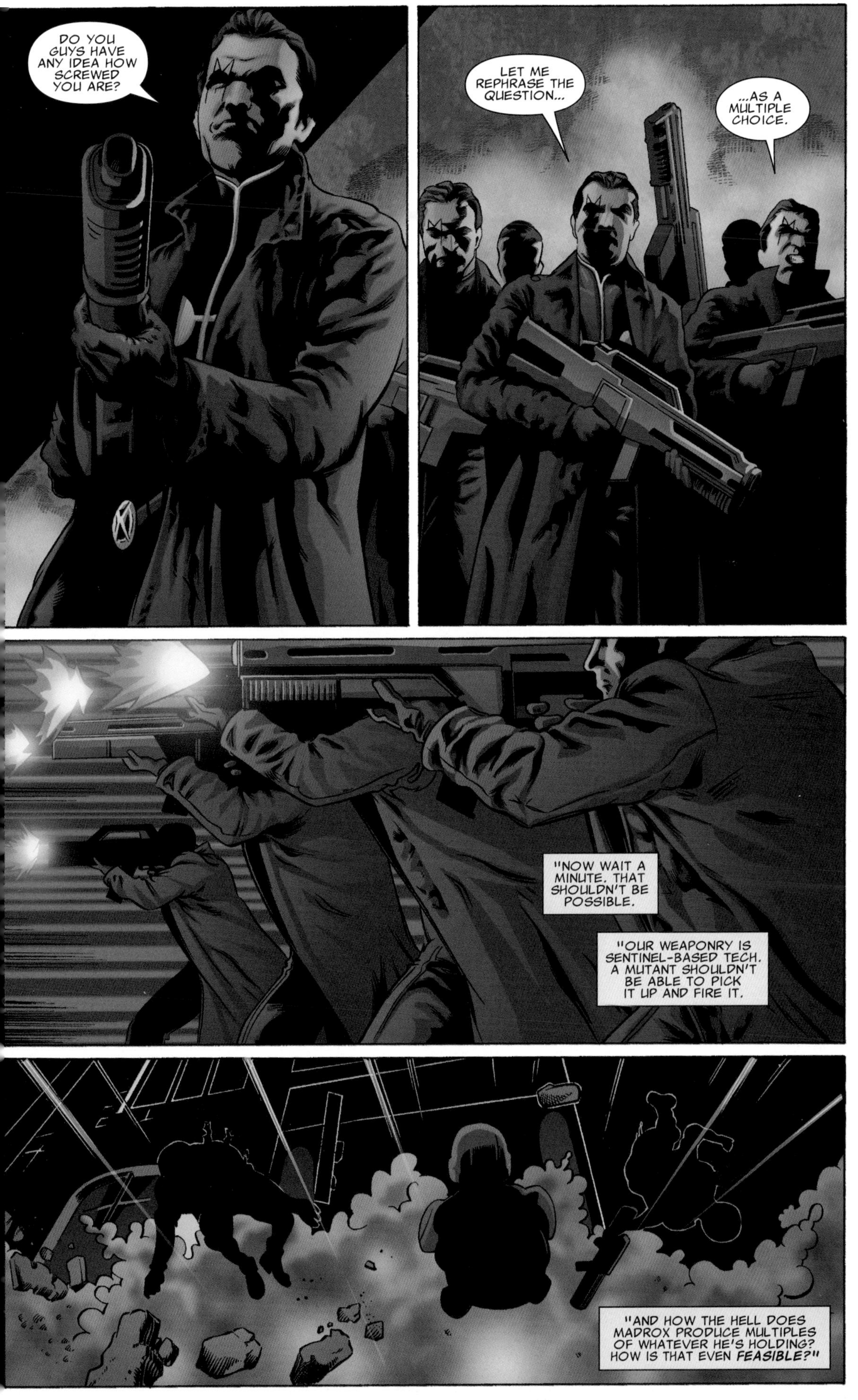

DO YOU GUYS HAVE ANY IDEA HOW SCREWED YOU ARE?
LET ME REPHRASE THE QUESTION...
...AS A MULTIPLE CHOICE.
"NOW WAIT A MINUTE. THAT SHOULDN'T BE POSSIBLE.
"OUR WEAPONRY IS SENTINEL-BASED TECH. A MUTANT SHOULDN'T BE ABLE TO PICK IT UP AND FIRE IT.
"AND HOW THE HELL DOES MADROX PRODUCE MULTIPLES OF WHATEVER HE'S HOLDING? HOW IS THAT EVEN FEASIBLE?"

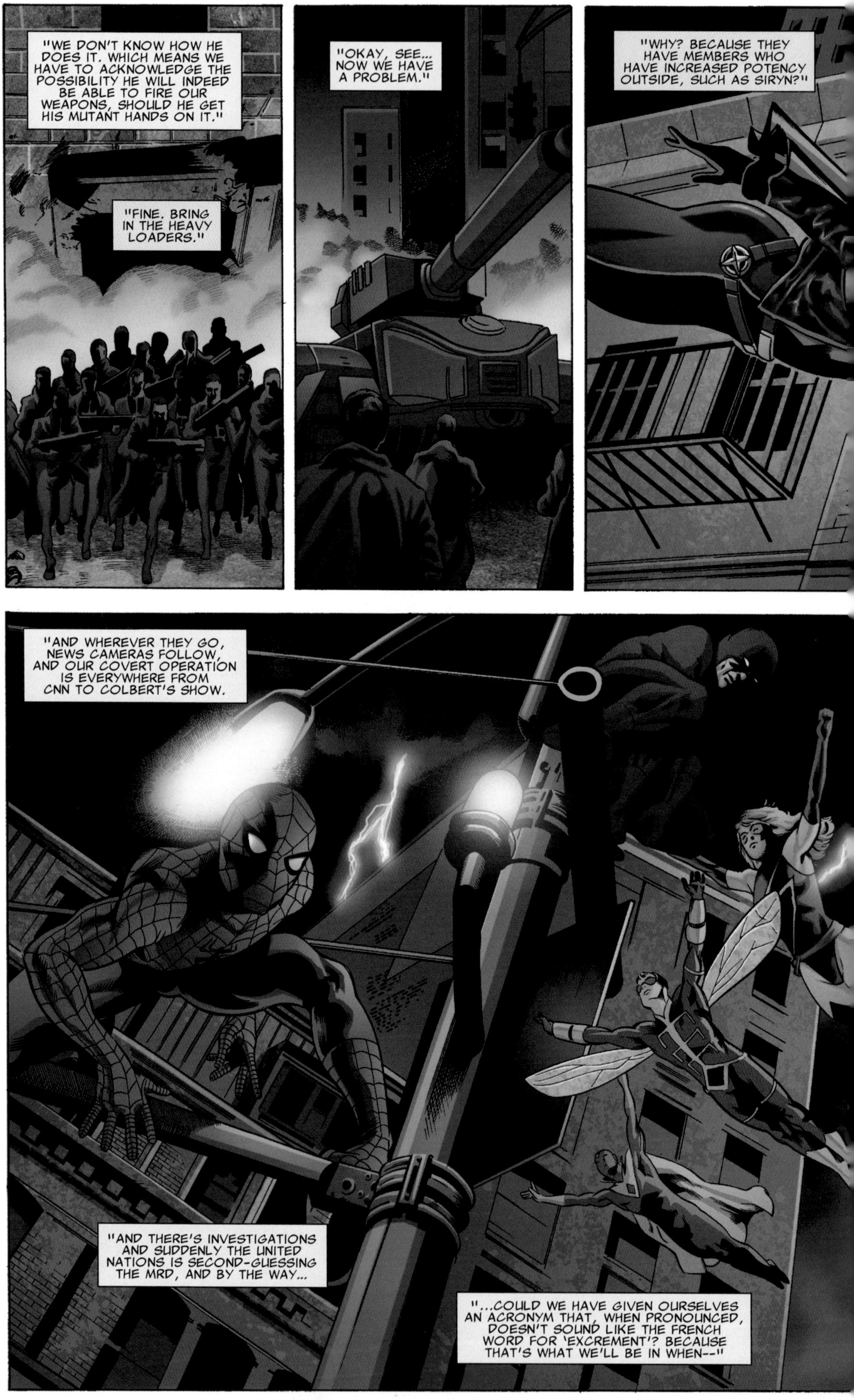
"WE DON'T KNOW HOW HE DOES IT. WHICH MEANS WE HAVE TO ACKNOWLEDGE THE POSSIBILITY HE WILL INDEED BE ABLE TO FIRE OUR WEAPONS, SHOULD HE GET HIS MUTANT HANDS ON IT."
"FINE. BRING IN THE HEAVY LOADERS."
"OKAY, SEE... NOW WE HAVE A PROBLEM."
"WHY? BECAUSE THEY HAVE MEMBERS WHO HAVE INCREASED POTENCY OUTSIDE, SUCH AS SIRYN?"
"AND WHEREVER THEY GO, NEWS CAMERAS FOLLOW, AND OUR COVERT OPERATION IS EVERYWHERE FROM CNN TO COLBERT'S SHOW.
"AND THERE'S INVESTIGATIONS AND SUDDENLY THE UNITED NATIONS IS SECOND-GUESSING THE MRD, AND BY THE WAY...
"...COULD WE HAVE GIVEN OURSELVES AN ACRONYM THAT, WHEN PRONOUNCED, DOESN'T SOUND LIKE THE FRENCH WORD FOR 'EXCREMENT'? BECAUSE THAT'S WHAT WE'LL BE IN WHEN--"

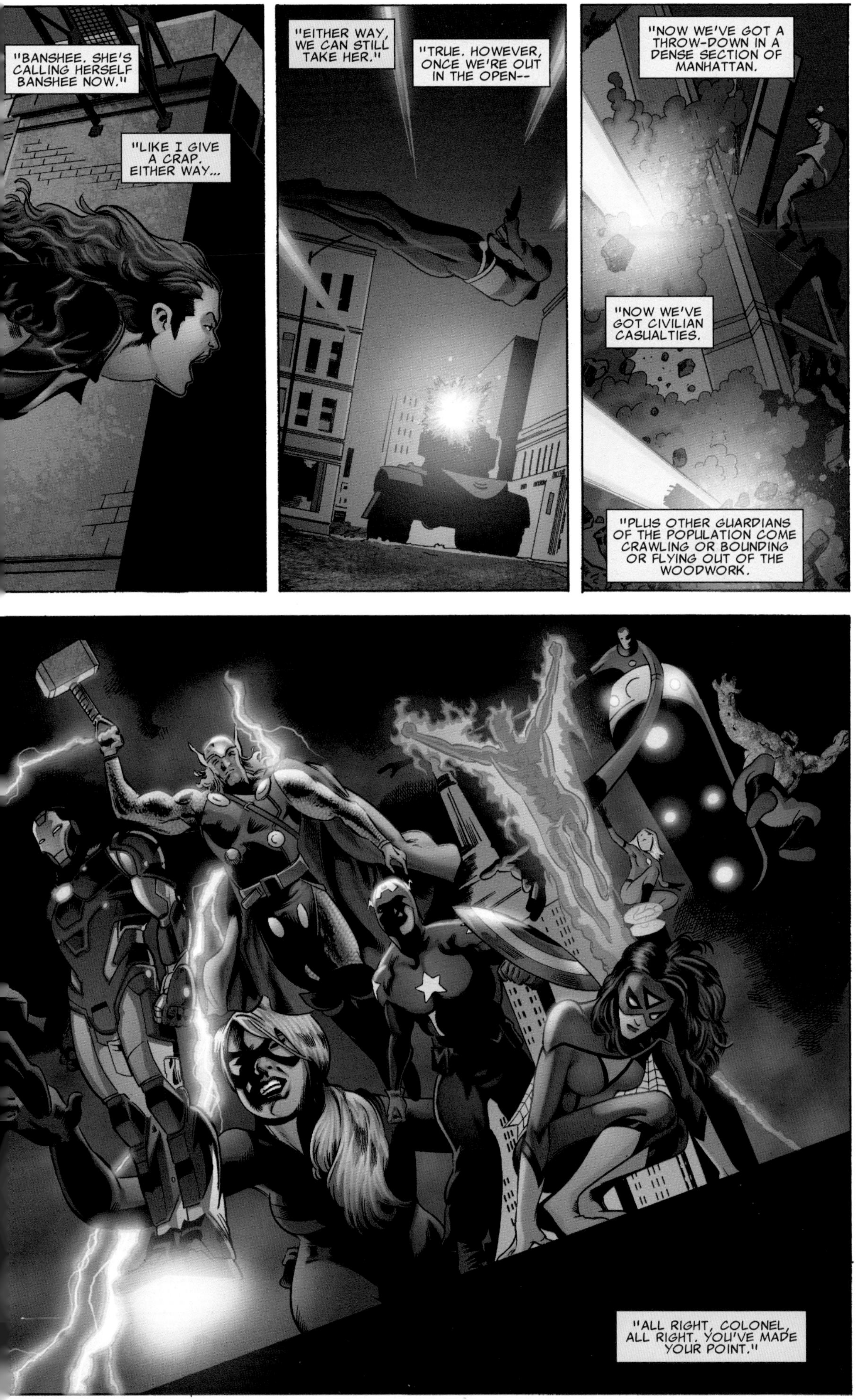
"BANSHEE. SHE'S CALLING HERSELF BANSHEE NOW."
"LIKE I GIVE A CRAP. EITHER WAY...
"EITHER WAY, WE CAN STILL TAKE HER."
"TRUE. HOWEVER, ONCE WE'RE OUT IN THE OPEN--
"NOW WE'VE GOT A THROW-DOWN IN A DENSE SECTION OF MANHATTAN.
"NOW WE'VE GOT CIVILIAN CASUALTIES.
"PLUS OTHER GUARDIANS OF THE POPULATION COME CRAWLING OR BOUNDING OR FLYING OUT OF THE WOODWORK.
"ALL RIGHT, COLONEL, ALL RIGHT. YOU'VE MADE YOUR POINT."

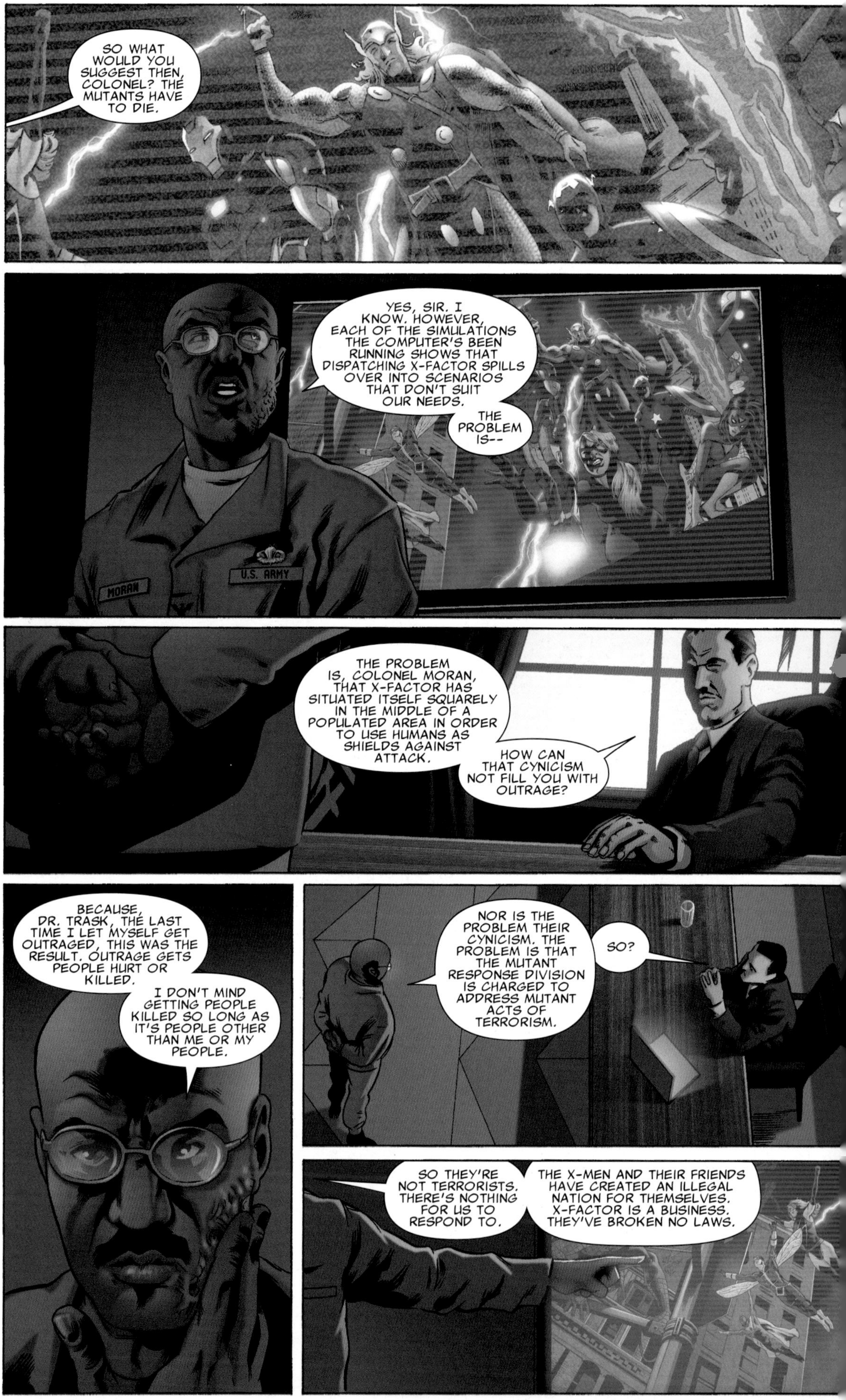
SO WHAT WOULD YOU SUGGEST THEN, COLONEL? THE MUTANTS HAVE TO DIE.
YES, SIR. I KNOW. HOWEVER, EACH OF THE SIMULATIONS THE COMPUTER'S BEEN RUNNING SHOWS THAT DISPATCHING X-FACTOR SPILLS OVER INTO SCENARIOS THAT DON'T SUIT OUR NEEDS.
THE PROBLEM IS--
U.S. ARMY
MORAN
THE PROBLEM IS, COLONEL MORAN, THAT X-FACTOR HAS SITUATED ITSELF SQUARELY IN THE MIDDLE OF A POPULATED AREA IN ORDER TO USE HUMANS AS SHIELDS AGAINST ATTACK.
HOW CAN THAT CYNICISM NOT FILL YOU WITH OUTRAGE?
BECAUSE, DR. TRASK, THE LAST TIME I LET MYSELF GET OUTRAGED, THIS WAS THE RESULT. OUTRAGE GETS PEOPLE HURT OR KILLED.
I DON'T MIND GETTING PEOPLE KILLED SO LONG AS IT'S PEOPLE OTHER THAN ME OR MY PEOPLE.
NOR IS THE PROBLEM THEIR CYNICISM. THE PROBLEM IS THAT THE MUTANT RESPONSE DIVISION IS CHARGED TO ADDRESS MUTANT ACTS OF TERRORISM.
SO?
SO THEY'RE NOT TERRORISTS. THERE'S NOTHING FOR US TO RESPOND TO.
THE X-MEN AND THEIR FRIENDS HAVE CREATED AN ILLEGAL NATION FOR THEMSELVES. X-FACTOR IS A BUSINESS. THEY'VE BROKEN NO LAWS.

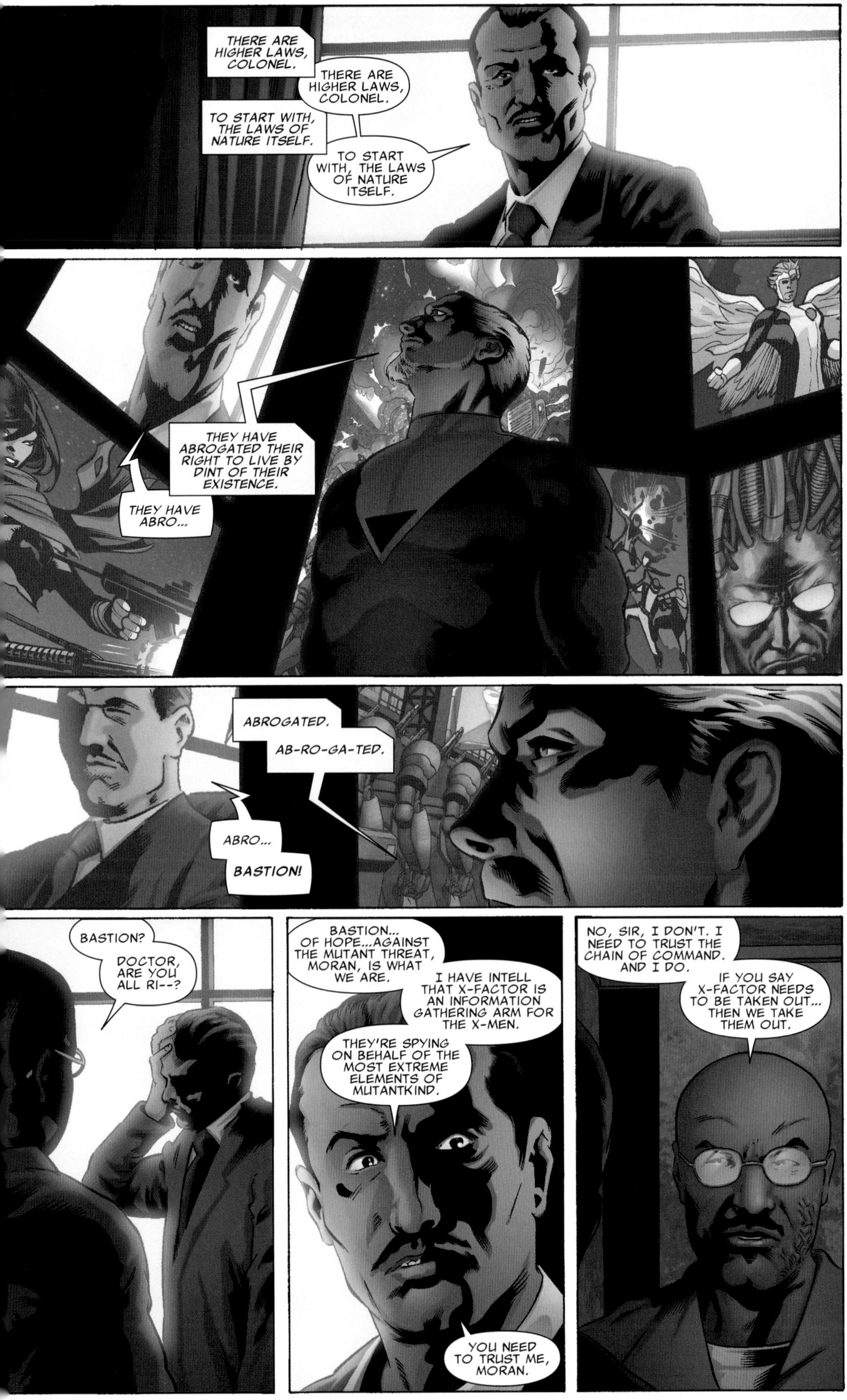

THERE ARE HIGHER LAWS, COLONEL.
THERE ARE HIGHER LAWS, COLONEL.
TO START WITH, THE LAWS OF NATURE ITSELF.
TO START WITH, THE LAWS OF NATURE ITSELF.
THEY HAVE ABROGATED THEIR RIGHT TO LIVE BY DINT OF THEIR EXISTENCE.
THEY HAVE ABRO...
ABROGATED.
AB-RO-GA-TED.
ABRO...
BASTION!
BASTION?
DOCTOR, ARE YOU ALL RI--?
BASTION... OF HOPE...AGAINST THE MUTANT THREAT, MORAN, IS WHAT WE ARE.
I HAVE INTELL THAT X-FACTOR IS AN INFORMATION GATHERING ARM FOR THE X-MEN.
THEY'RE SPYING ON BEHALF OF THE MOST EXTREME ELEMENTS OF MUTANTKIND.
YOU NEED TO TRUST ME, MORAN.
NO, SIR, I DON'T. I NEED TO TRUST THE CHAIN OF COMMAND. AND I DO.
IF YOU SAY X-FACTOR NEEDS TO BE TAKEN OUT... THEN WE TAKE THEM OUT.

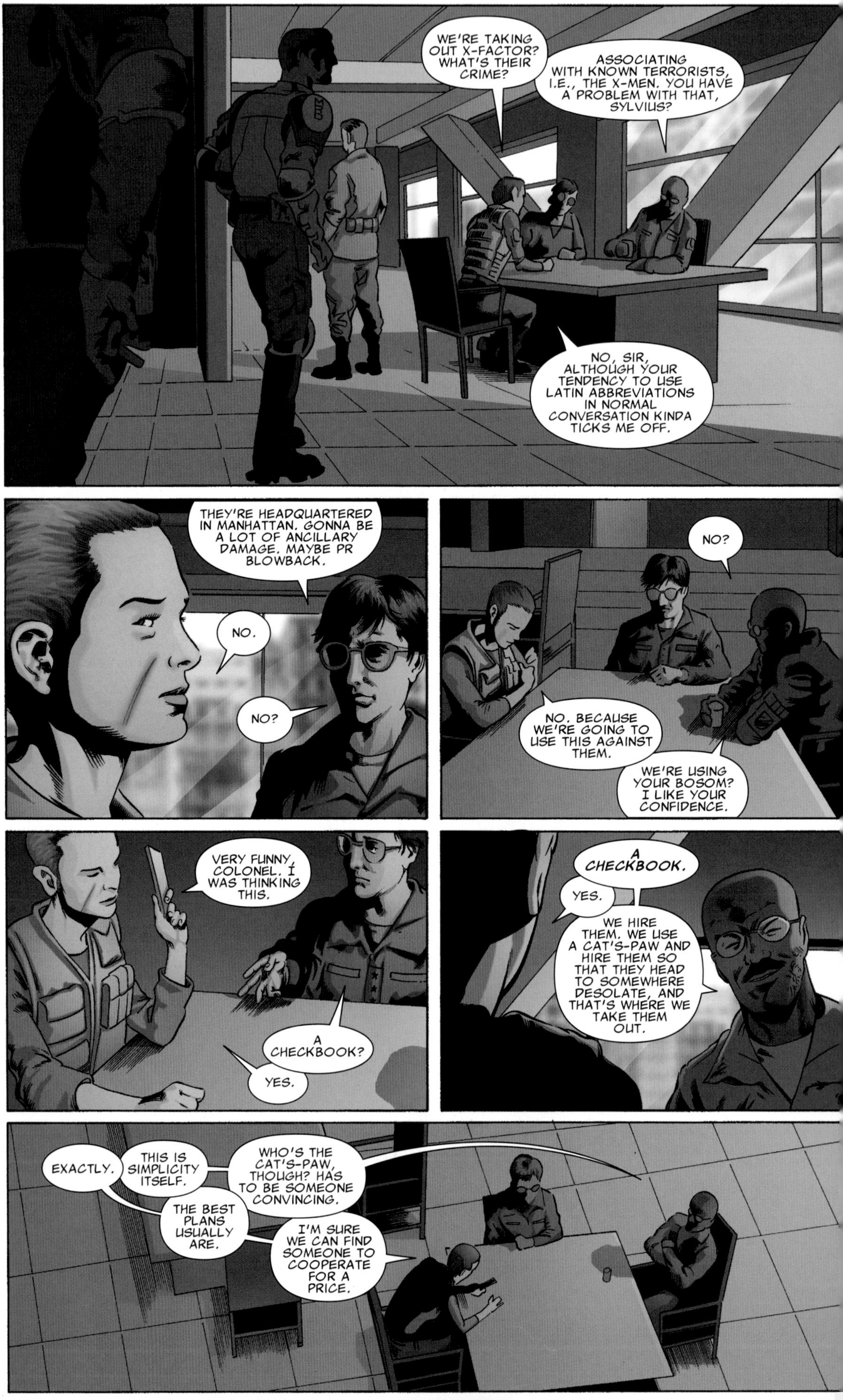
WE'RE TAKING OUT X-FACTOR? WHAT'S THEIR CRIME?
ASSOCIATING WITH KNOWN TERRORISTS, I.E., THE X-MEN. YOU HAVE A PROBLEM WITH THAT, SYLVIUS?
NO, SIR, ALTHOUGH YOUR TENDENCY TO USE LATIN ABBREVIATIONS IN NORMAL CONVERSATION KINDA TICKS ME OFF.
THEY'RE HEADQUARTERED IN MANHATTAN. GONNA BE A LOT OF ANCILLARY DAMAGE. MAYBE PR BLOWBACK.
NO.
NO?
NO?
NO. BECAUSE WE'RE GOING TO USE THIS AGAINST THEM.
WE'RE USING YOUR BOSOM? I LIKE YOUR CONFIDENCE.
VERY FUNNY, COLONEL. I WAS THINKING THIS.
A CHECKBOOK?
YES.
A CHECKBOOK.
YES.
WE HIRE THEM. WE USE A CAT'S-PAW AND HIRE THEM SO THAT THEY HEAD TO SOMEWHERE DESOLATE, AND THAT'S WHERE WE TAKE THEM OUT.
EXACTLY.
THIS IS SIMPLICITY ITSELF.
WHO'S THE CAT'S-PAW, THOUGH? HAS TO BE SOMEONE CONVINCING.
THE BEST PLANS USUALLY ARE.
I'M SURE WE CAN FIND SOMEONE TO COOPERATE FOR A PRICE.

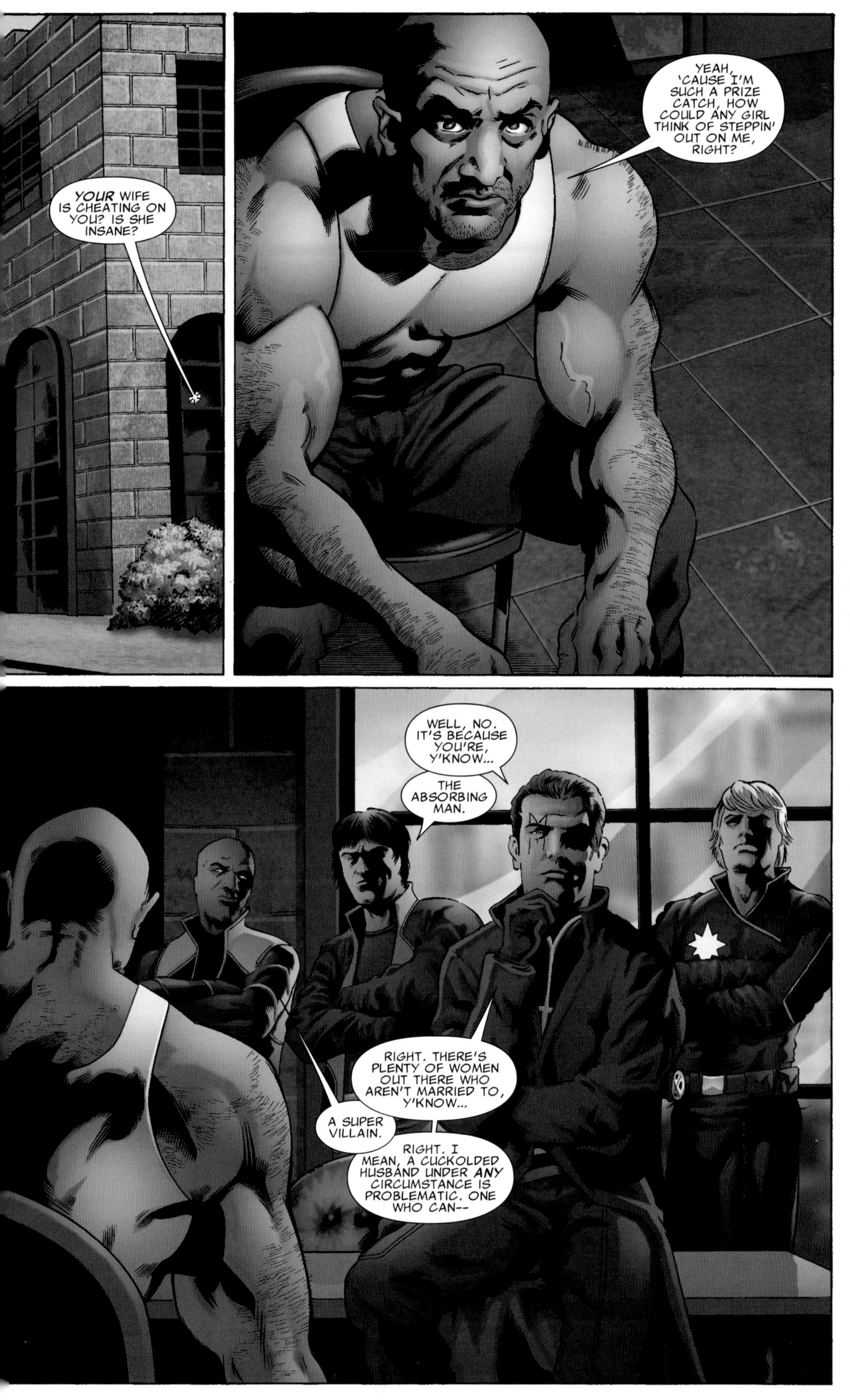
YOUR WIFE IS CHEATING ON YOU? IS SHE INSANE?
YEAH, 'CAUSE I'M SUCH A PRIZE CATCH, HOW COULD ANY GIRL THINK OF STEPPIN' OUT ON ME, RIGHT?
WELL, NO. IT'S BECAUSE YOU'RE, Y'KNOW...
THE ABSORBING MAN.
RIGHT. THERE'S PLENTY OF WOMEN OUT THERE WHO AREN'T MARRIED TO, Y'KNOW...
A SUPER VILLAIN.
RIGHT. I MEAN, A CUCKOLDED HUSBAND UNDER ANY CIRCUMSTANCE IS PROBLEMATIC. ONE WHO CAN--

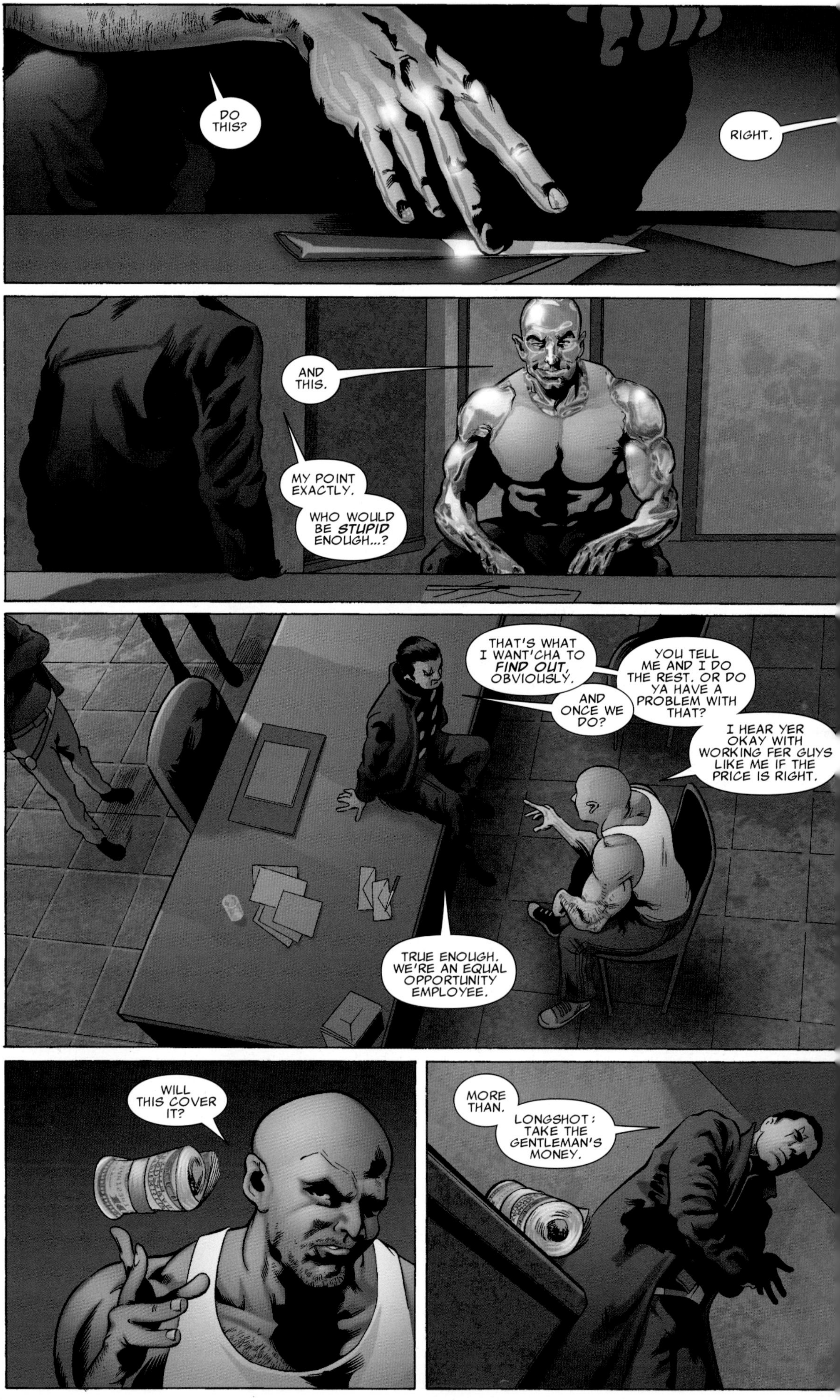
DO THIS?
RIGHT.
AND THIS.
MY POINT EXACTLY.
WHO WOULD BE **STUPID** ENOUGH...?
THAT'S WHAT I WANT'CHA TO **FIND OUT**, OBVIOUSLY.
YOU TELL ME AND I DO THE REST. OR DO YA HAVE A PROBLEM WITH THAT?
AND ONCE WE DO?
I HEAR YER OKAY WITH WORKING FER GUYS LIKE ME IF THE PRICE IS RIGHT.
TRUE ENOUGH. WE'RE AN EQUAL OPPORTUNITY EMPLOYEE.
WILL THIS COVER IT?
MORE THAN.
LONGSHOT: TAKE THE GENTLEMAN'S MONEY.

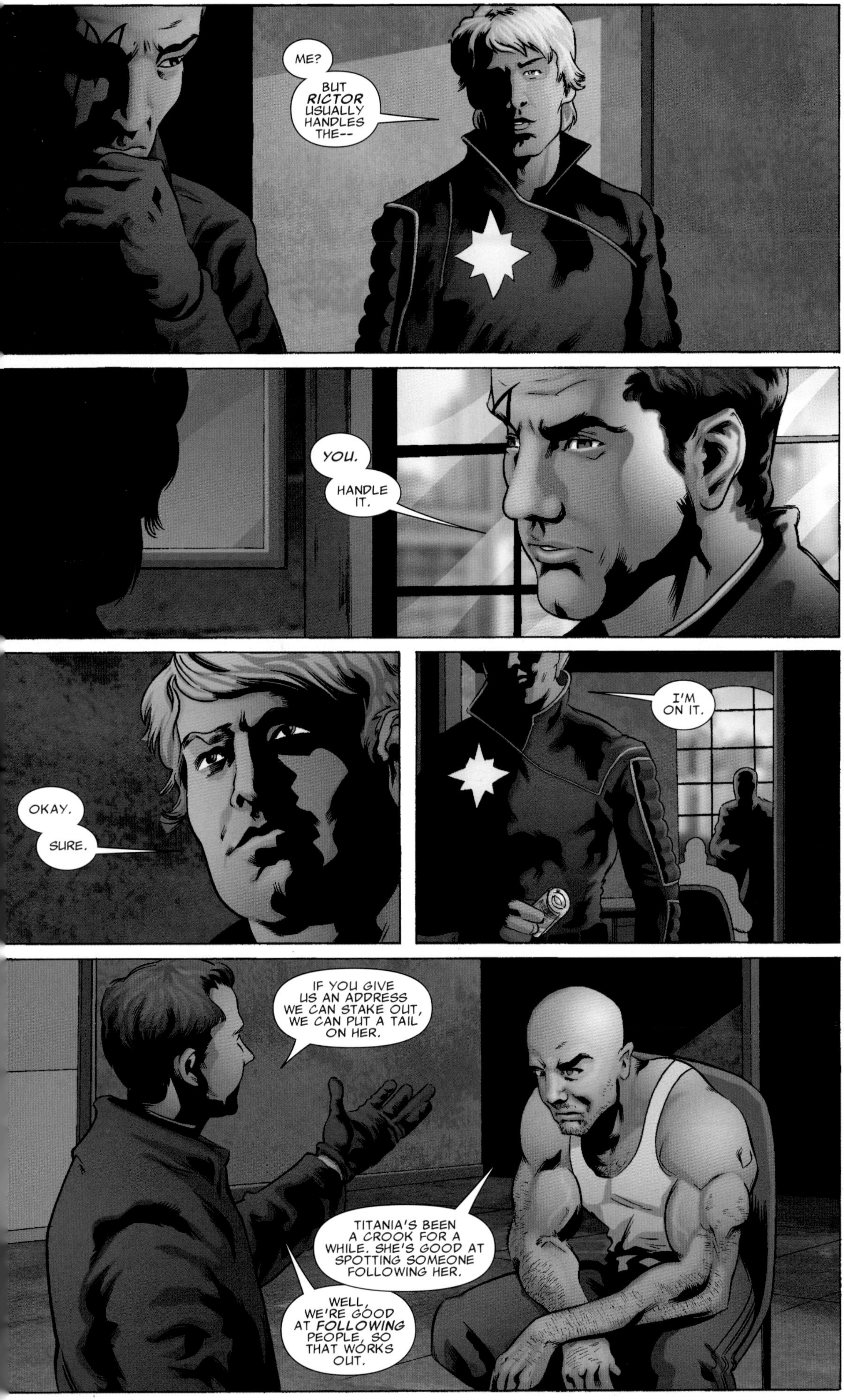

ME?
BUT RICTOR USUALLY HANDLES THE--
YOU.
HANDLE IT.
OKAY.
SURE.
I'M ON IT.
IF YOU GIVE US AN ADDRESS WE CAN STAKE OUT, WE CAN PUT A TAIL ON HER.
TITANIA'S BEEN A CROOK FOR A WHILE. SHE'S GOOD AT SPOTTING SOMEONE FOLLOWING HER.
WELL, WE'RE GOOD AT FOLLOWING PEOPLE, SO THAT WORKS OUT.

DO NOT DO THAT AGAIN.

IT WAS JUST FOR A MOMENT.

NO MOMENTS.

EVER.

BUT...X-FACTOR ISN'T EVEN JOINING THE X-MEN IN UTOPIA. WITH THEIR RACE FIGHTING FOR SURVIVAL, X-FACTOR IS ON THE SIDELINES.

IRRELEVANT.

EXTERMINATION IS MANDATORY. UNDERSTOOD?

YES, BASTION... OF *COURSE* I UNDERSTAND.

DOCTOR TRASK.

YES!

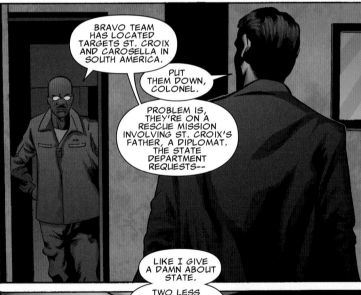

BRAVO TEAM HAS LOCATED TARGETS ST. CROIX AND CAROSELLA IN SOUTH AMERICA.

PUT THEM DOWN, COLONEL.

PROBLEM IS, THEY'RE ON A RESCUE MISSION INVOLVING ST. CROIX'S FATHER, A DIPLOMAT. THE STATE DEPARTMENT REQUESTS--

LIKE I GIVE A DAMN ABOUT STATE.

TWO LESS MUTANTS IS TWO LESS MUTANTS, COLONEL. THAT'S JUST MATH.

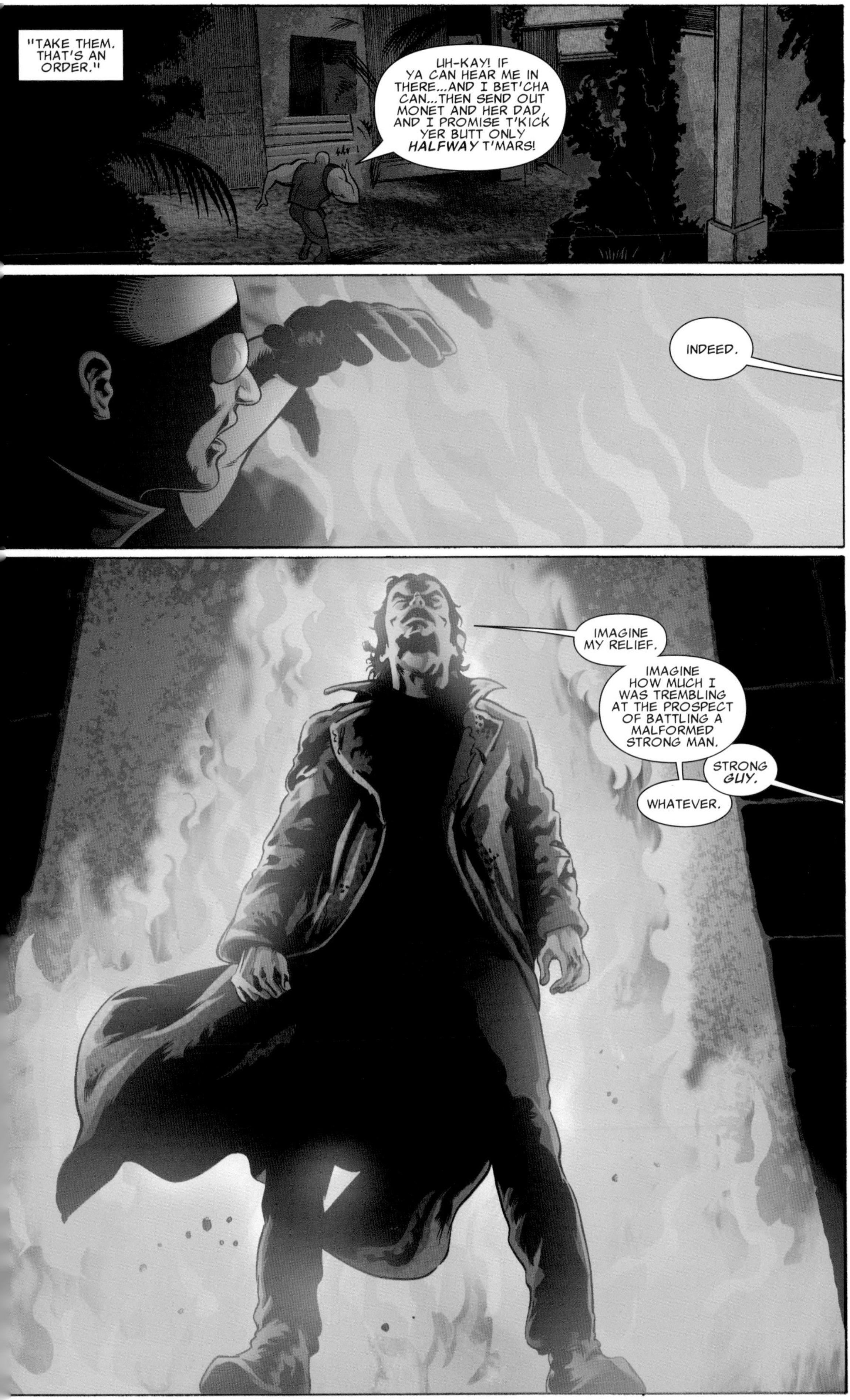
"TAKE THEM. THAT'S AN ORDER."
UH-KAY! IF YA CAN HEAR ME IN THERE...AND I BET'CHA CAN...THEN SEND OUT MONET AND HER DAD, AND I PROMISE T'KICK YER BUTT ONLY HALFWAY T'MARS!
INDEED.
IMAGINE MY RELIEF.
IMAGINE HOW MUCH I WAS TREMBLING AT THE PROSPECT OF BATTLING A MALFORMED STRONG MAN.
STRONG GUY.
WHATEVER.

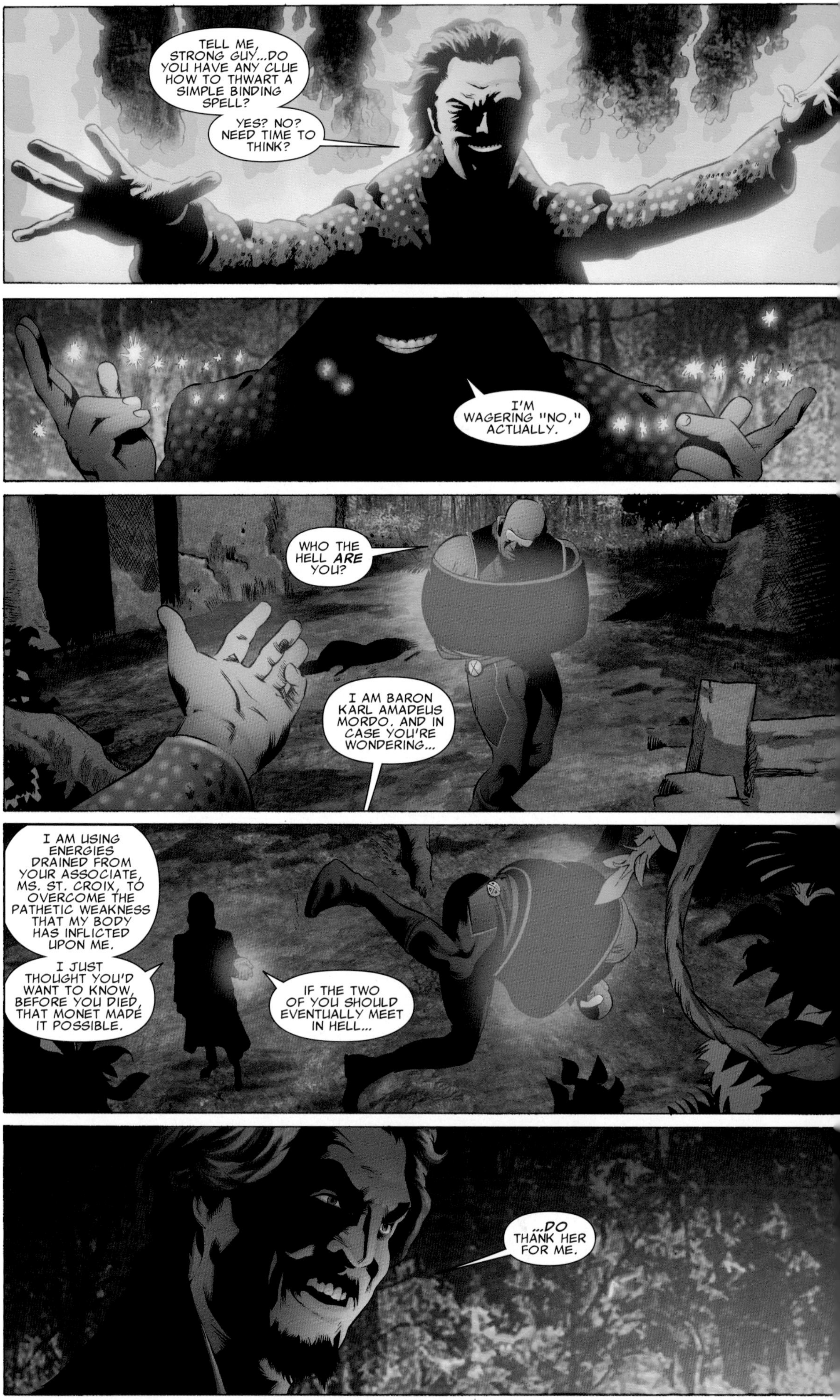
TELL ME, STRONG GUY...DO YOU HAVE ANY CLUE HOW TO THWART A SIMPLE BINDING SPELL?
YES? NO? NEED TIME TO THINK?
I'M WAGERING "NO," ACTUALLY.
WHO THE HELL ARE YOU?
I AM BARON KARL AMADEUS MORDO. AND IN CASE YOU'RE WONDERING...
I AM USING ENERGIES DRAINED FROM YOUR ASSOCIATE, MS. ST. CROIX, TO OVERCOME THE PATHETIC WEAKNESS THAT MY BODY HAS INFLICTED UPON ME.
I JUST THOUGHT YOU'D WANT TO KNOW, BEFORE YOU DIED, THAT MONET MADE IT POSSIBLE.
IF THE TWO OF YOU SHOULD EVENTUALLY MEET IN HELL...
...DO THANK HER FOR ME.

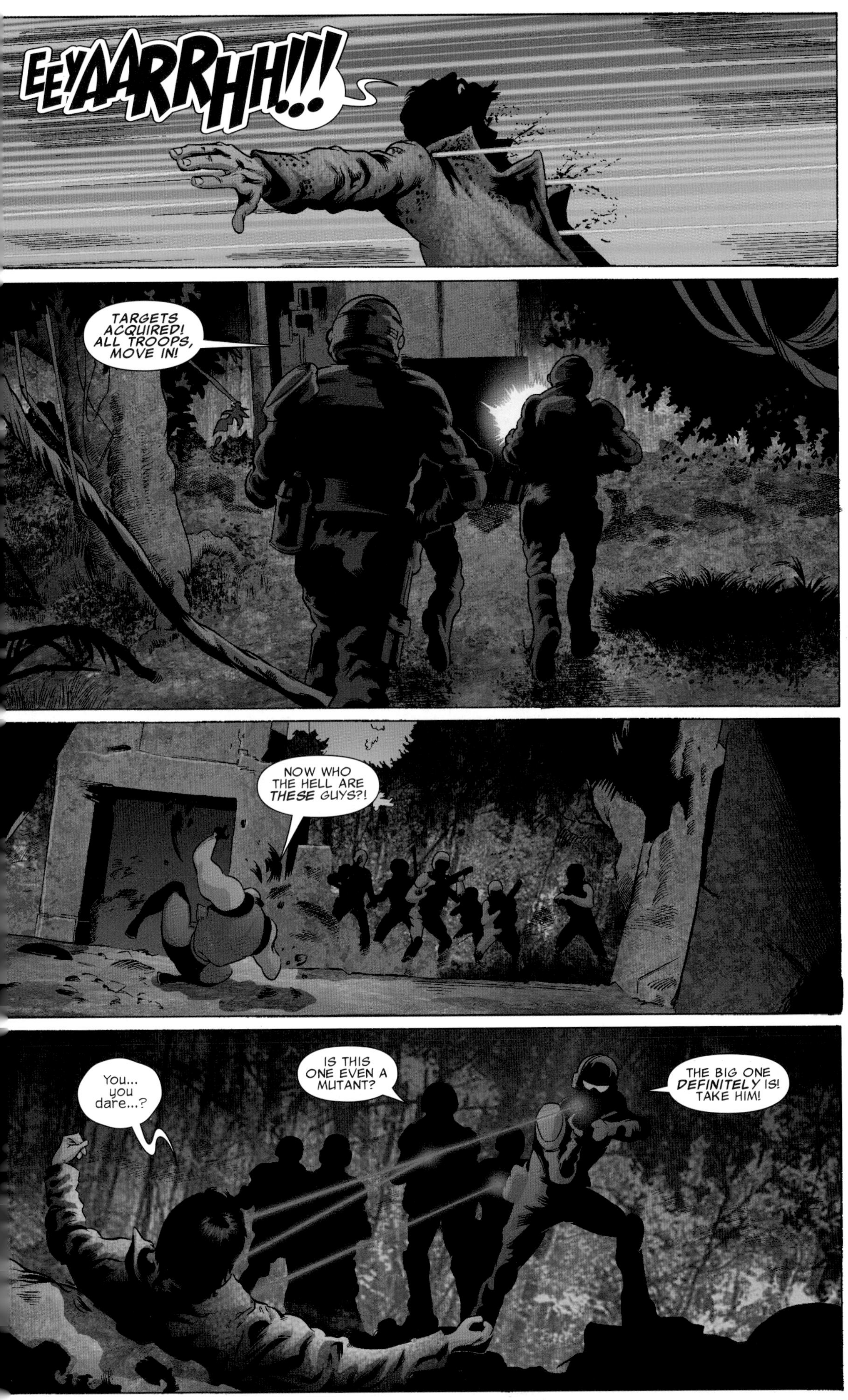
EEYAARRHH!!!
TARGETS ACQUIRED! ALL TROOPS, MOVE IN!
NOW WHO THE HELL ARE *THESE* GUYS?!
You... you dare...?
IS THIS ONE EVEN A MUTANT?
THE BIG ONE *DEFINITELY* IS! TAKE HIM!

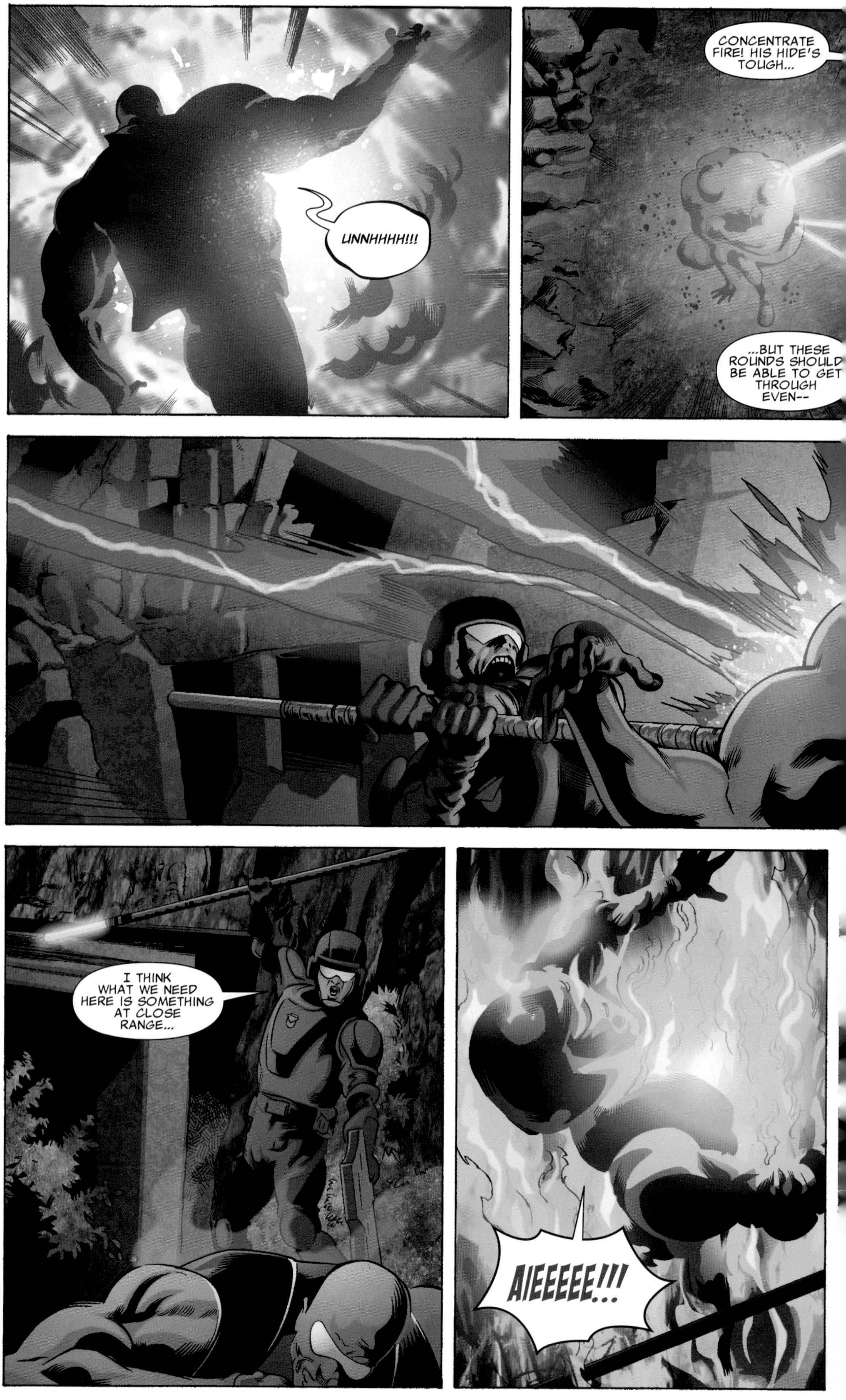
UNNHHHH!!!
CONCENTRATE FIRE! HIS HIDE'S TOUGH...
...BUT THESE ROUNDS SHOULD BE ABLE TO GET THROUGH EVEN--
I THINK WHAT WE NEED HERE IS SOMETHING AT CLOSE RANGE...
AIEEEEE!!!...

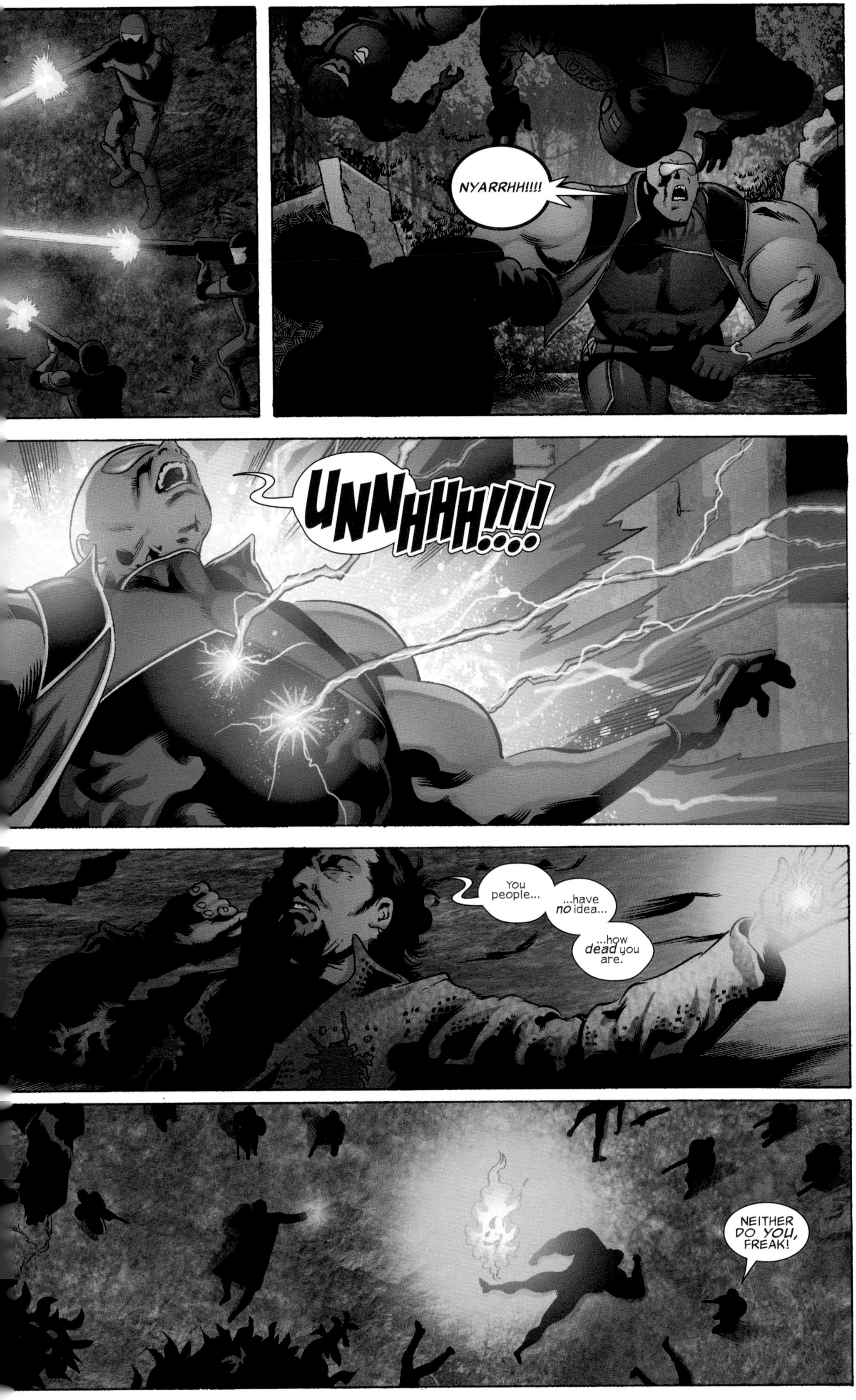
NYARRHH!!!!
UNNHHH!!!!...
You people...
...have no idea...
...how dead you are.
NEITHER DO YOU, FREAK!

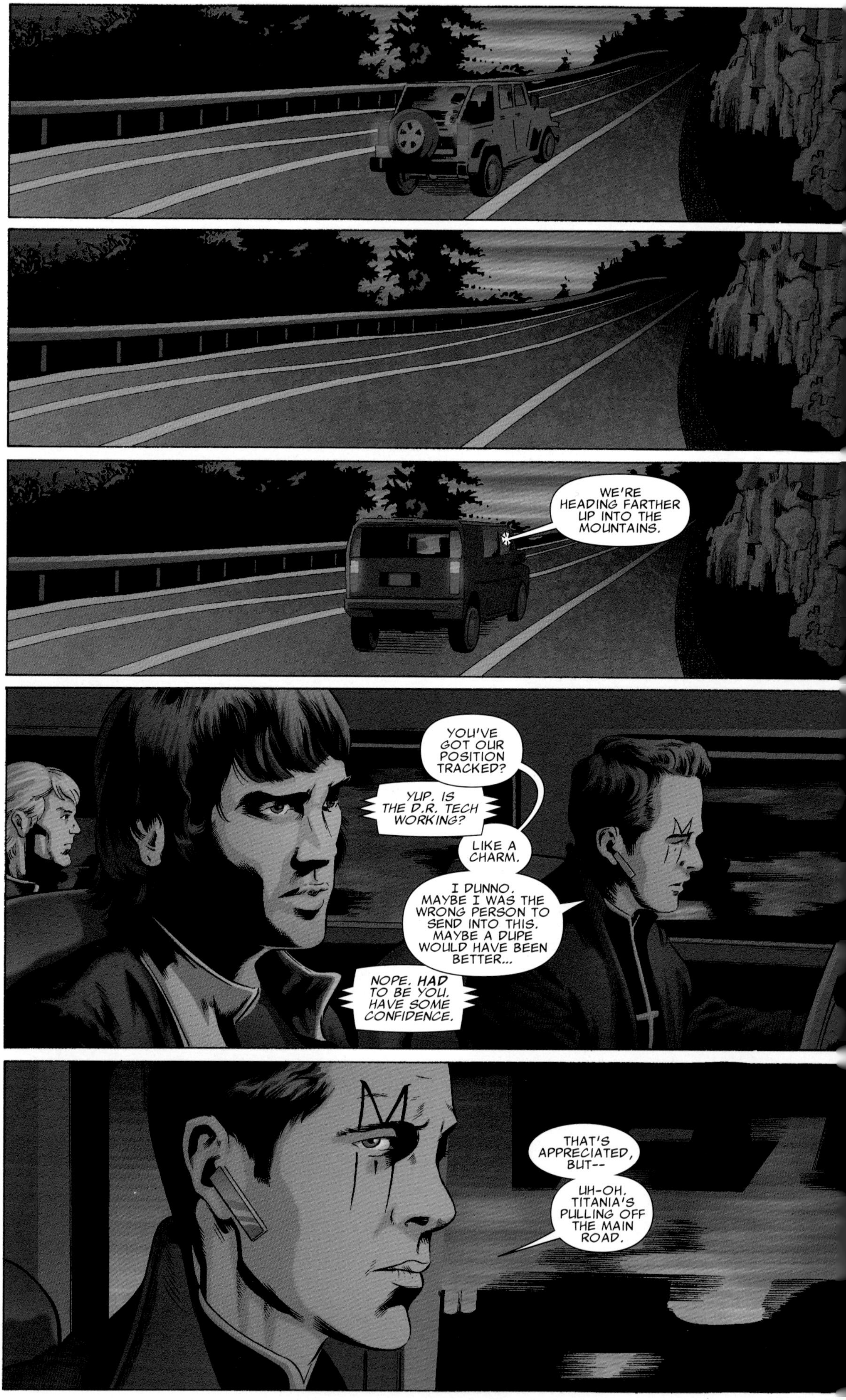
WE'RE HEADING FARTHER UP INTO THE MOUNTAINS.
YOU'VE GOT OUR POSITION TRACKED?
YUP. IS THE D.R. TECH WORKING?
LIKE A CHARM.
I DUNNO. MAYBE I WAS THE WRONG PERSON TO SEND INTO THIS. MAYBE A DUPE WOULD HAVE BEEN BETTER...
NOPE. **HAD** TO BE YOU. HAVE SOME CONFIDENCE.
THAT'S APPRECIATED, BUT--
UH-OH. TITANIA'S PULLING OFF THE MAIN ROAD.

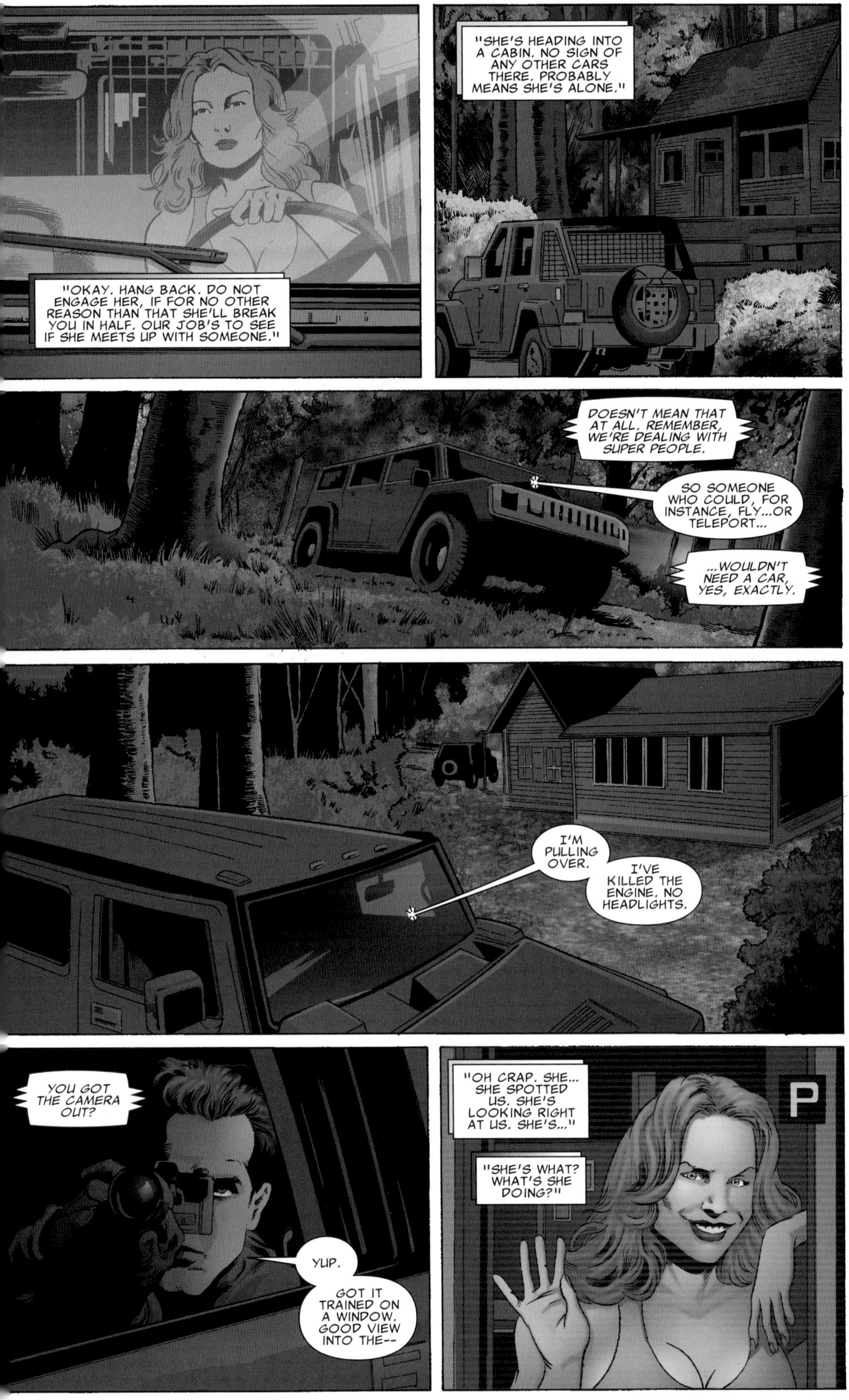
"OKAY. HANG BACK. DO NOT ENGAGE HER, IF FOR NO OTHER REASON THAN THAT SHE'LL BREAK YOU IN HALF. OUR JOB'S TO SEE IF SHE MEETS UP WITH SOMEONE."
"SHE'S HEADING INTO A CABIN. NO SIGN OF ANY OTHER CARS THERE. PROBABLY MEANS SHE'S ALONE."
DOESN'T MEAN THAT AT ALL. REMEMBER, WE'RE DEALING WITH SUPER PEOPLE.
SO SOMEONE WHO COULD, FOR INSTANCE, FLY...OR TELEPORT...
...WOULDN'T NEED A CAR, YES, EXACTLY.
I'M PULLING OVER.
I'VE KILLED THE ENGINE. NO HEADLIGHTS.
YOU GOT THE CAMERA OUT?
YUP.
GOT IT TRAINED ON A WINDOW. GOOD VIEW INTO THE--
"OH CRAP. SHE... SHE SPOTTED US. SHE'S LOOKING RIGHT AT US. SHE'S..."
"SHE'S WHAT? WHAT'S SHE DOING?"
P

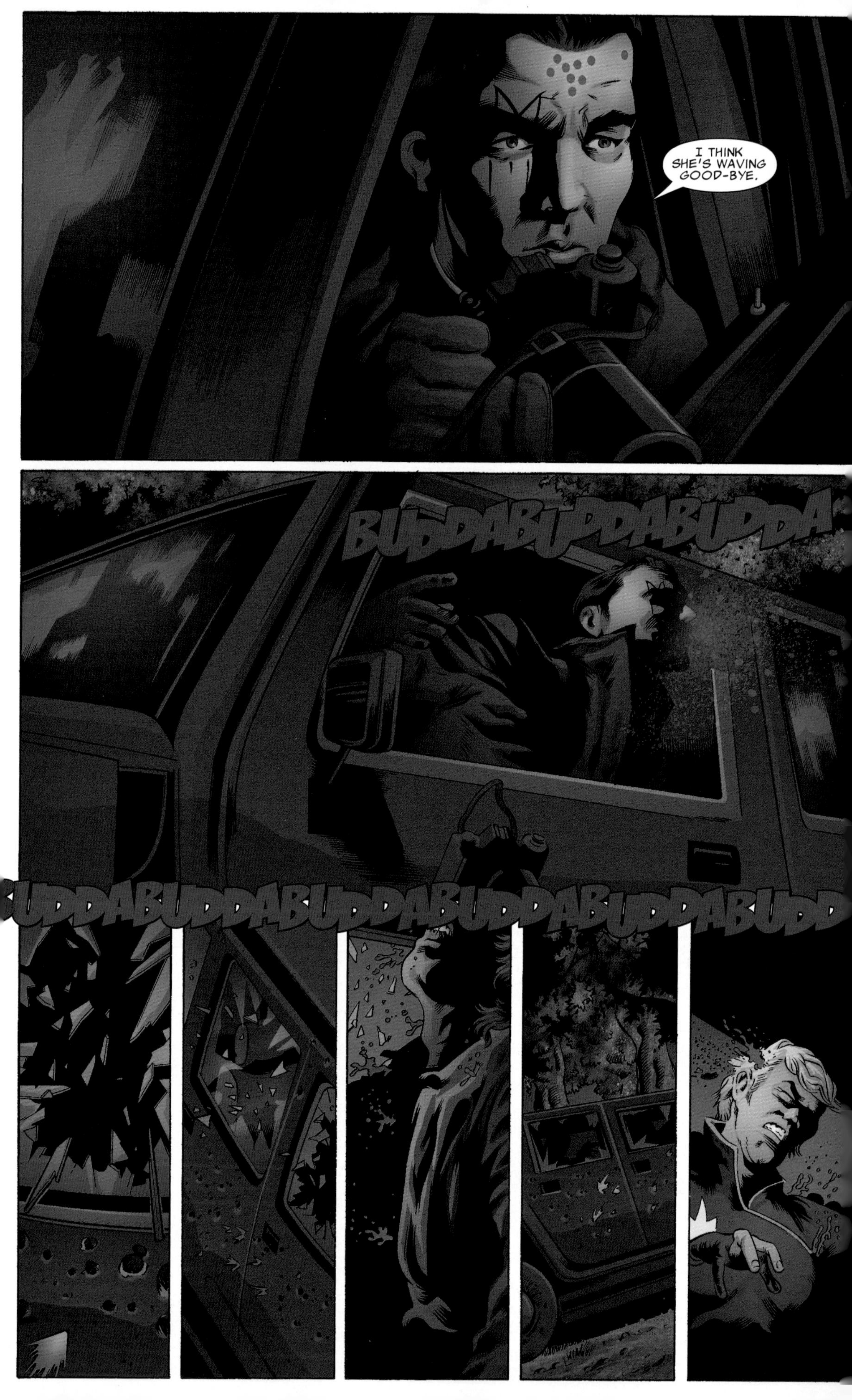
I THINK SHE'S WAVING GOOD-BYE.
BUDDABUDDABUDDA
BUDDABUDDABUDDABUDDABUDDABUDD

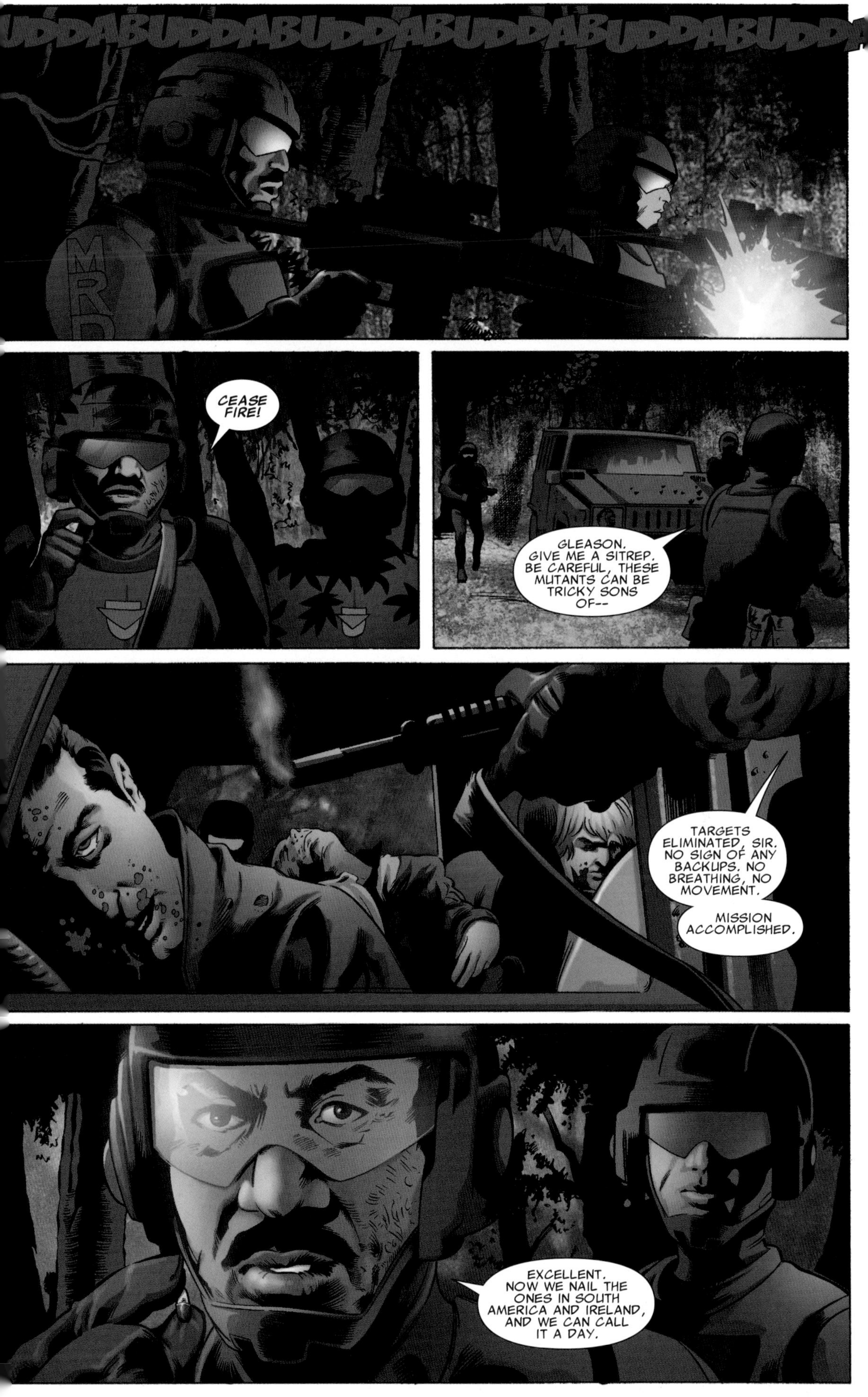
UDDABUDDABUDDABUDDABUDDA
CEASE FIRE!
GLEASON. GIVE ME A SITREP. BE CAREFUL, THESE MUTANTS CAN BE TRICKY SONS OF--
TARGETS ELIMINATED, SIR. NO SIGN OF ANY BACKUPS. NO BREATHING, NO MOVEMENT.
MISSION ACCOMPLISHED.
EXCELLENT. NOW WE NAIL THE ONES IN SOUTH AMERICA AND IRELAND, AND WE CAN CALL IT A DAY.

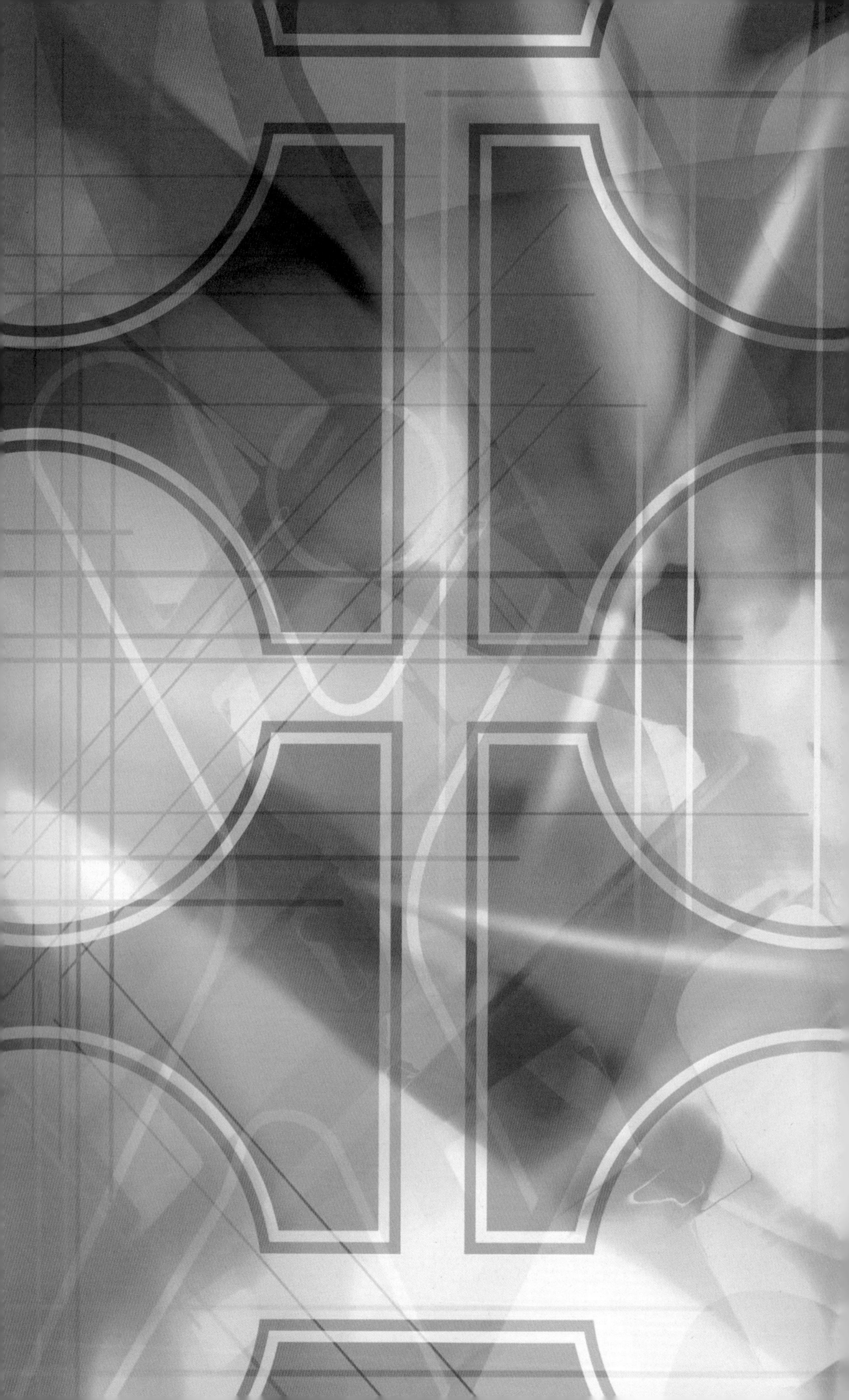

#205

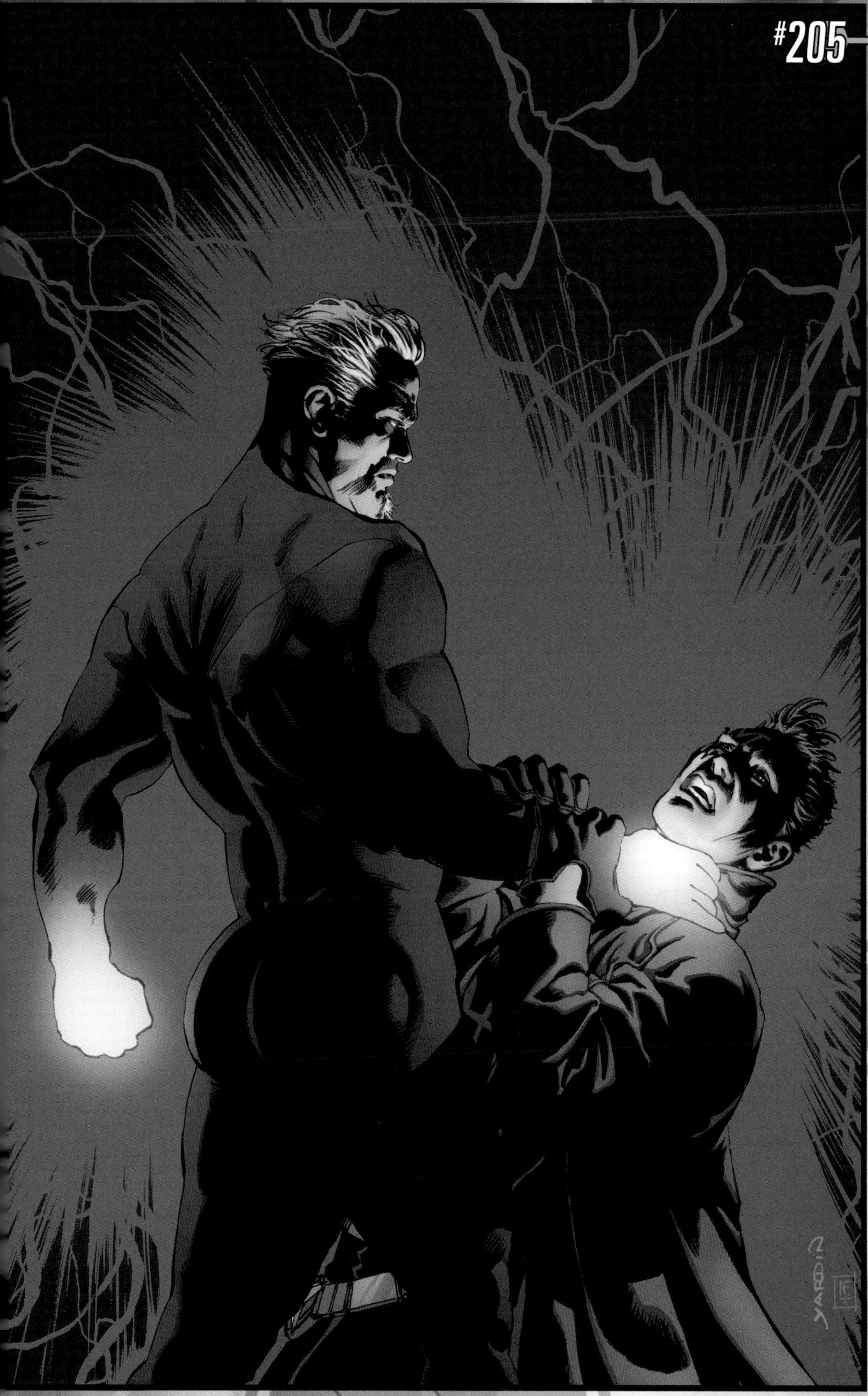

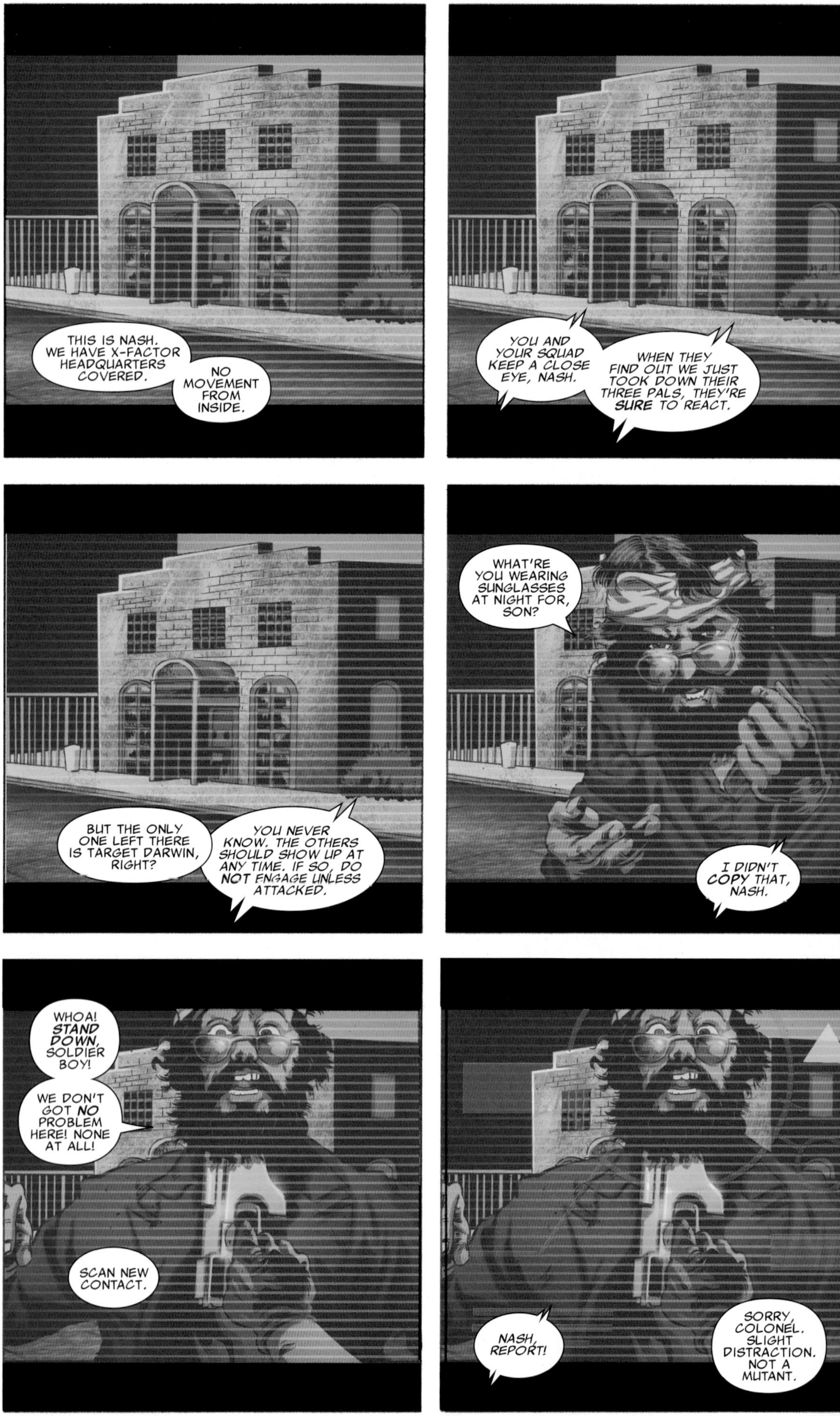
THIS IS NASH. WE HAVE X-FACTOR HEADQUARTERS COVERED.
NO MOVEMENT FROM INSIDE.
YOU AND YOUR SQUAD KEEP A CLOSE EYE, NASH.
WHEN THEY FIND OUT WE JUST TOOK DOWN THEIR THREE PALS, THEY'RE SURE TO REACT.
BUT THE ONLY ONE LEFT THERE IS TARGET DARWIN, RIGHT?
YOU NEVER KNOW. THE OTHERS SHOULD SHOW UP AT ANY TIME. IF SO, DO NOT ENGAGE UNLESS ATTACKED.
WHAT'RE YOU WEARING SUNGLASSES AT NIGHT FOR, SON?
I DIDN'T COPY THAT, NASH.
WHOA! STAND DOWN, SOLDIER BOY!
WE DON'T GOT NO PROBLEM HERE! NONE AT ALL!
SCAN NEW CONTACT.
NASH, REPORT!
SORRY, COLONEL. SLIGHT DISTRACTION. NOT A MUTANT.

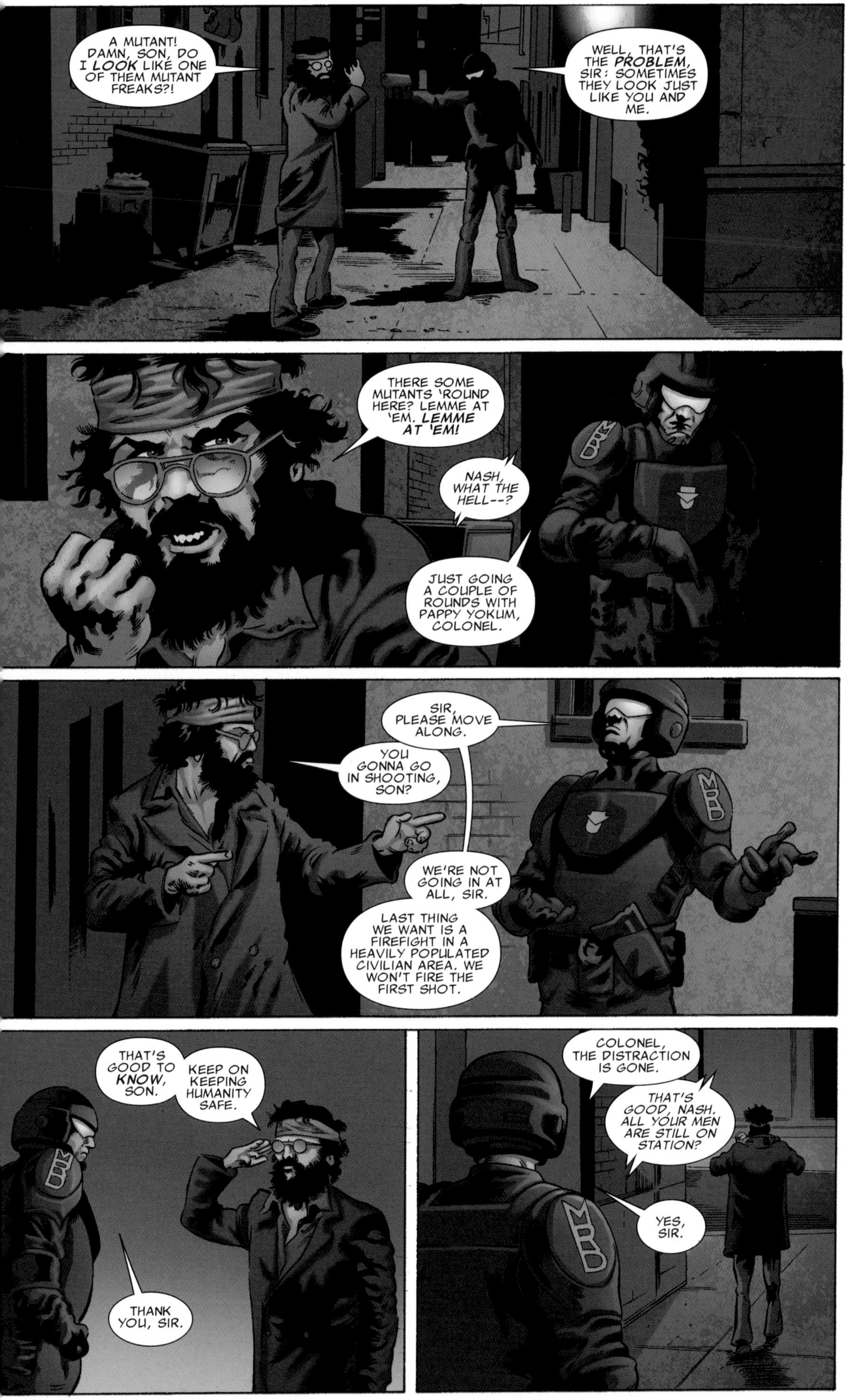
A MUTANT! DAMN, SON, DO I **LOOK** LIKE ONE OF THEM MUTANT FREAKS?!
WELL, THAT'S THE **PROBLEM**, SIR: SOMETIMES THEY LOOK JUST LIKE YOU AND ME.
THERE SOME MUTANTS 'ROUND HERE? LEMME AT 'EM. **LEMME AT 'EM!**
NASH, WHAT THE HELL--?
JUST GOING A COUPLE OF ROUNDS WITH PAPPY YOKUM, COLONEL.
MBD
SIR, PLEASE MOVE ALONG.
YOU GONNA GO IN SHOOTING, SON?
WE'RE NOT GOING IN AT ALL, SIR.
LAST THING WE WANT IS A FIREFIGHT IN A HEAVILY POPULATED CIVILIAN AREA. WE WON'T FIRE THE FIRST SHOT.
THAT'S GOOD TO **KNOW**, SON.
KEEP ON KEEPING HUMANITY SAFE.
THANK YOU, SIR.
COLONEL, THE DISTRACTION IS GONE.
THAT'S GOOD, NASH. ALL YOUR MEN ARE STILL ON STATION?
YES, SIR.

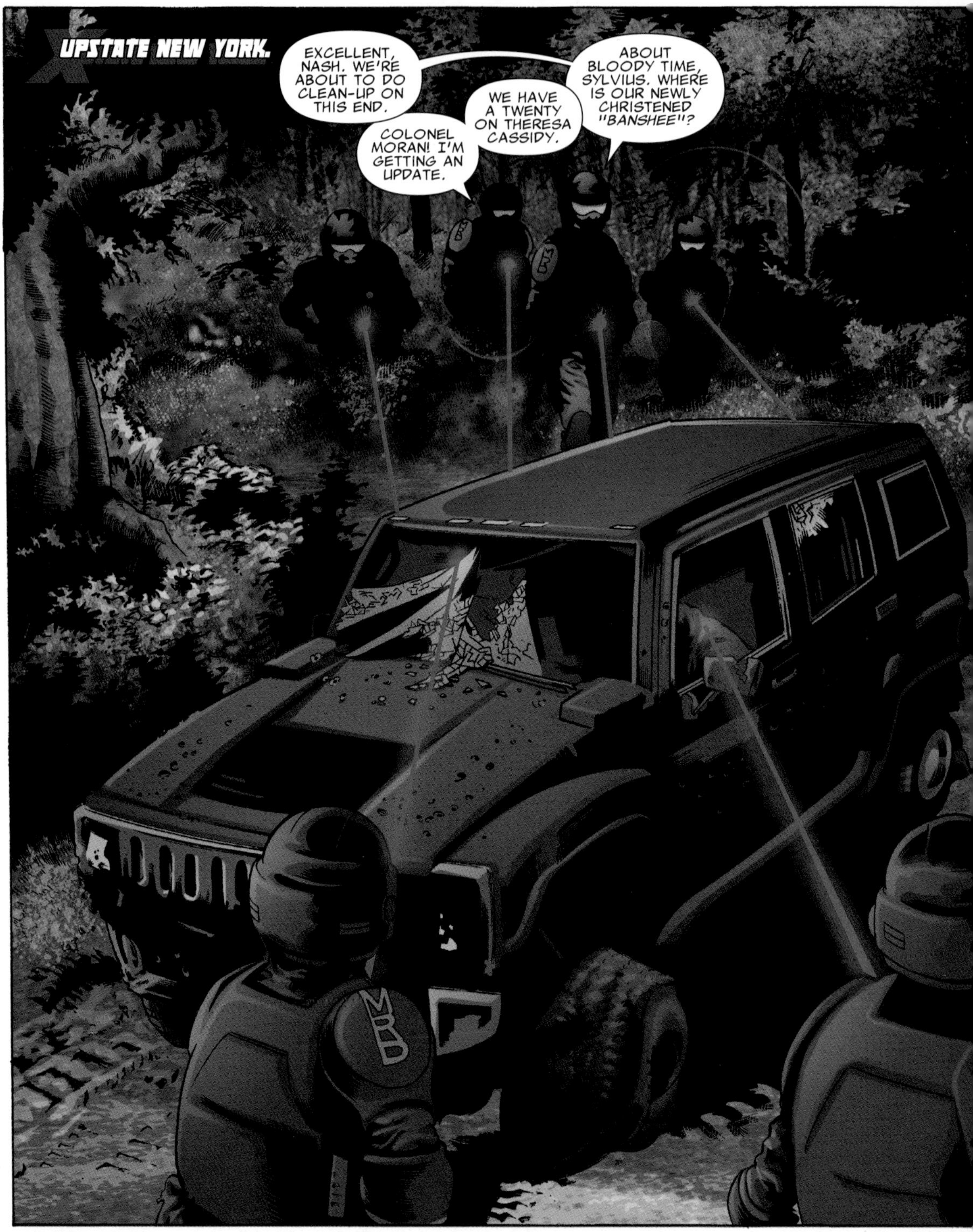
UPSTATE NEW YORK.
COLONEL MORAN! I'M GETTING AN UPDATE.
ABOUT BLOODY TIME, SYLVIUS. WHERE IS OUR NEWLY CHRISTENED "BANSHEE"?
WE HAVE A TWENTY ON THERESA CASSIDY.
EXCELLENT, NASH. WE'RE ABOUT TO DO CLEAN-UP ON THIS END.

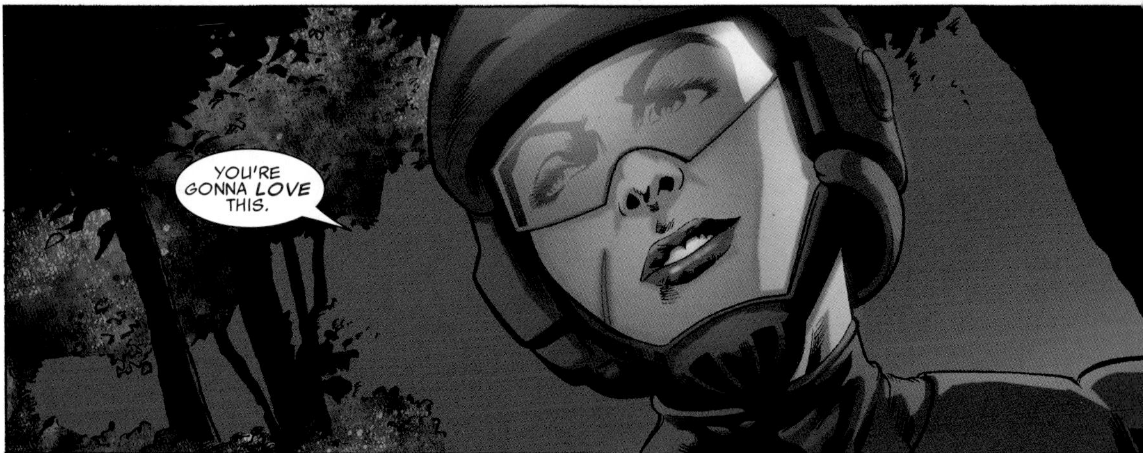
YOU'RE GONNA LOVE THIS.

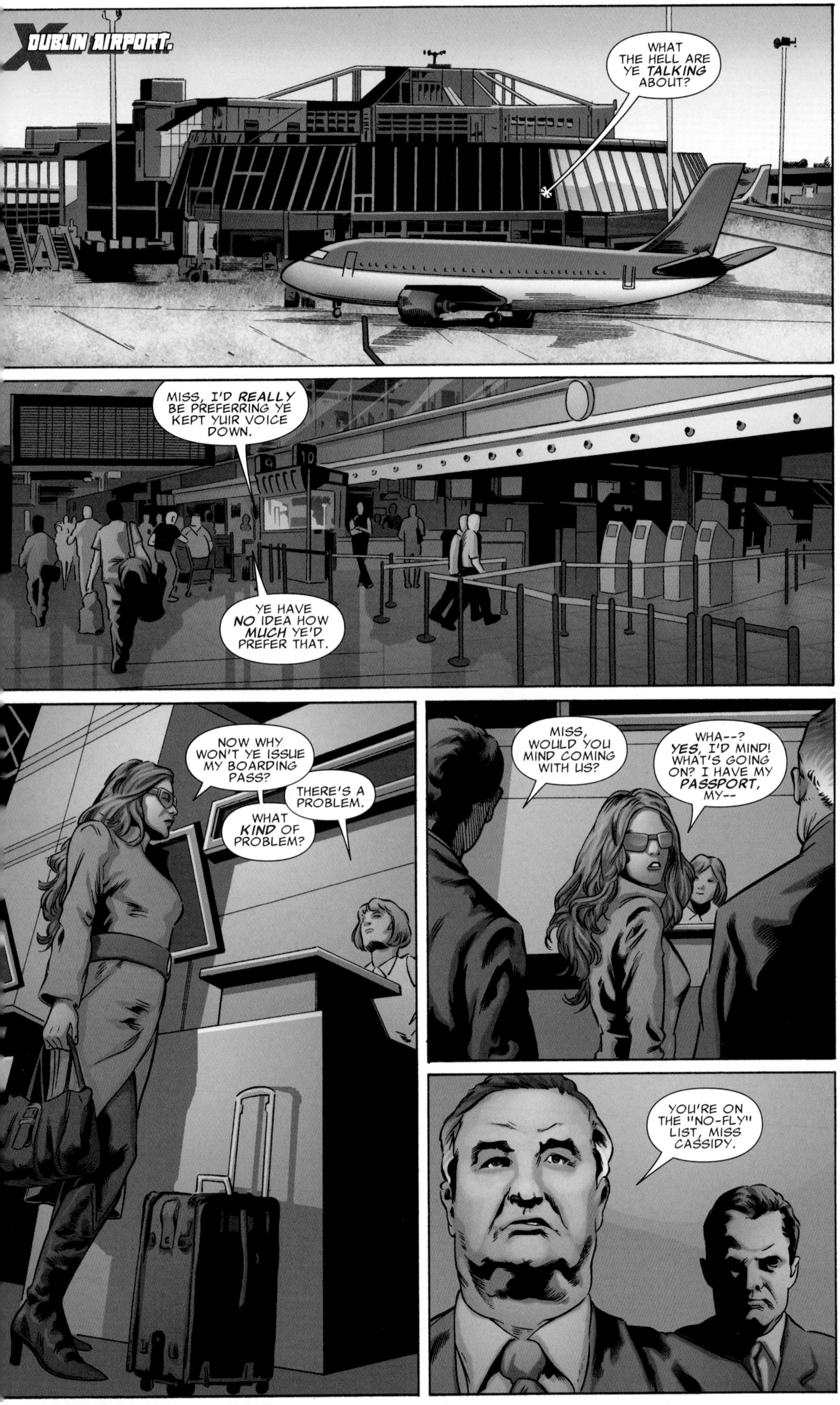
DUBLIN AIRPORT.
WHAT THE HELL ARE YE TALKING ABOUT?
MISS, I'D REALLY BE PREFERRING YE KEPT YUIR VOICE DOWN.
YE HAVE NO IDEA HOW MUCH YE'D PREFER THAT.
NOW WHY WON'T YE ISSUE MY BOARDING PASS?
THERE'S A PROBLEM.
WHAT KIND OF PROBLEM?
MISS, WOULD YOU MIND COMING WITH US?
WHA--? YES, I'D MIND! WHAT'S GOING ON? I HAVE MY PASSPORT, MY--
YOU'RE ON THE "NO-FLY" LIST, MISS CASSIDY.

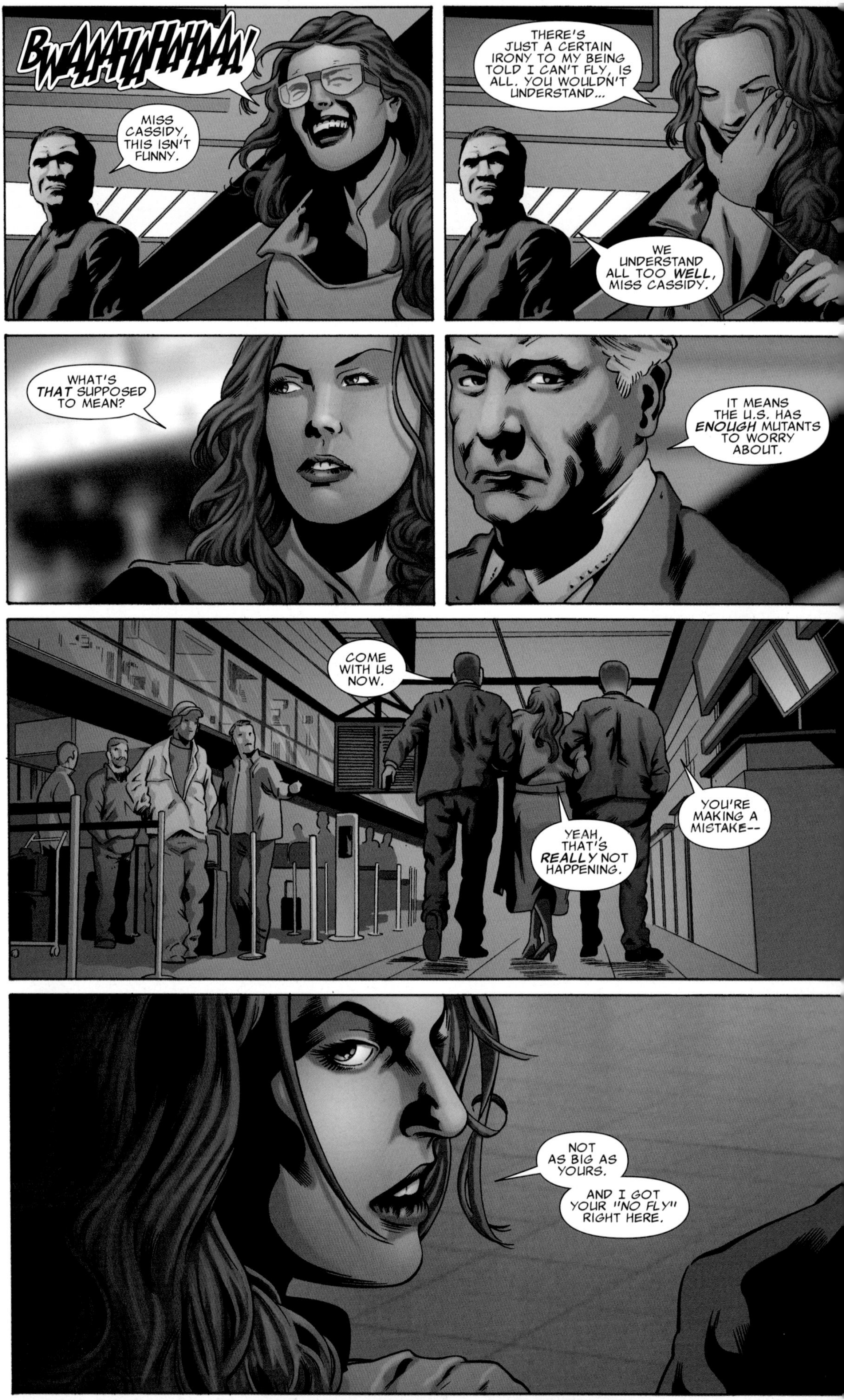
BWAAAHAHAHAA!
MISS CASSIDY, THIS ISN'T FUNNY.
THERE'S JUST A CERTAIN IRONY TO MY BEING TOLD I CAN'T FLY, IS ALL. YOU WOULDN'T UNDERSTAND...
WE UNDERSTAND ALL TOO WELL, MISS CASSIDY.
WHAT'S THAT SUPPOSED TO MEAN?
IT MEANS THE U.S. HAS ENOUGH MUTANTS TO WORRY ABOUT.
COME WITH US NOW.
YEAH, THAT'S REALLY NOT HAPPENING.
YOU'RE MAKING A MISTAKE--
NOT AS BIG AS YOURS.
AND I GOT YOUR "NO FLY" RIGHT HERE.

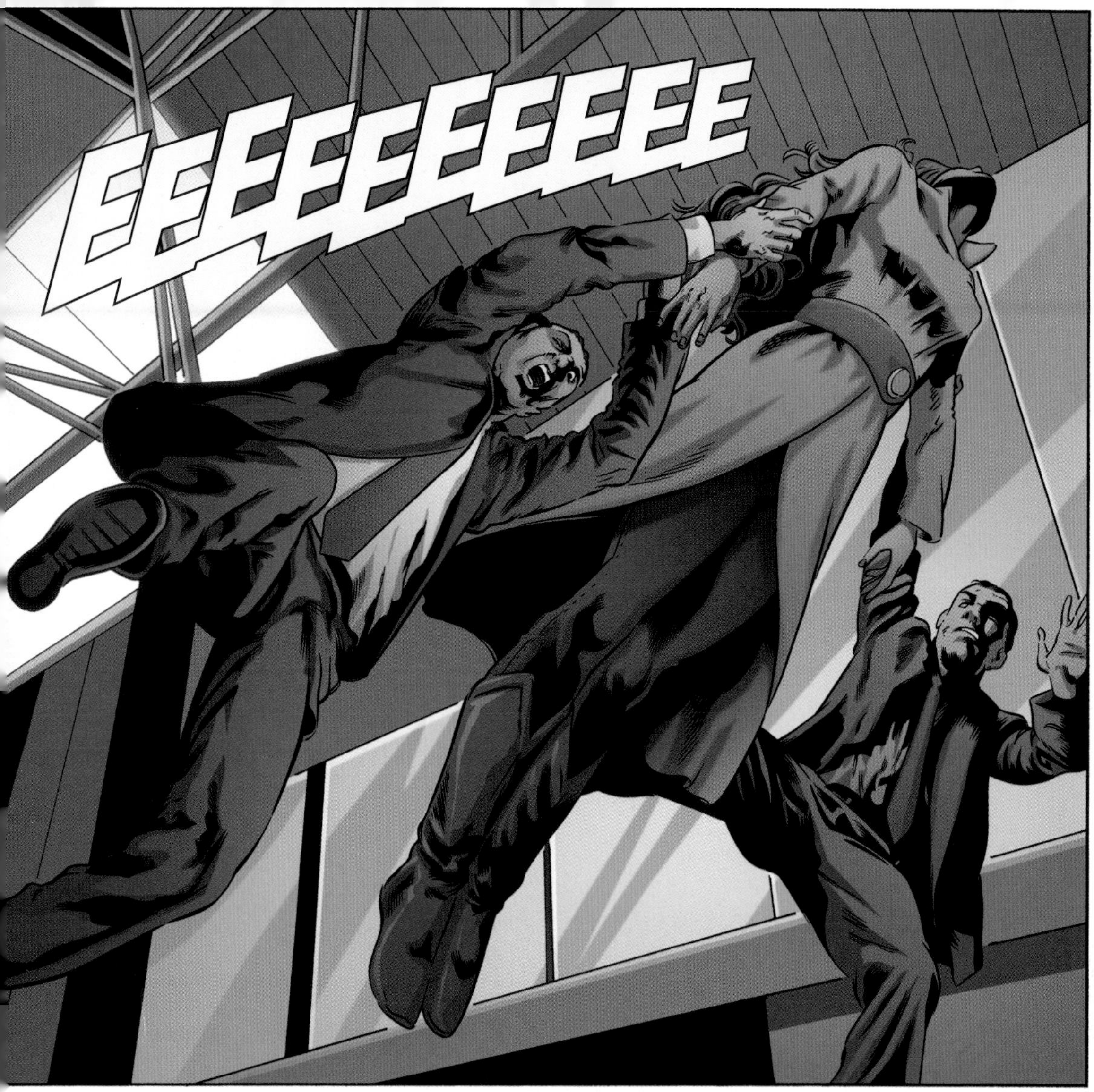
EEEEEEEEEE

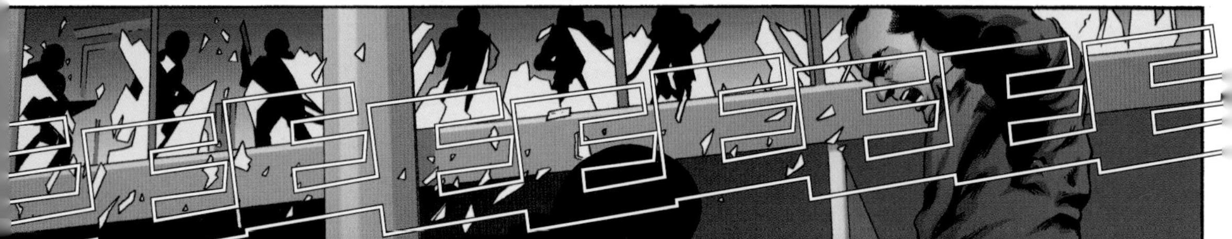

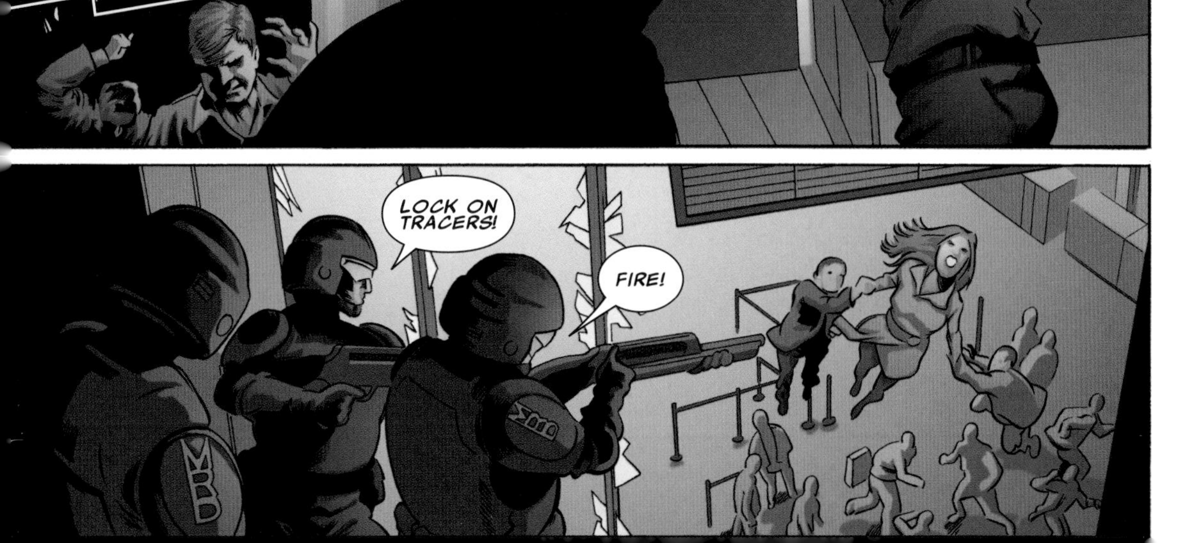
LOCK ON TRACERS!
FIRE!

BUDDABUDDABUDDABUDDA

EEE

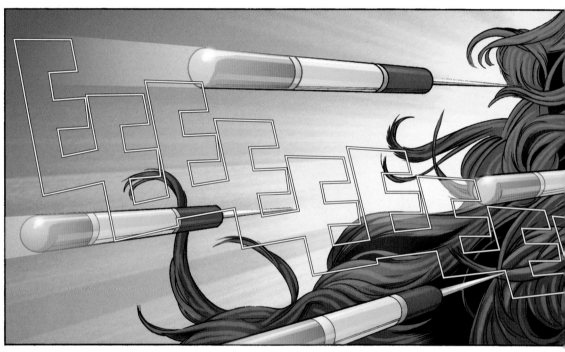

EEEEEE

--UNNFFFFFF!!!

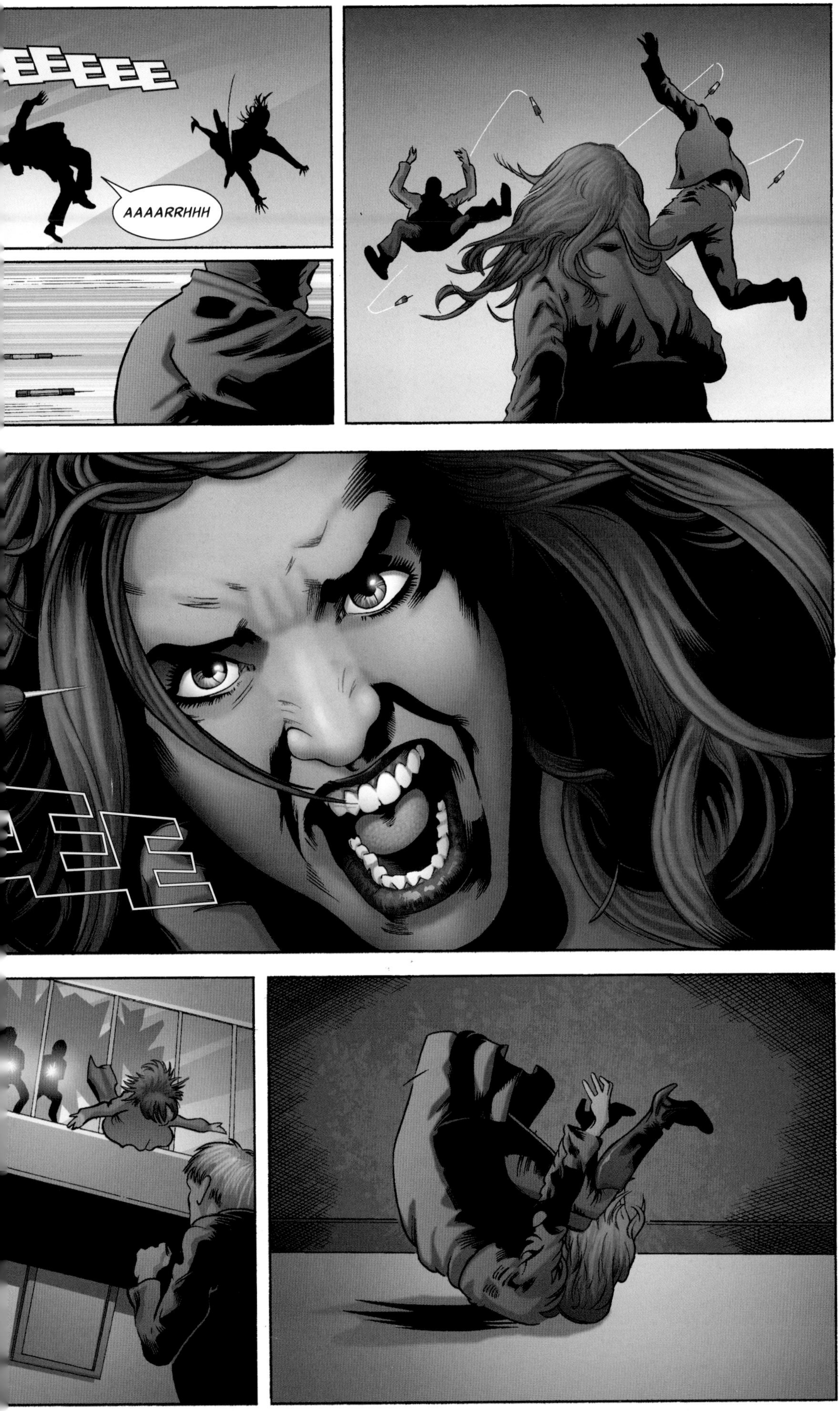
EEEEEE
AAAARRHHH
EEE

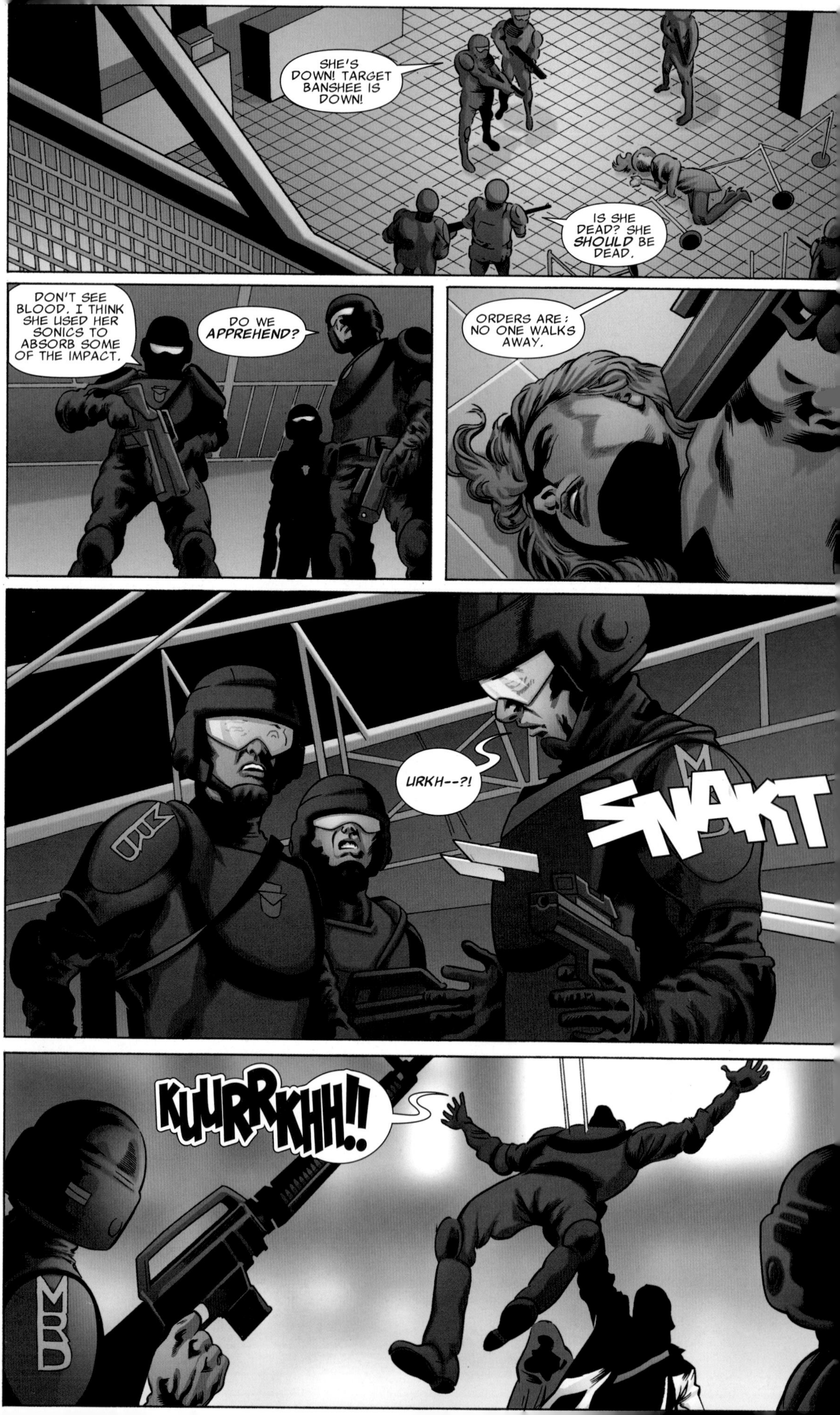

SHE'S DOWN! TARGET BANSHEE IS DOWN!
IS SHE DEAD? SHE SHOULD BE DEAD.
DON'T SEE BLOOD. I THINK SHE USED HER SONICS TO ABSORB SOME OF THE IMPACT.
DO WE APPREHEND?
ORDERS ARE: NO ONE WALKS AWAY.
URKH--?!
SNAKT
KUURRKHH!!

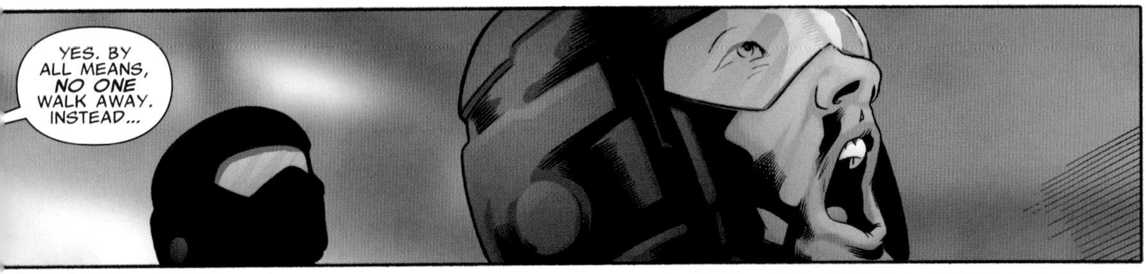
YES. BY ALL MEANS, NO ONE WALK AWAY. INSTEAD...

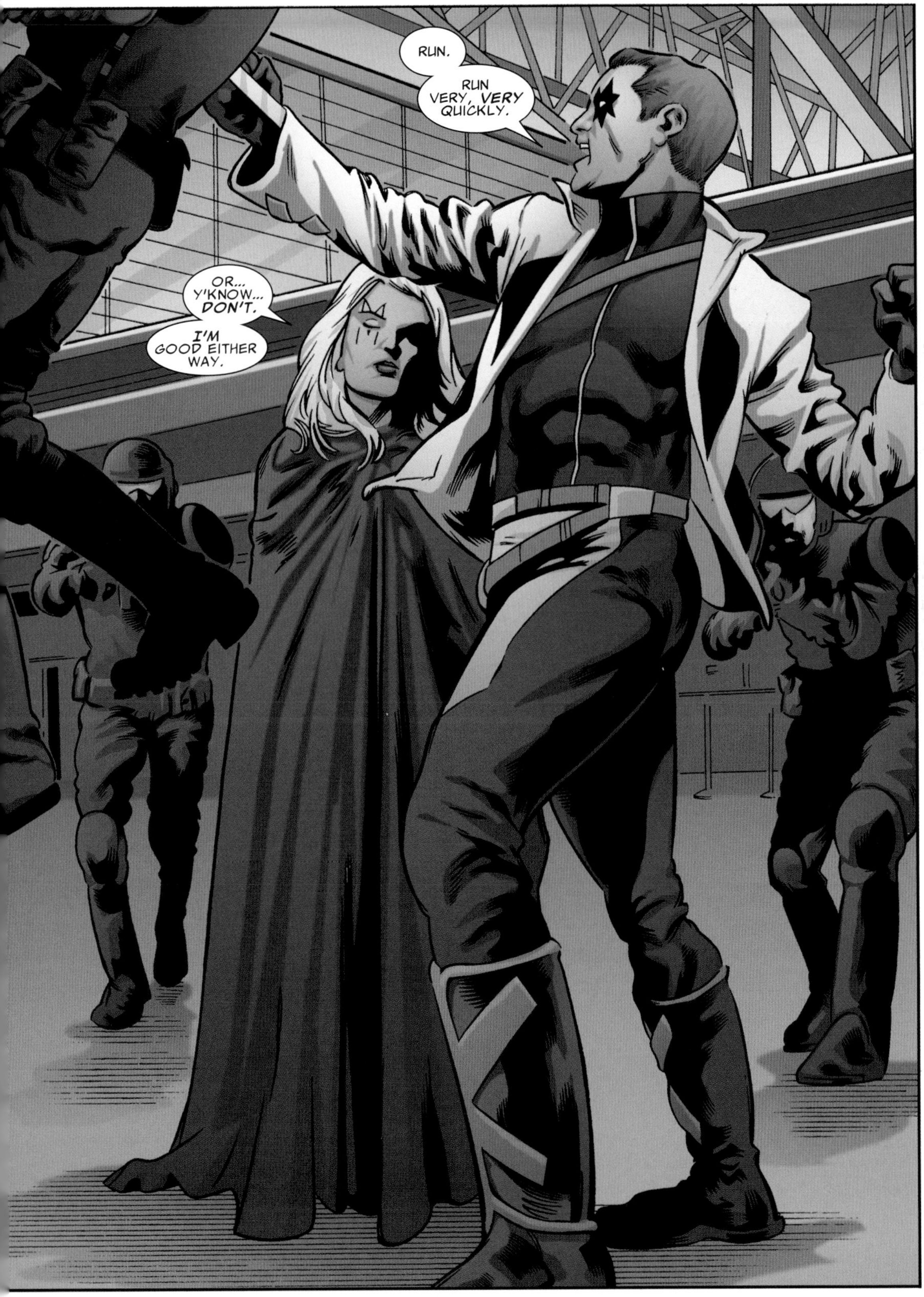
RUN.
RUN VERY, VERY QUICKLY.
OR... Y'KNOW... DON'T.
I'M GOOD EITHER WAY.

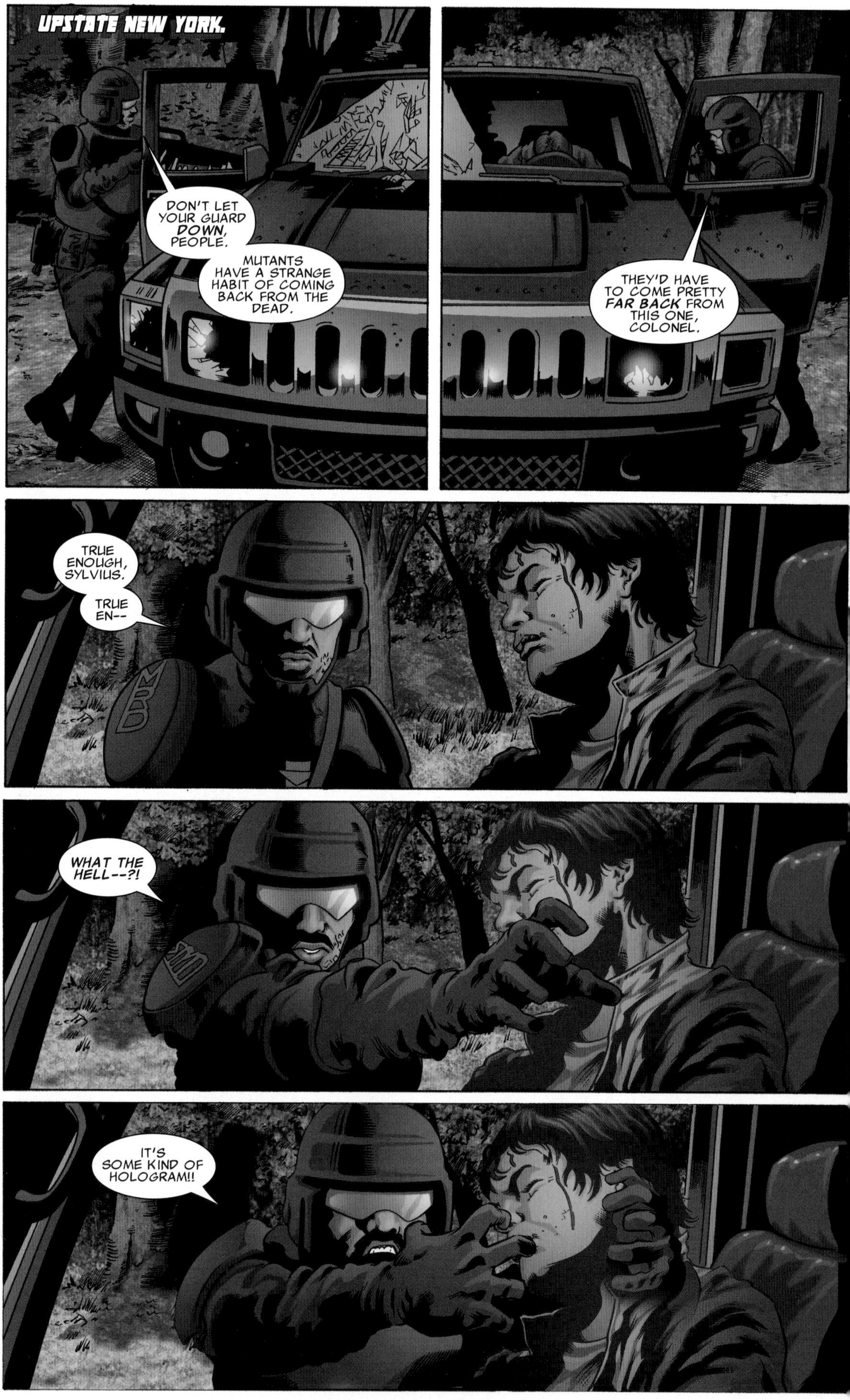
UPSTATE NEW YORK.
DON'T LET YOUR GUARD DOWN, PEOPLE.
MUTANTS HAVE A STRANGE HABIT OF COMING BACK FROM THE DEAD.
THEY'D HAVE TO COME PRETTY FAR BACK FROM THIS ONE, COLONEL.
TRUE ENOUGH, SYLVIUS.
TRUE EN--
WHAT THE HELL--?!
IT'S SOME KIND OF HOLOGRAM!!

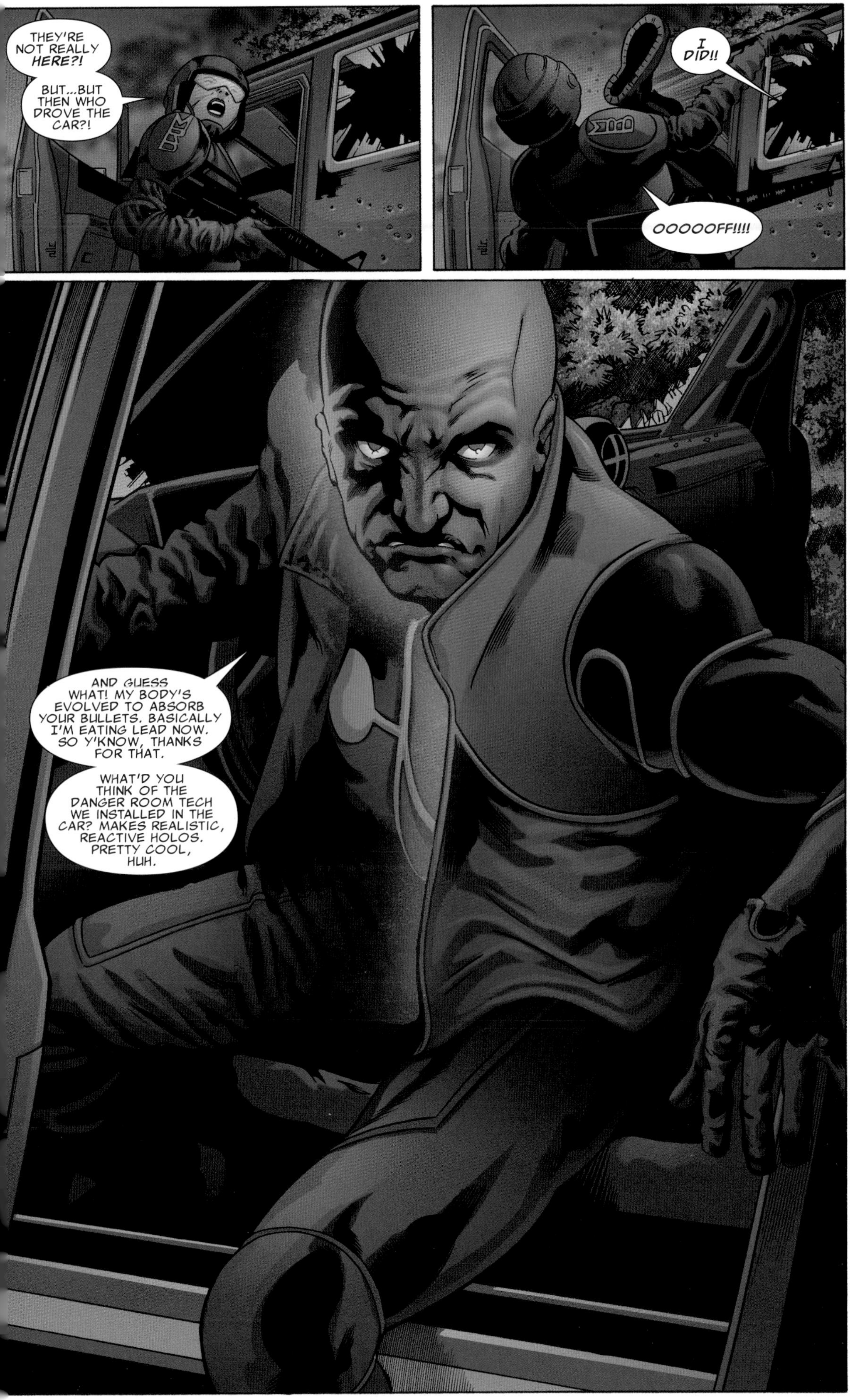
THEY'RE NOT REALLY *HERE?!*
BUT...BUT THEN WHO DROVE THE CAR?!
I DID!!
OOOOOFF!!!!
AND GUESS WHAT! MY BODY'S EVOLVED TO ABSORB YOUR BULLETS. BASICALLY I'M EATING LEAD NOW. SO Y'KNOW, THANKS FOR THAT.
WHAT'D YOU THINK OF THE DANGER ROOM TECH WE INSTALLED IN THE CAR? MAKES REALISTIC, REACTIVE HOLOS. PRETTY COOL, HUH.

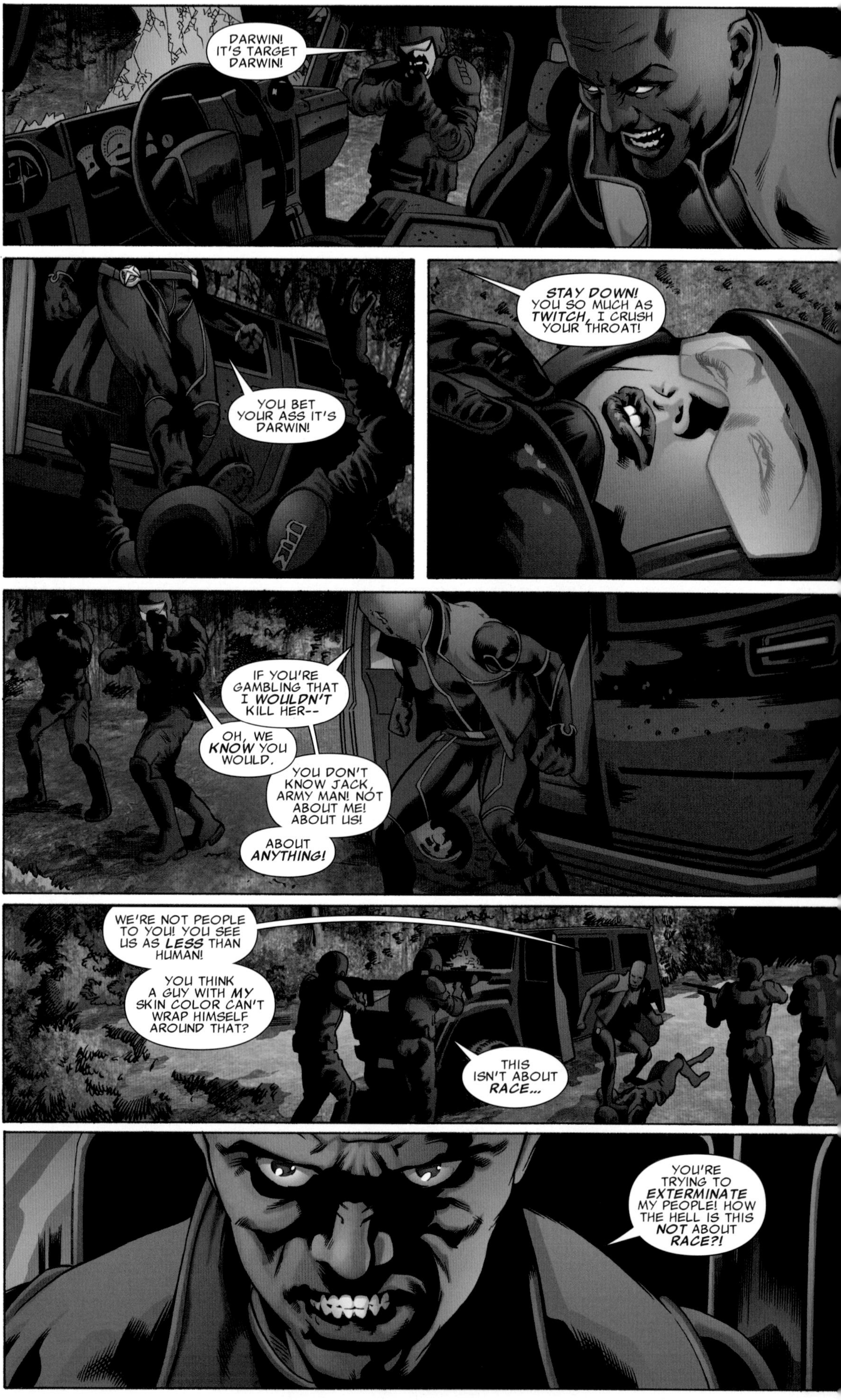
DARWIN! IT'S TARGET DARWIN!
YOU BET YOUR ASS IT'S DARWIN!
STAY DOWN! YOU SO MUCH AS TWITCH, I CRUSH YOUR THROAT!
IF YOU'RE GAMBLING THAT I WOULDN'T KILL HER--
OH, WE KNOW YOU WOULD.
YOU DON'T KNOW JACK, ARMY MAN! NOT ABOUT ME! ABOUT US!
ABOUT ANYTHING!
WE'RE NOT PEOPLE TO YOU! YOU SEE US AS LESS THAN HUMAN!
YOU THINK A GUY WITH MY SKIN COLOR CAN'T WRAP HIMSELF AROUND THAT?
THIS ISN'T ABOUT RACE...
YOU'RE TRYING TO EXTERMINATE MY PEOPLE! HOW THE HELL IS THIS NOT ABOUT RACE?!

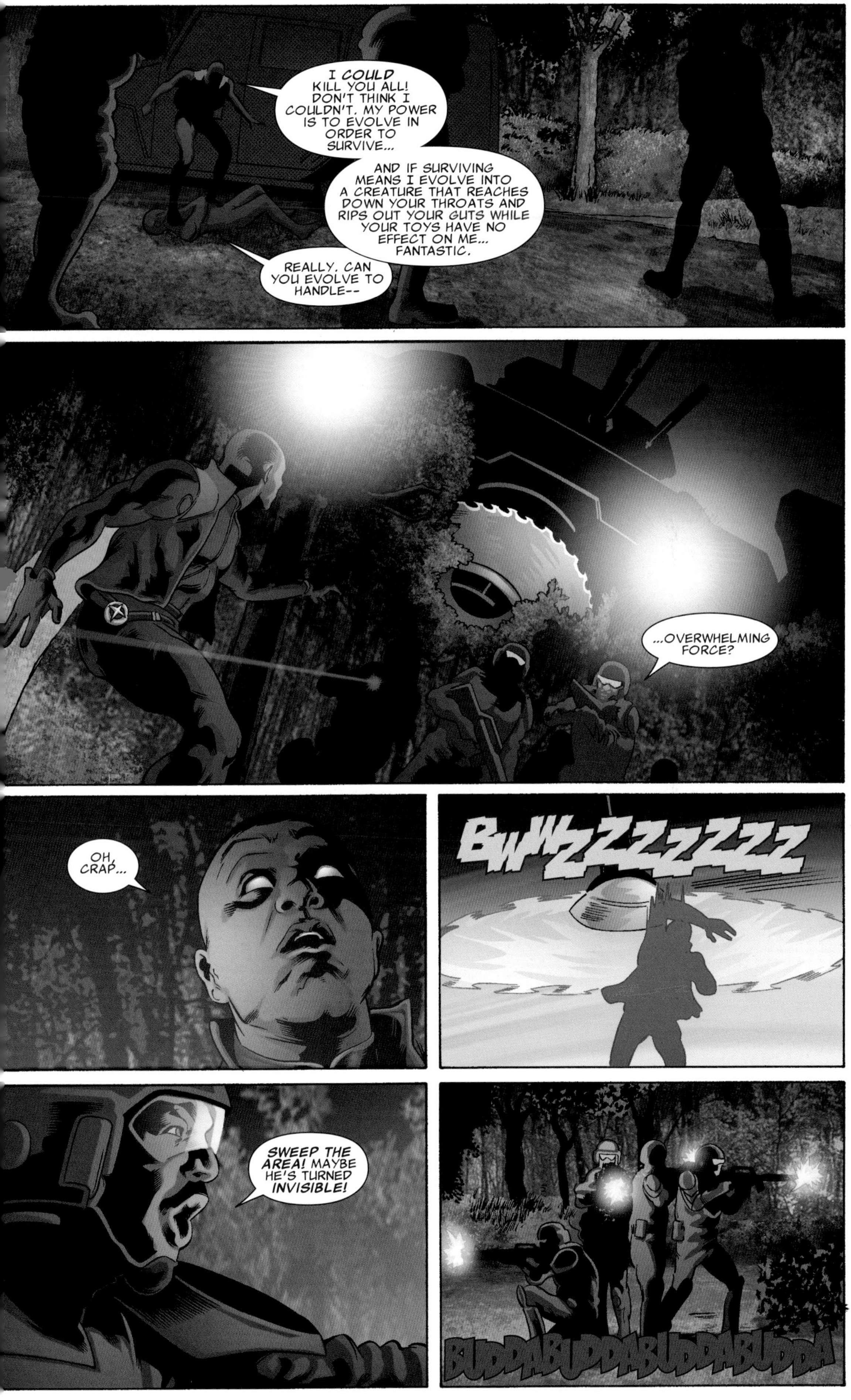
I COULD KILL YOU ALL! DON'T THINK I COULDN'T. MY POWER IS TO EVOLVE IN ORDER TO SURVIVE...
AND IF SURVIVING MEANS I EVOLVE INTO A CREATURE THAT REACHES DOWN YOUR THROATS AND RIPS OUT YOUR GUTS WHILE YOUR TOYS HAVE NO EFFECT ON ME... FANTASTIC.
REALLY. CAN YOU EVOLVE TO HANDLE--
...OVERWHELMING FORCE?
OH, CRAP...
BWWZZZZZZZ
SWEEP THE AREA! MAYBE HE'S TURNED INVISIBLE!
BUDDABUDDABUDDABUDDA

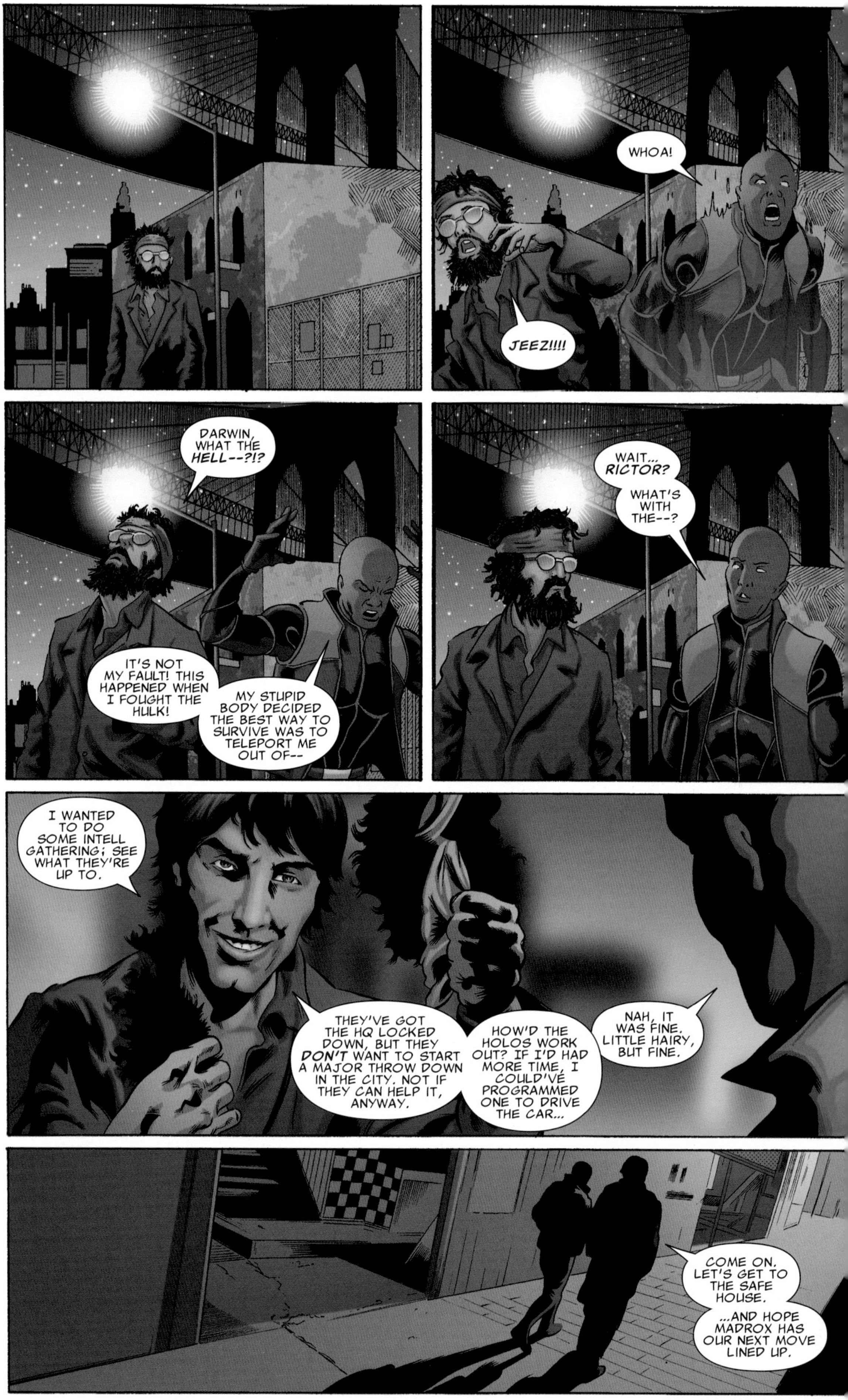
WHOA!
JEEZ!!!!
DARWIN, WHAT THE HELL--?!?
IT'S NOT MY FAULT! THIS HAPPENED WHEN I FOUGHT THE HULK!
MY STUPID BODY DECIDED THE BEST WAY TO SURVIVE WAS TO TELEPORT ME OUT OF--
WAIT... RICTOR?
WHAT'S WITH THE--?
I WANTED TO DO SOME INTELL GATHERING; SEE WHAT THEY'RE UP TO.
THEY'VE GOT THE HQ LOCKED DOWN, BUT THEY DON'T WANT TO START A MAJOR THROW DOWN IN THE CITY. NOT IF THEY CAN HELP IT, ANYWAY.
HOW'D THE HOLOS WORK OUT? IF I'D HAD MORE TIME, I COULD'VE PROGRAMMED ONE TO DRIVE THE CAR...
NAH, IT WAS FINE. LITTLE HAIRY, BUT FINE.
COME ON. LET'S GET TO THE SAFE HOUSE.
...AND HOPE MADROX HAS OUR NEXT MOVE LINED UP.

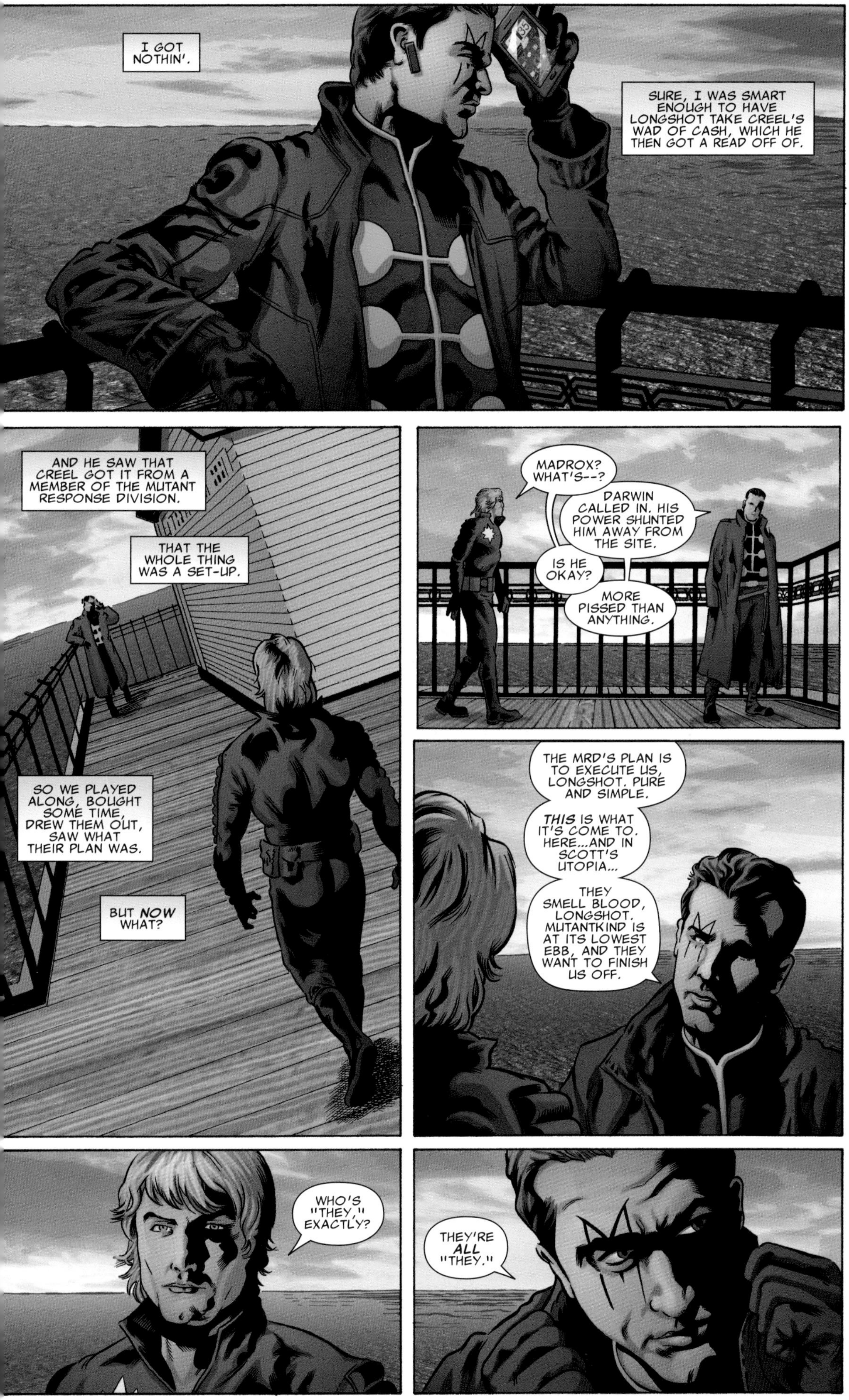
I GOT NOTHIN'.
SURE, I WAS SMART ENOUGH TO HAVE LONGSHOT TAKE CREEL'S WAD OF CASH, WHICH HE THEN GOT A READ OFF OF.
AND HE SAW THAT CREEL GOT IT FROM A MEMBER OF THE MUTANT RESPONSE DIVISION.
THAT THE WHOLE THING WAS A SET-UP.
SO WE PLAYED ALONG, BOUGHT SOME TIME, DREW THEM OUT, SAW WHAT THEIR PLAN WAS.
BUT *NOW* WHAT?
MADROX? WHAT'S--?
DARWIN CALLED IN. HIS POWER SHUNTED HIM AWAY FROM THE SITE.
IS HE OKAY?
MORE PISSED THAN ANYTHING.
THE MRD'S PLAN IS TO EXECUTE US, LONGSHOT. PURE AND SIMPLE.
THIS IS WHAT IT'S COME TO. HERE...AND IN SCOTT'S UTOPIA...
THEY SMELL BLOOD, LONGSHOT. MUTANTKIND IS AT ITS LOWEST EBB, AND THEY WANT TO FINISH US OFF.
WHO'S "THEY," EXACTLY?
THEY'RE *ALL* "THEY."

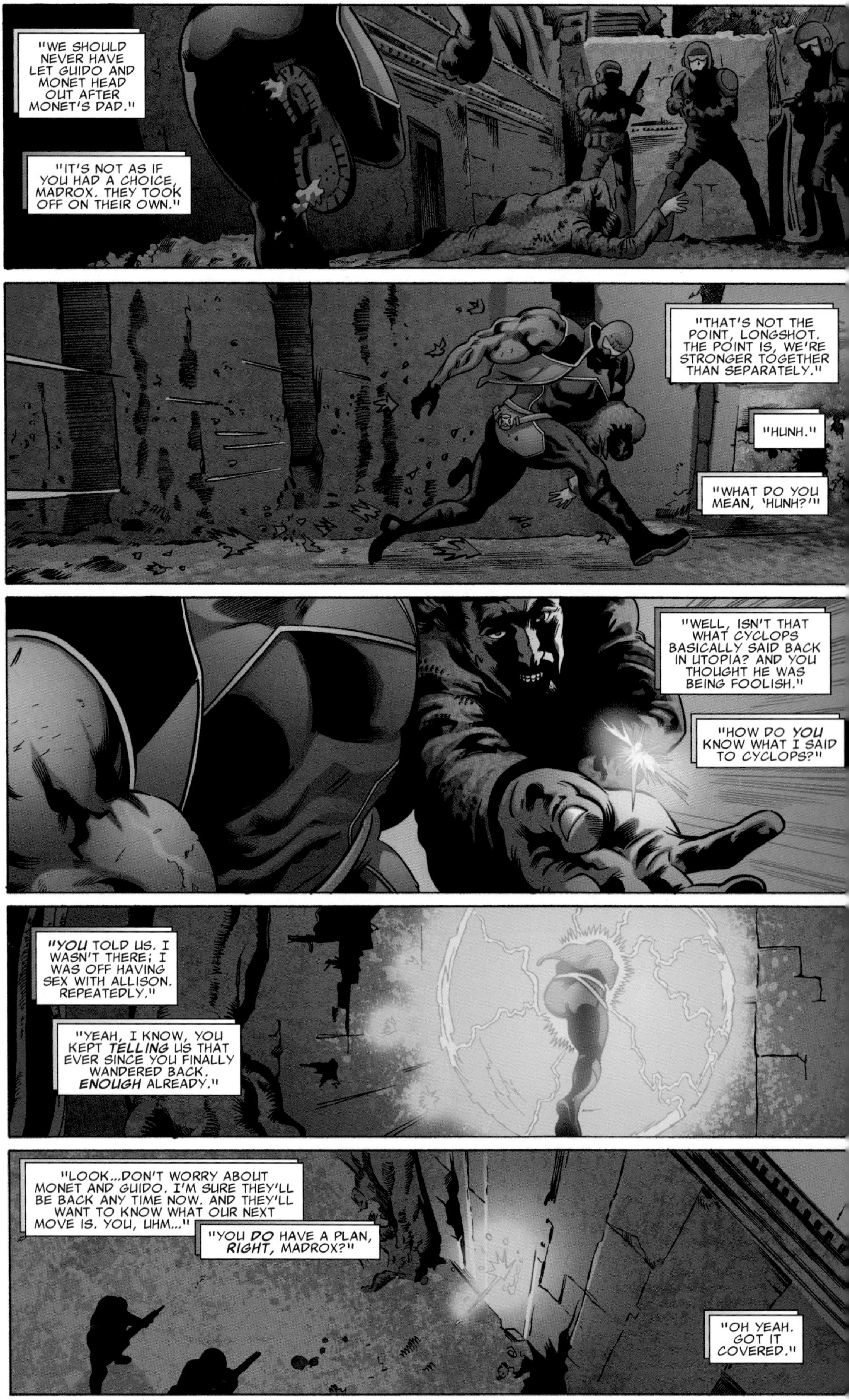
"WE SHOULD NEVER HAVE LET GUIDO AND MONET HEAD OUT AFTER MONET'S DAD."
"IT'S NOT AS IF YOU HAD A CHOICE, MADROX. THEY TOOK OFF ON THEIR OWN."
"THAT'S NOT THE POINT, LONGSHOT. THE POINT IS, WE'RE STRONGER TOGETHER THAN SEPARATELY."
"HUNH."
"WHAT DO YOU MEAN, 'HUNH?'"
"WELL, ISN'T THAT WHAT CYCLOPS BASICALLY SAID BACK IN UTOPIA? AND YOU THOUGHT HE WAS BEING FOOLISH."
"HOW DO *YOU* KNOW WHAT I SAID TO CYCLOPS?"
"*YOU* TOLD US. I WASN'T THERE; I WAS OFF HAVING SEX WITH ALLISON. REPEATEDLY."
"YEAH, I KNOW, YOU KEPT ***TELLING*** US THAT EVER SINCE YOU FINALLY WANDERED BACK. ***ENOUGH*** ALREADY."
"LOOK...DON'T WORRY ABOUT MONET AND GUIDO. I'M SURE THEY'LL BE BACK ANY TIME NOW. AND THEY'LL WANT TO KNOW WHAT OUR NEXT MOVE IS. YOU, UHM..."
"YOU ***DO*** HAVE A PLAN, ***RIGHT***, MADROX?"
"OH YEAH. GOT IT COVERED."

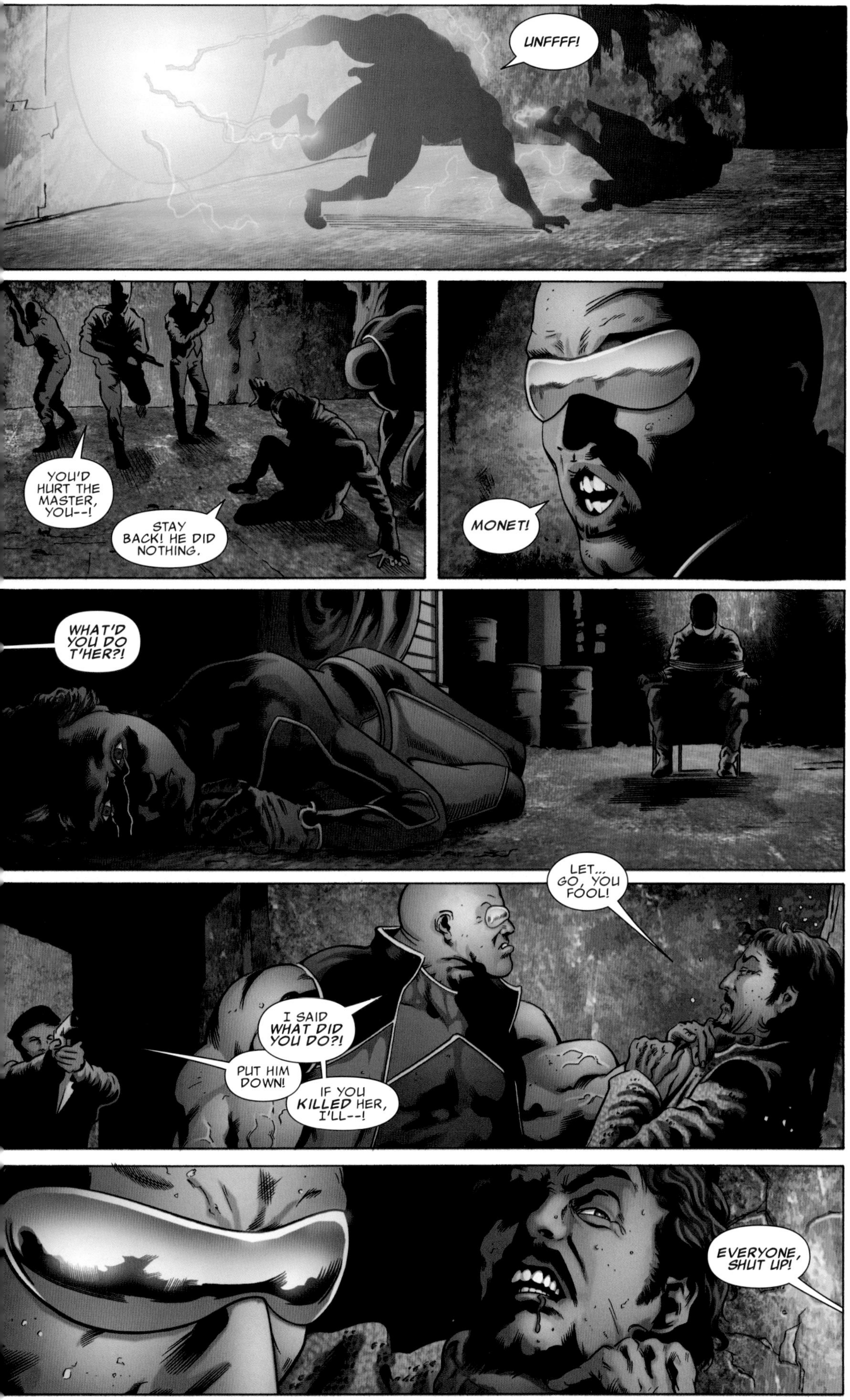
UNFFFF!
YOU'D HURT THE MASTER, YOU--!
STAY BACK! HE DID NOTHING.
MONET!
WHAT'D YOU DO T'HER?!
LET... GO, YOU FOOL!
I SAID WHAT DID YOU DO?!
PUT HIM DOWN!
IF YOU KILLED HER, I'LL--!
EVERYONE, SHUT UP!

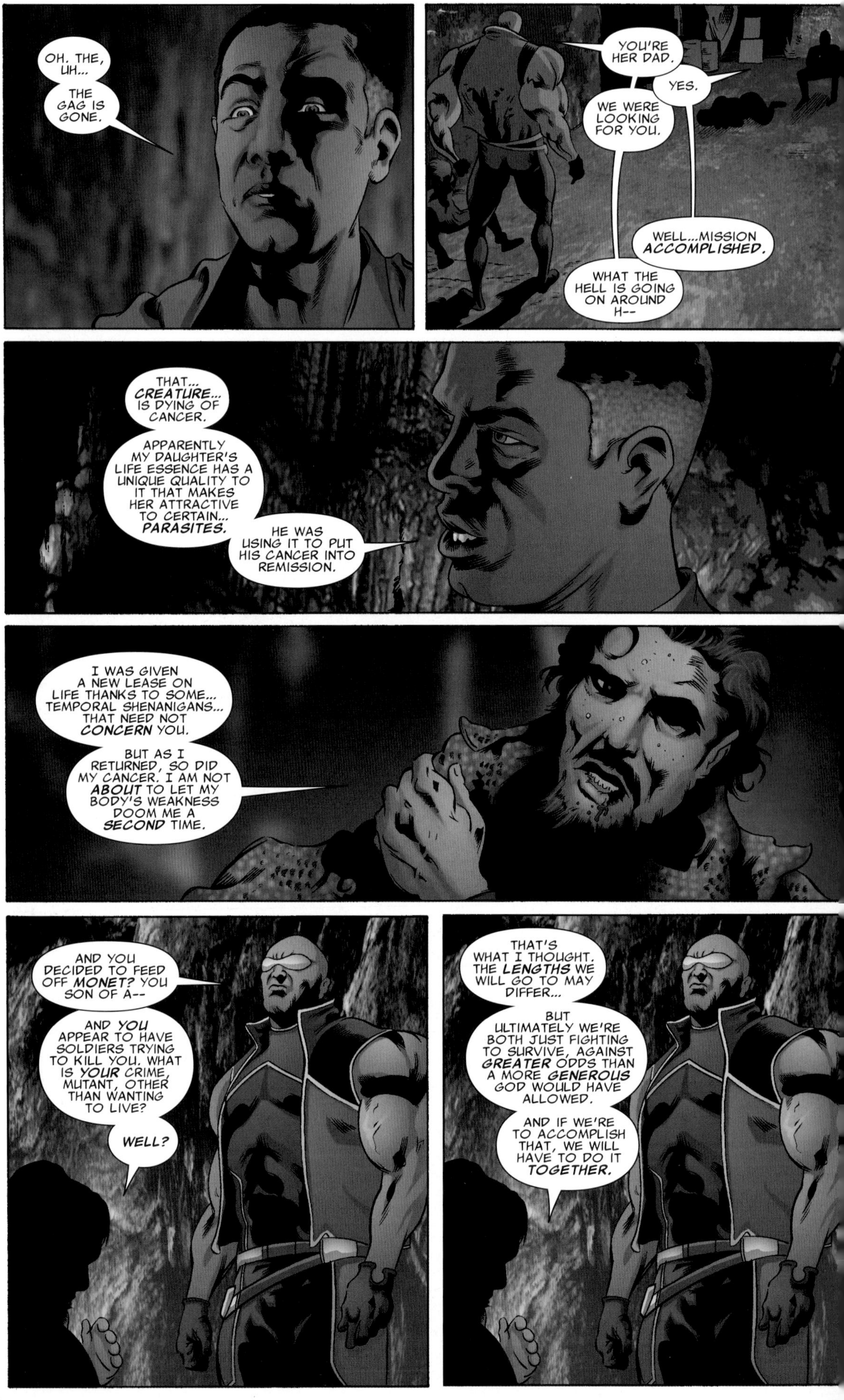
OH. THE, UH...
THE GAG IS GONE.
YOU'RE HER DAD.
YES.
WE WERE LOOKING FOR YOU.
WELL...MISSION ACCOMPLISHED.
WHAT THE HELL IS GOING ON AROUND H--
THAT... CREATURE... IS DYING OF CANCER.
APPARENTLY MY DAUGHTER'S LIFE ESSENCE HAS A UNIQUE QUALITY TO IT THAT MAKES HER ATTRACTIVE TO CERTAIN... PARASITES.
HE WAS USING IT TO PUT HIS CANCER INTO REMISSION.
I WAS GIVEN A NEW LEASE ON LIFE THANKS TO SOME... TEMPORAL SHENANIGANS... THAT NEED NOT CONCERN YOU.
BUT AS I RETURNED, SO DID MY CANCER. I AM NOT ABOUT TO LET MY BODY'S WEAKNESS DOOM ME A SECOND TIME.
AND YOU DECIDED TO FEED OFF MONET? YOU SON OF A--
AND YOU APPEAR TO HAVE SOLDIERS TRYING TO KILL YOU. WHAT IS YOUR CRIME, MUTANT, OTHER THAN WANTING TO LIVE?
WELL?
THAT'S WHAT I THOUGHT. THE LENGTHS WE WILL GO TO MAY DIFFER...
BUT ULTIMATELY WE'RE BOTH JUST FIGHTING TO SURVIVE, AGAINST GREATER ODDS THAN A MORE GENEROUS GOD WOULD HAVE ALLOWED.
AND IF WE'RE TO ACCOMPLISH THAT, WE WILL HAVE TO DO IT TOGETHER.

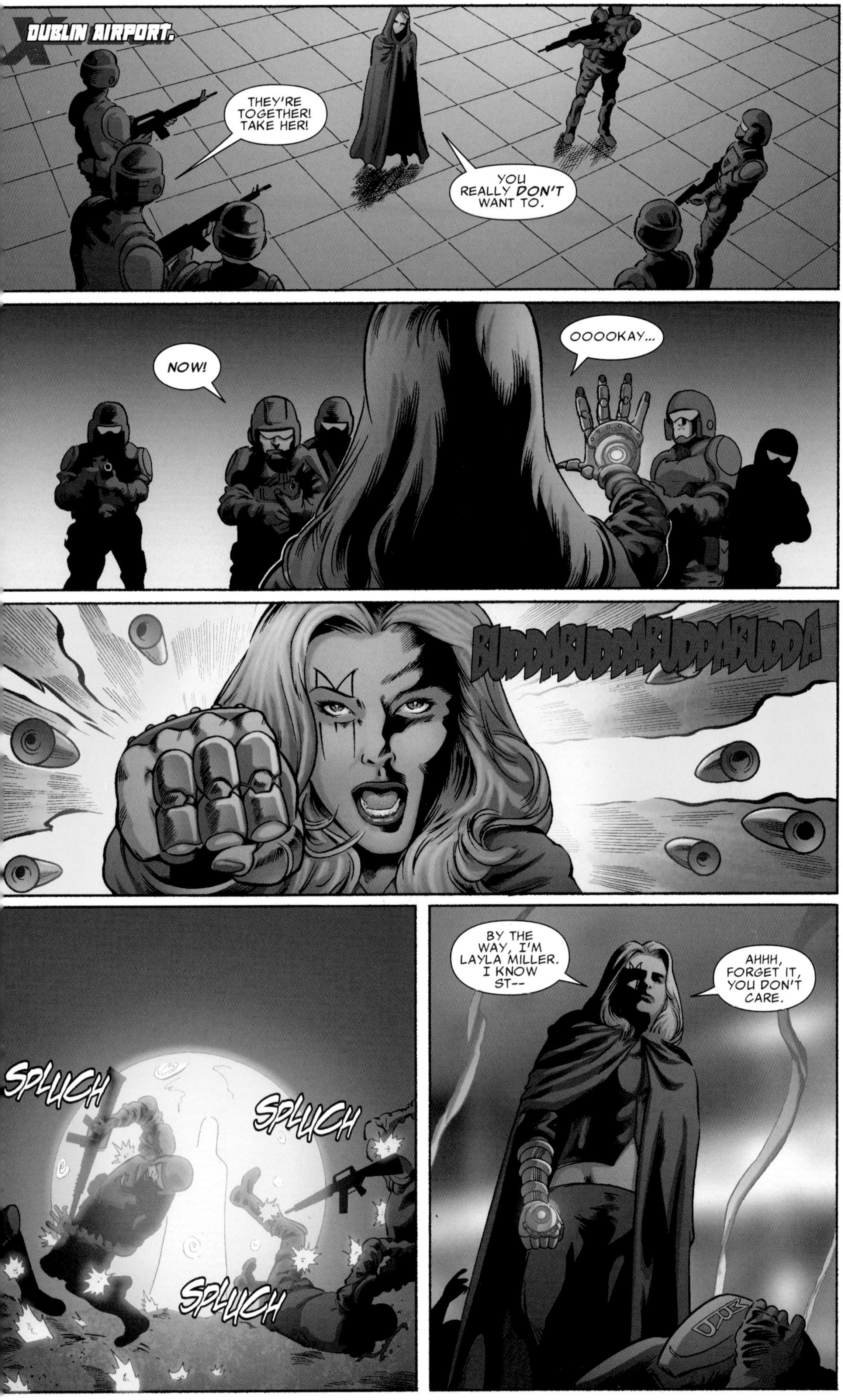
DUBLIN AIRPORT.
THEY'RE TOGETHER! TAKE HER!
YOU REALLY DON'T WANT TO.
NOW!
OOOOKAY...
BUDDABUDDABUDDABUDDA
SPLUCH
SPLUCH
SPLUCH
BY THE WAY, I'M LAYLA MILLER. I KNOW ST--
AHHH, FORGET IT, YOU DON'T CARE.

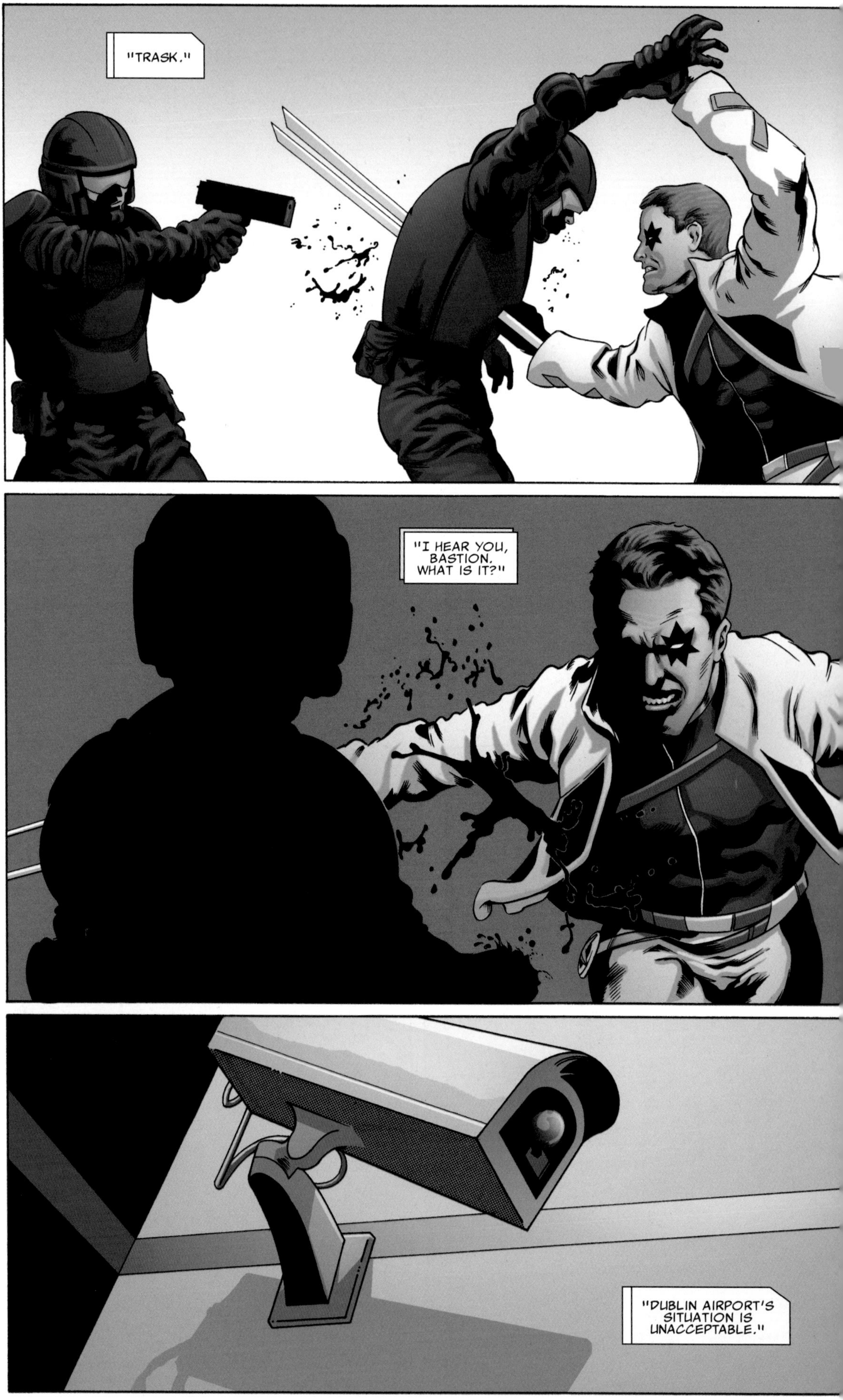
"TRASK."
"I HEAR YOU, BASTION. WHAT IS IT?"
"DUBLIN AIRPORT'S SITUATION IS UNACCEPTABLE."

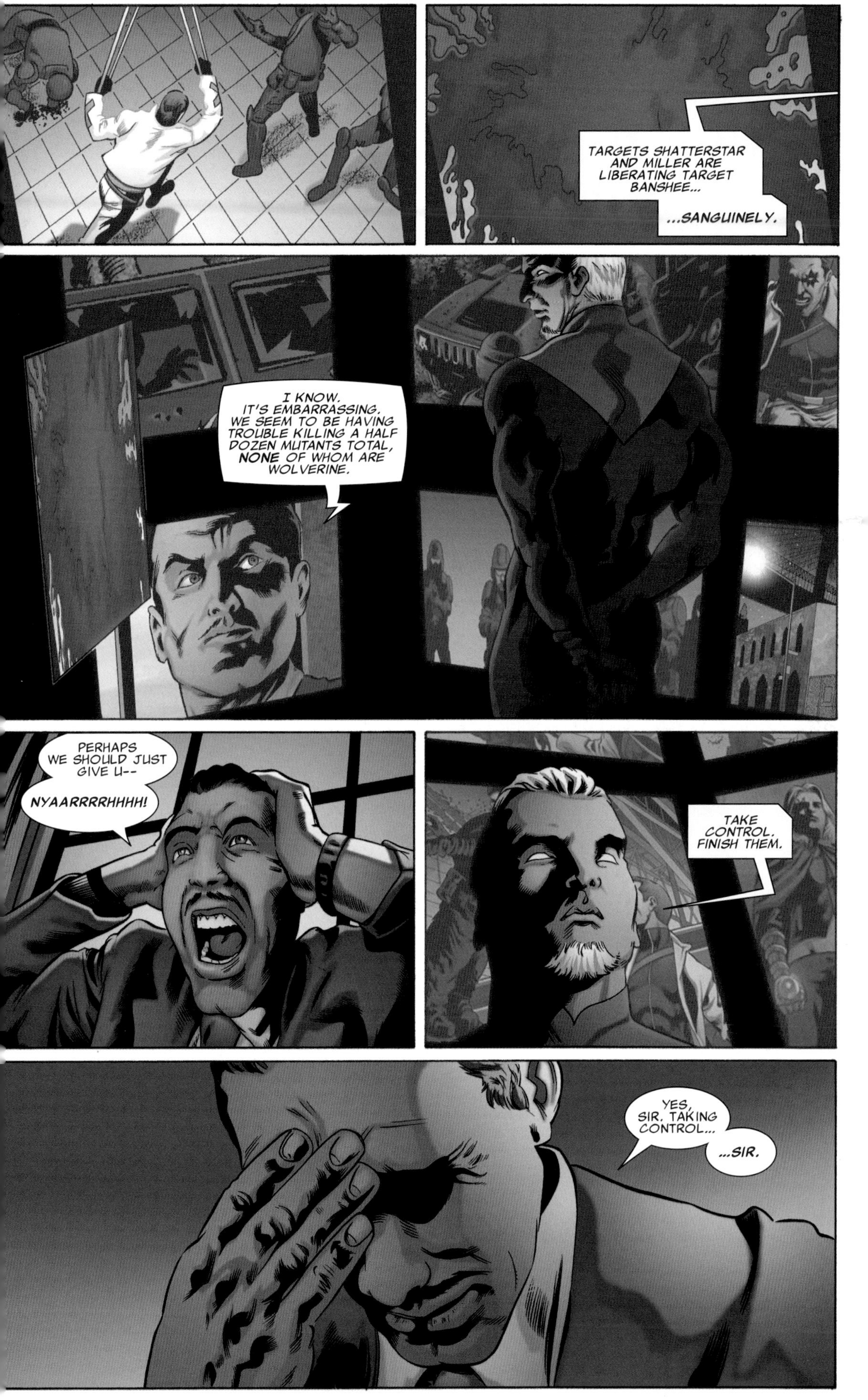
TARGETS SHATTERSTAR AND MILLER ARE LIBERATING TARGET BANSHEE...
...SANGUINELY.
I KNOW. IT'S EMBARRASSING. WE SEEM TO BE HAVING TROUBLE KILLING A HALF DOZEN MUTANTS TOTAL, NONE OF WHOM ARE WOLVERINE.
PERHAPS WE SHOULD JUST GIVE U--
NYAARRRRHHHH!
TAKE CONTROL. FINISH THEM.
YES, SIR. TAKING CONTROL...
...SIR.

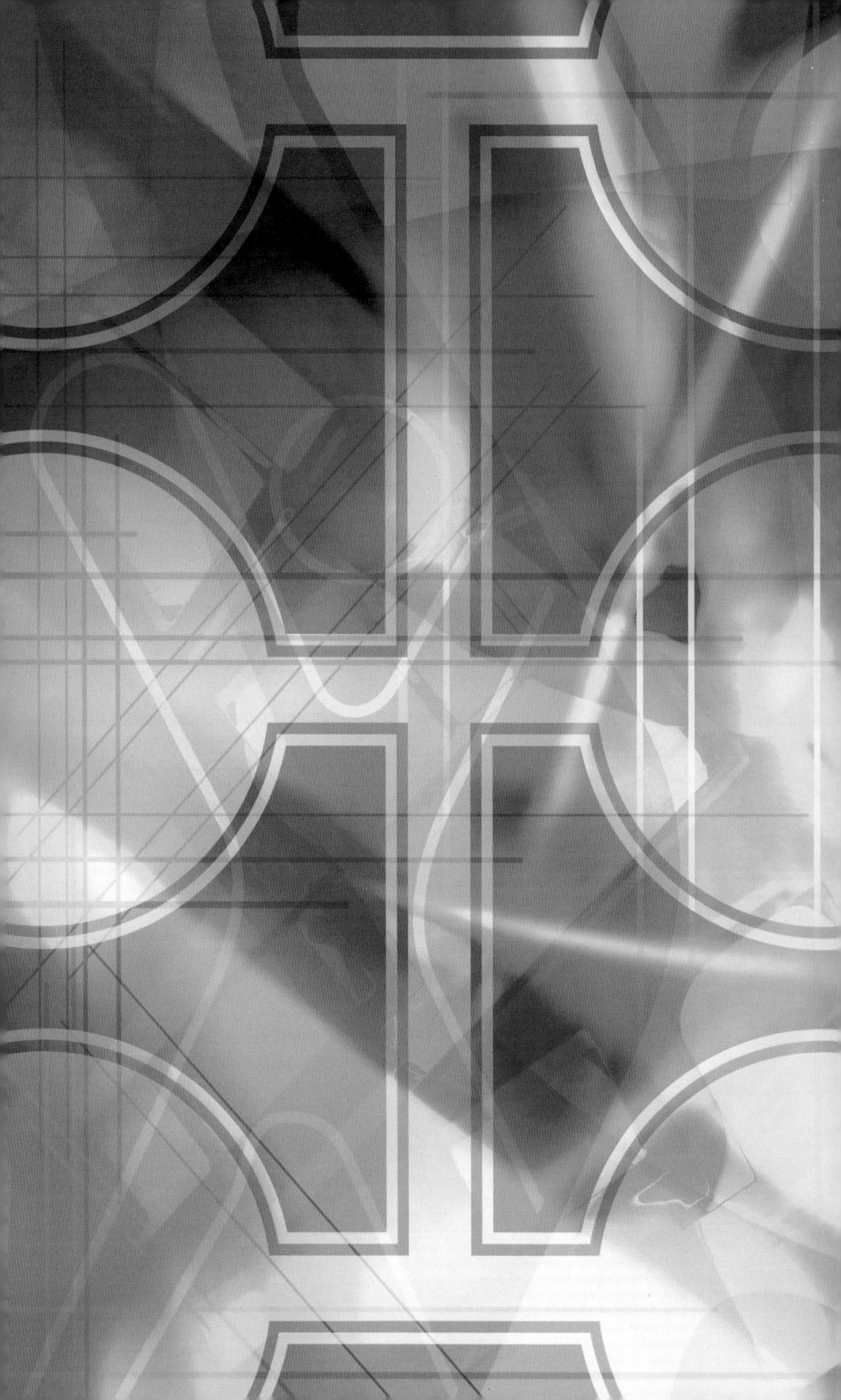

#206

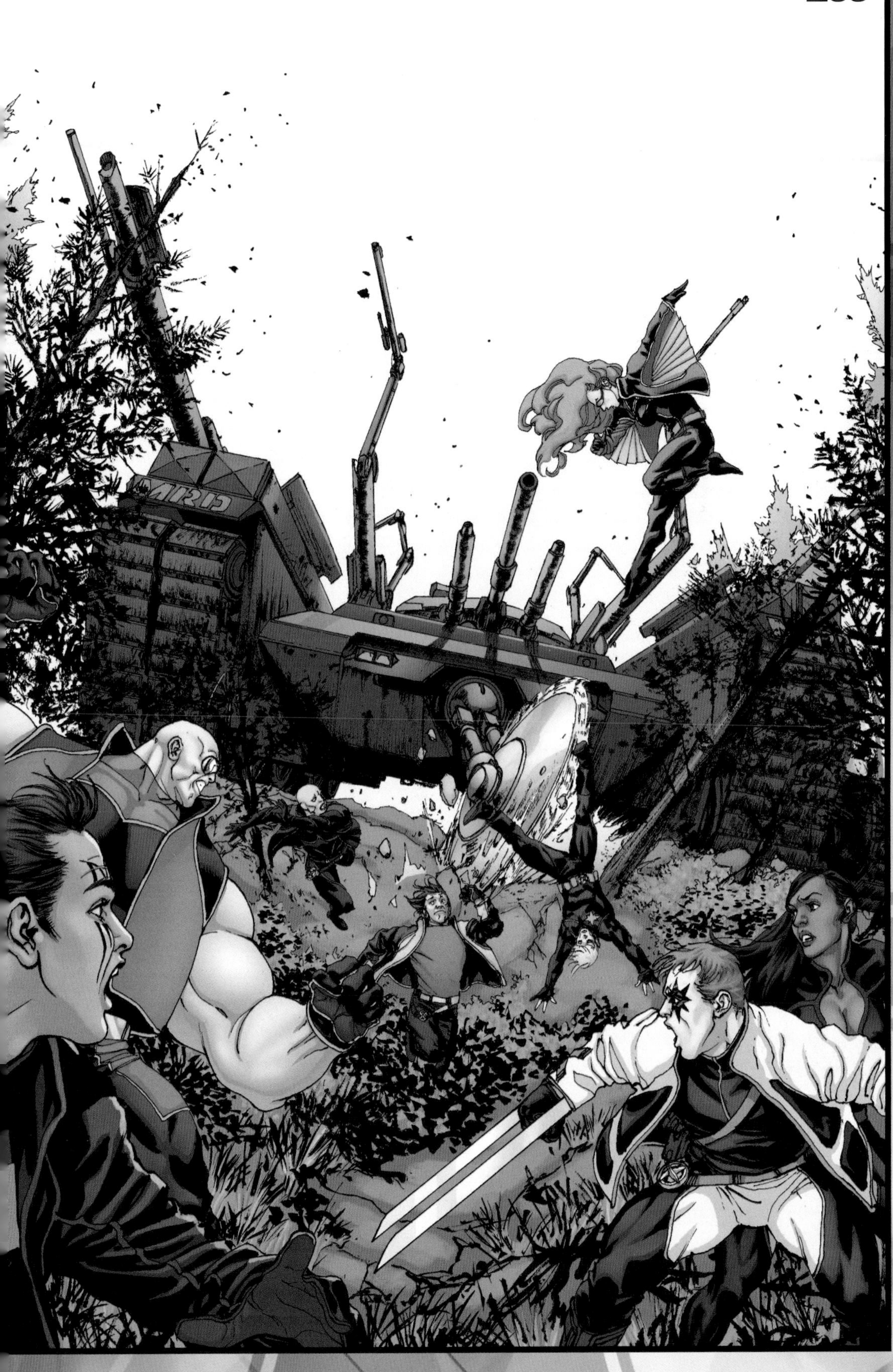

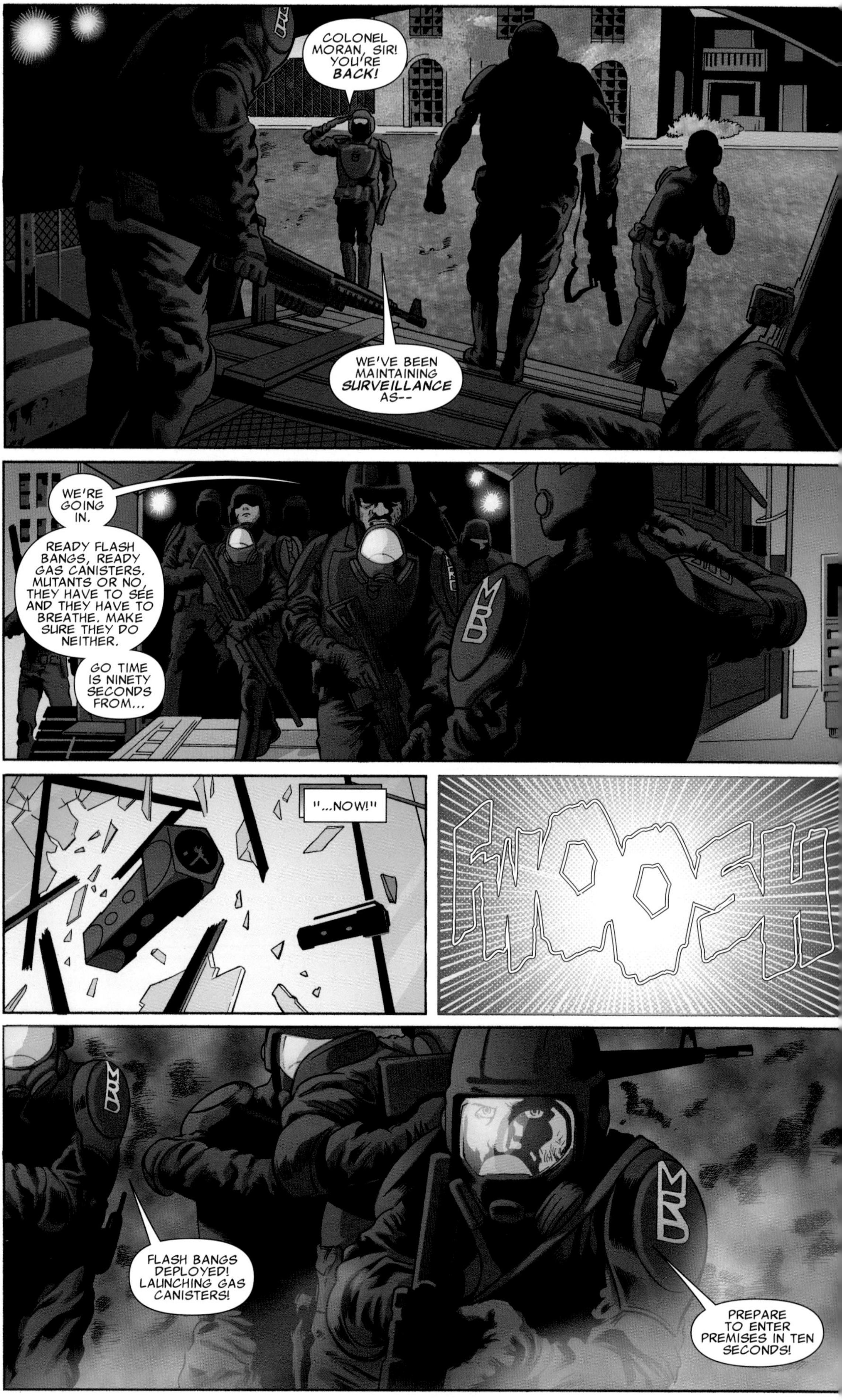
COLONEL MORAN, SIR! YOU'RE BACK!
WE'VE BEEN MAINTAINING SURVEILLANCE AS--
WE'RE GOING IN.
READY FLASH BANGS, READY GAS CANISTERS. MUTANTS OR NO, THEY HAVE TO SEE AND THEY HAVE TO BREATHE. MAKE SURE THEY DO NEITHER.
GO TIME IS NINETY SECONDS FROM...
"...NOW!"
FLASH BANGS DEPLOYED! LAUNCHING GAS CANISTERS!
PREPARE TO ENTER PREMISES IN TEN SECONDS!

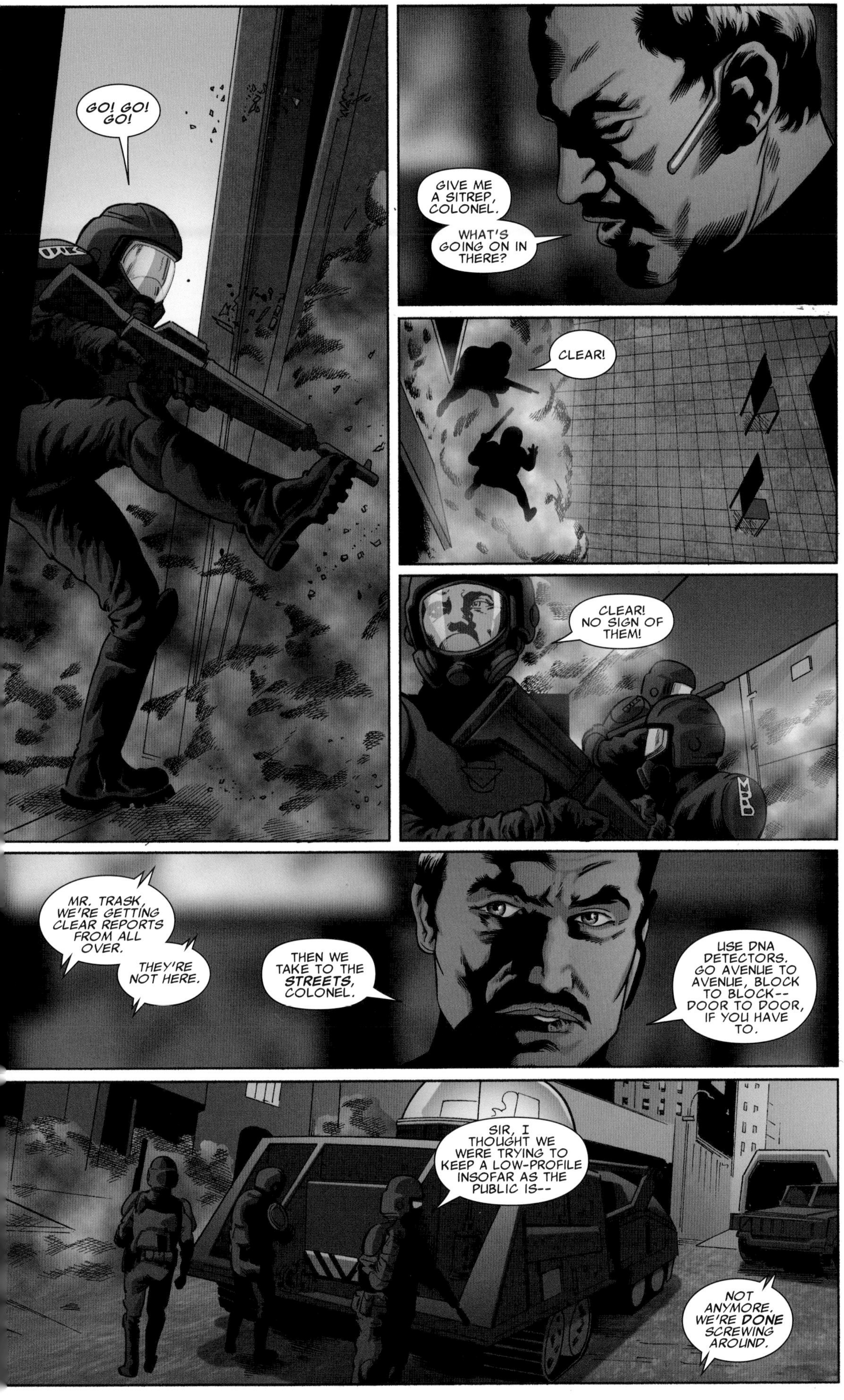
GO! GO! GO!
GIVE ME A SITREP, COLONEL.
WHAT'S GOING ON IN THERE?
CLEAR!
CLEAR! NO SIGN OF THEM!
MR. TRASK, WE'RE GETTING CLEAR REPORTS FROM ALL OVER.
THEY'RE NOT HERE.
THEN WE TAKE TO THE STREETS, COLONEL.
USE DNA DETECTORS. GO AVENUE TO AVENUE, BLOCK TO BLOCK-- DOOR TO DOOR, IF YOU HAVE TO.
SIR, I THOUGHT WE WERE TRYING TO KEEP A LOW-PROFILE INSOFAR AS THE PUBLIC IS--
NOT ANYMORE. WE'RE DONE SCREWING AROUND.

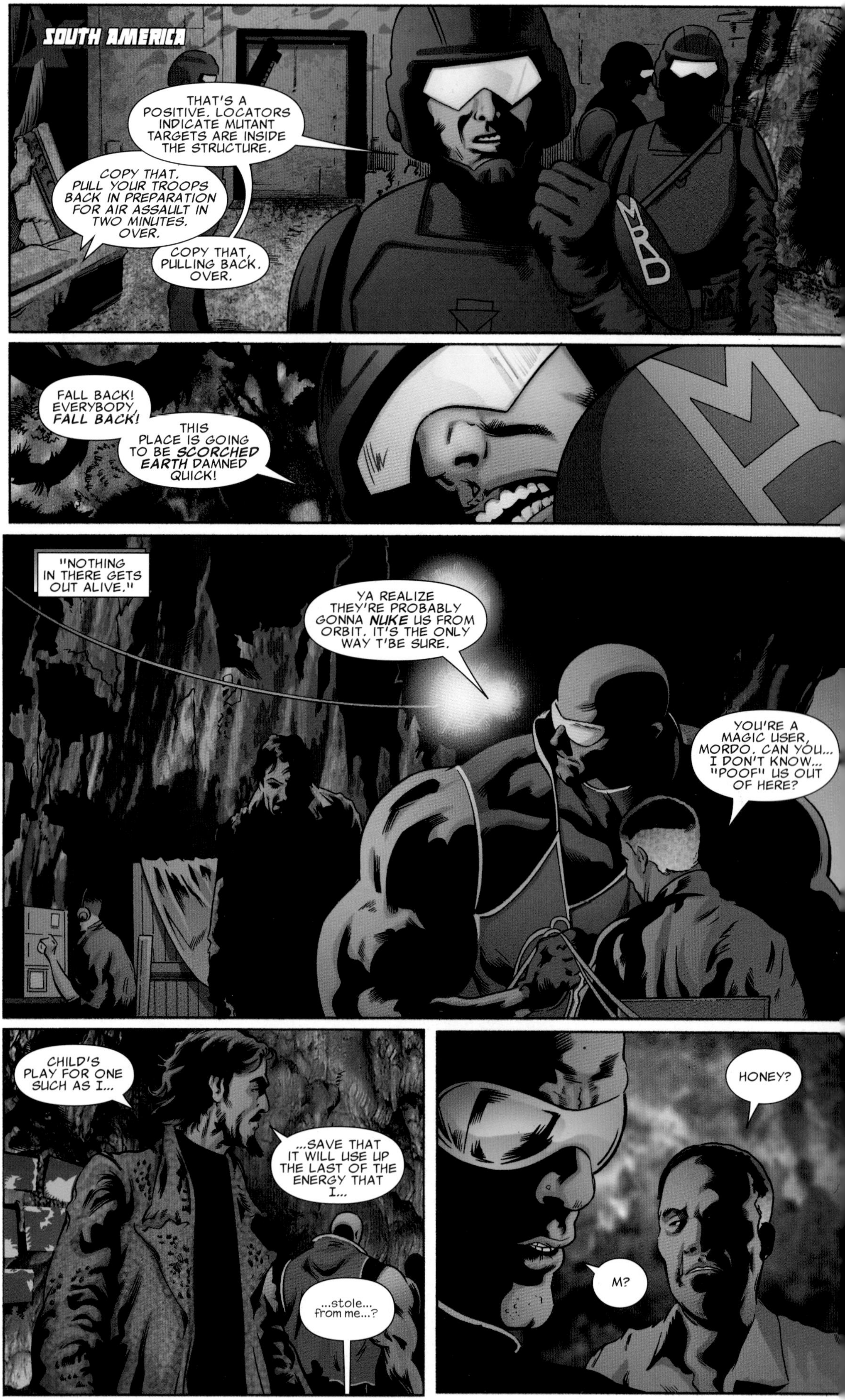
SOUTH AMERICA
THAT'S A POSITIVE. LOCATORS INDICATE MUTANT TARGETS ARE INSIDE THE STRUCTURE.
COPY THAT. PULL YOUR TROOPS BACK IN PREPARATION FOR AIR ASSAULT IN TWO MINUTES. OVER.
COPY THAT, PULLING BACK. OVER.
FALL BACK! EVERYBODY, FALL BACK!
THIS PLACE IS GOING TO BE SCORCHED EARTH DAMNED QUICK!
"NOTHING IN THERE GETS OUT ALIVE."
YA REALIZE THEY'RE PROBABLY GONNA NUKE US FROM ORBIT. IT'S THE ONLY WAY T'BE SURE.
YOU'RE A MAGIC USER, MORDO. CAN YOU... I DON'T KNOW... "POOF" US OUT OF HERE?
CHILD'S PLAY FOR ONE SUCH AS I...
...SAVE THAT IT WILL USE UP THE LAST OF THE ENERGY THAT I...
...stole... from me...?
HONEY?
M?

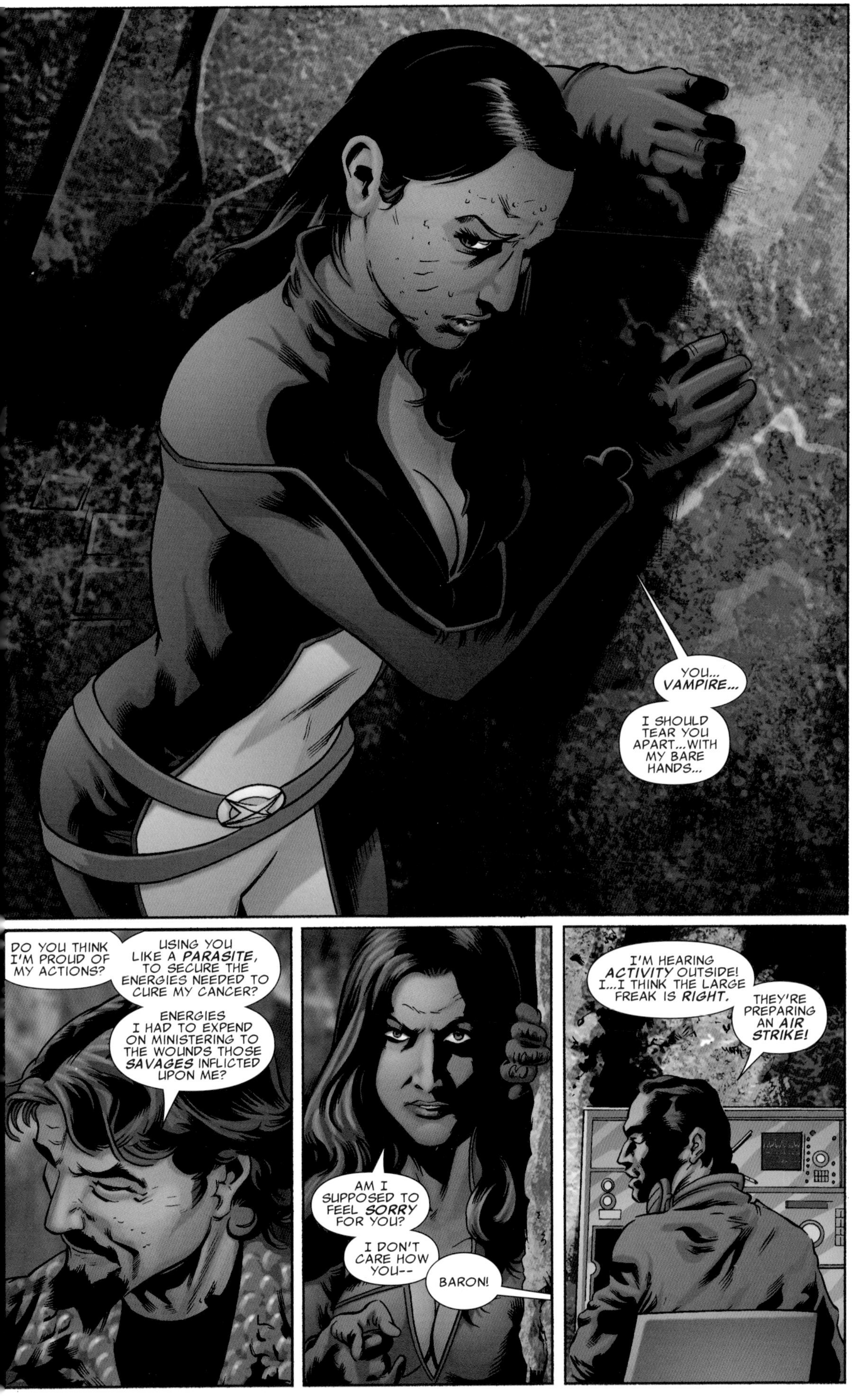

YOU... VAMPIRE...
I SHOULD TEAR YOU APART...WITH MY BARE HANDS...
DO YOU THINK I'M PROUD OF MY ACTIONS?
USING YOU LIKE A PARASITE, TO SECURE THE ENERGIES NEEDED TO CURE MY CANCER?
ENERGIES I HAD TO EXPEND ON MINISTERING TO THE WOUNDS THOSE SAVAGES INFLICTED UPON ME?
AM I SUPPOSED TO FEEL SORRY FOR YOU?
I DON'T CARE HOW YOU--
BARON!
I'M HEARING ACTIVITY OUTSIDE! I...I THINK THE LARGE FREAK IS RIGHT.
THEY'RE PREPARING AN AIR STRIKE!

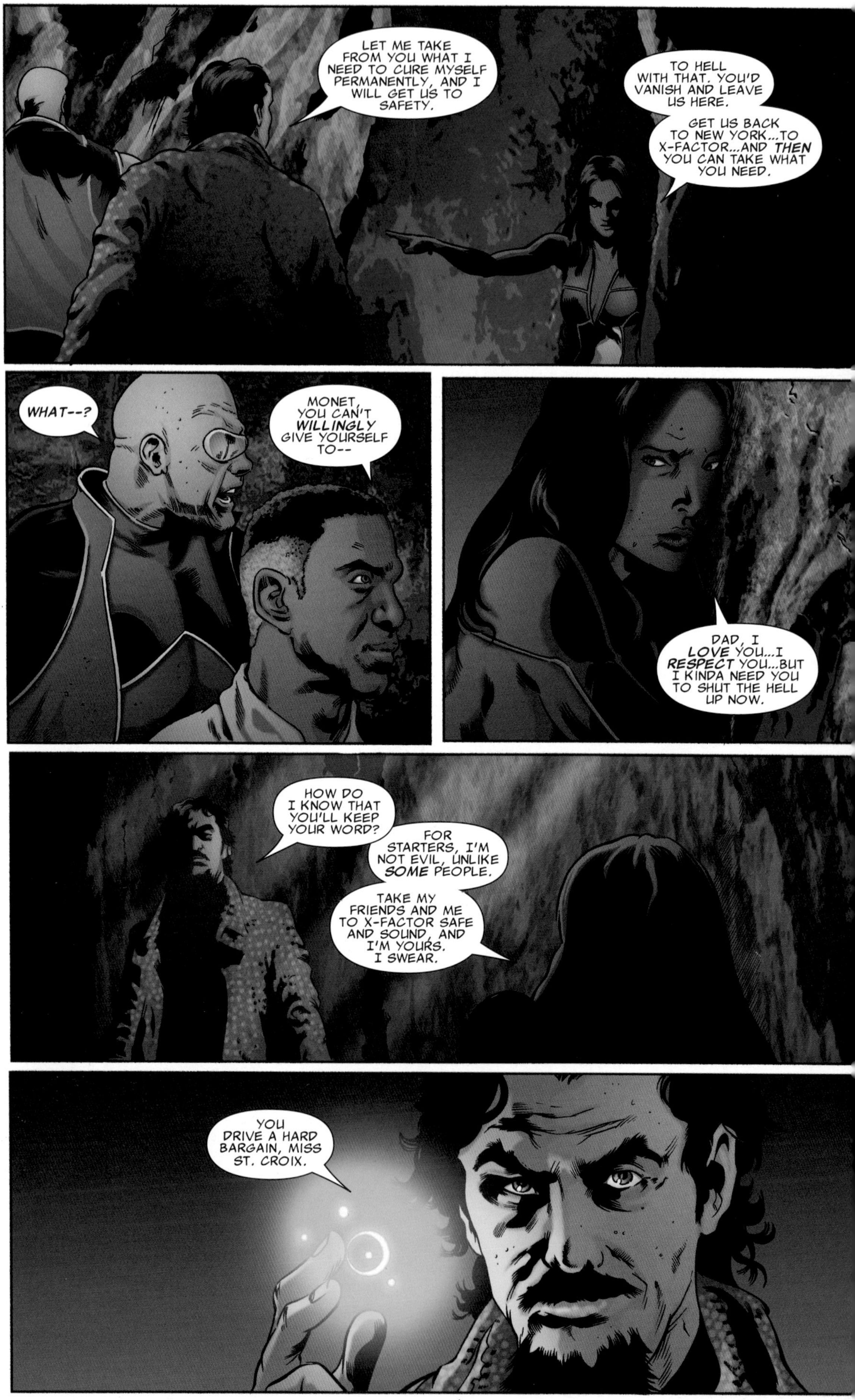
LET ME TAKE FROM YOU WHAT I NEED TO CURE MYSELF PERMANENTLY, AND I WILL GET US TO SAFETY.
TO HELL WITH THAT. YOU'D VANISH AND LEAVE US HERE.
GET US BACK TO NEW YORK...TO X-FACTOR...AND *THEN* YOU CAN TAKE WHAT YOU NEED.
WHAT--?
MONET, YOU CAN'T *WILLINGLY* GIVE YOURSELF TO--
DAD, I *LOVE* YOU...I *RESPECT* YOU...BUT I KINDA NEED YOU TO SHUT THE HELL UP NOW.
HOW DO I KNOW THAT YOU'LL KEEP YOUR WORD?
FOR STARTERS, I'M NOT EVIL, UNLIKE *SOME* PEOPLE.
TAKE MY FRIENDS AND ME TO X-FACTOR SAFE AND SOUND, AND I'M YOURS. I SWEAR.
YOU DRIVE A HARD BARGAIN, MISS ST. CROIX.

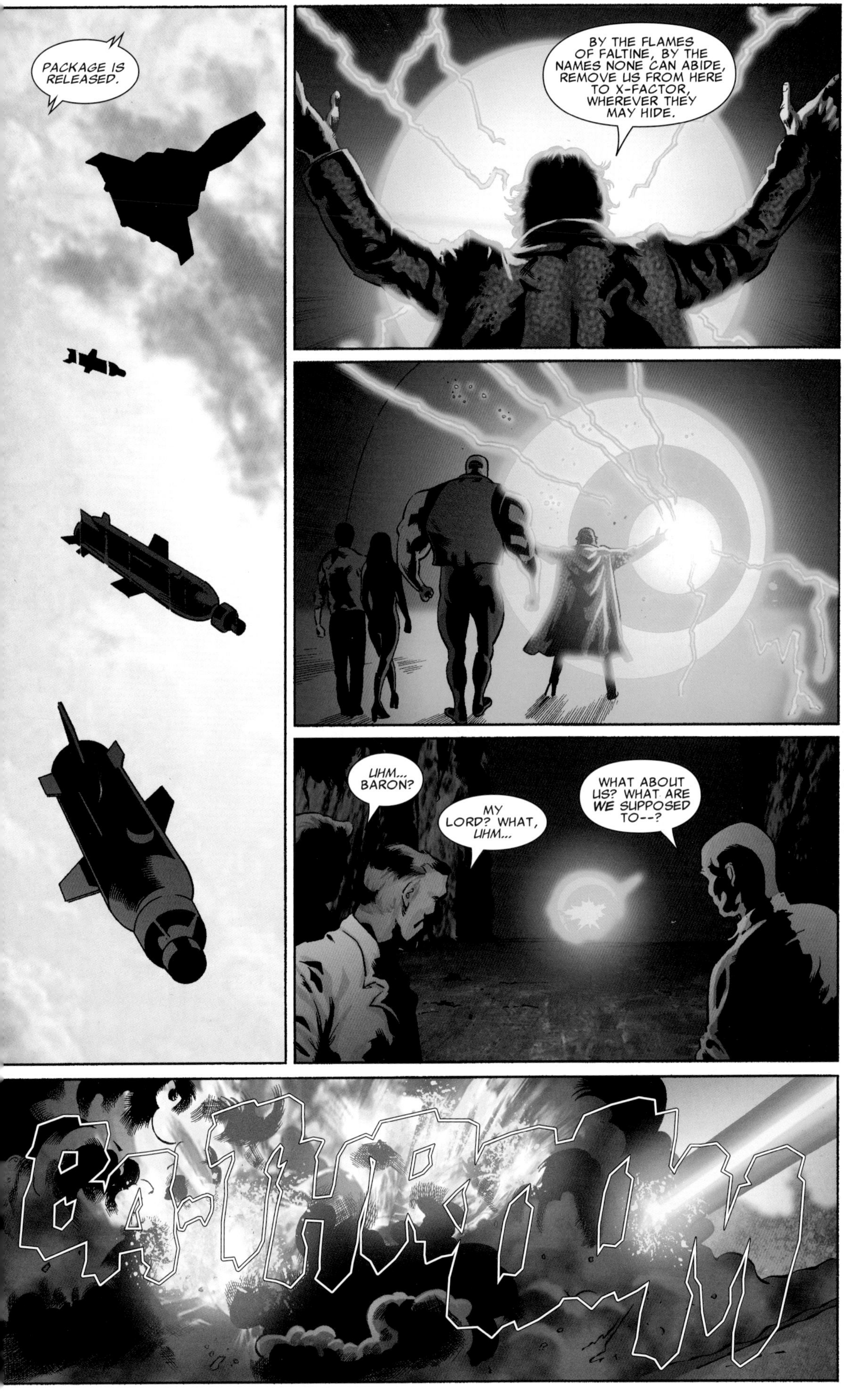
PACKAGE IS RELEASED.
BY THE FLAMES OF FALTINE, BY THE NAMES NONE CAN ABIDE, REMOVE US FROM HERE TO X-FACTOR, WHEREVER THEY MAY HIDE.
UHM... BARON?
MY LORD? WHAT, UHM...
WHAT ABOUT US? WHAT ARE WE SUPPOSED TO--?

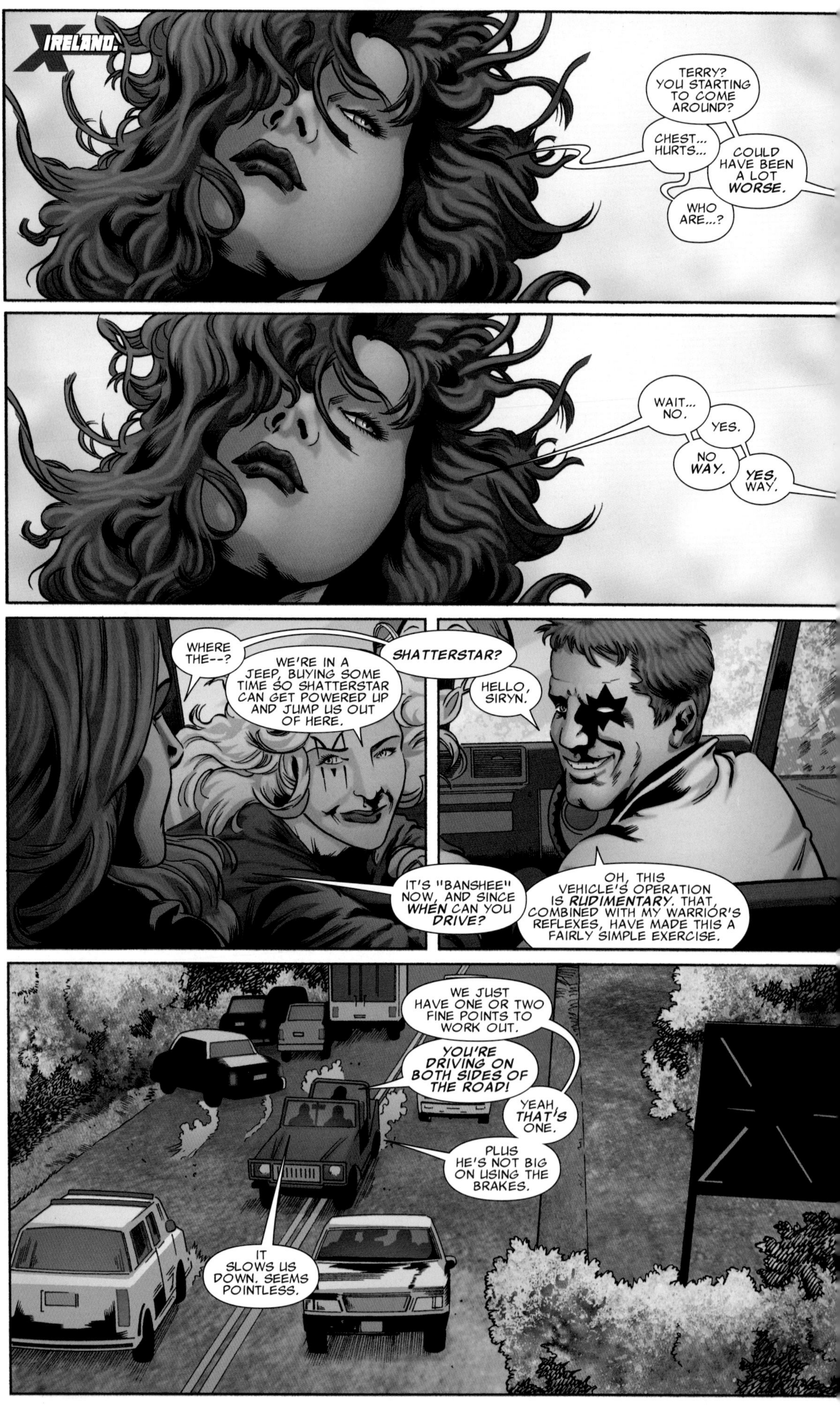
IRELAND.
TERRY? YOU STARTING TO COME AROUND?
CHEST... HURTS...
COULD HAVE BEEN A LOT WORSE.
WHO ARE...?
WAIT... NO.
YES.
NO WAY.
YES, WAY.
WHERE THE--?
WE'RE IN A JEEP, BUYING SOME TIME SO SHATTERSTAR CAN GET POWERED UP AND JUMP US OUT OF HERE.
SHATTERSTAR?
HELLO, SIRYN.
IT'S "BANSHEE" NOW, AND SINCE WHEN CAN YOU DRIVE?
OH, THIS VEHICLE'S OPERATION IS RUDIMENTARY. THAT, COMBINED WITH MY WARRIOR'S REFLEXES, HAVE MADE THIS A FAIRLY SIMPLE EXERCISE.
WE JUST HAVE ONE OR TWO FINE POINTS TO WORK OUT.
YOU'RE DRIVING ON BOTH SIDES OF THE ROAD!
YEAH, THAT'S ONE.
PLUS HE'S NOT BIG ON USING THE BRAKES.
IT SLOWS US DOWN. SEEMS POINTLESS.

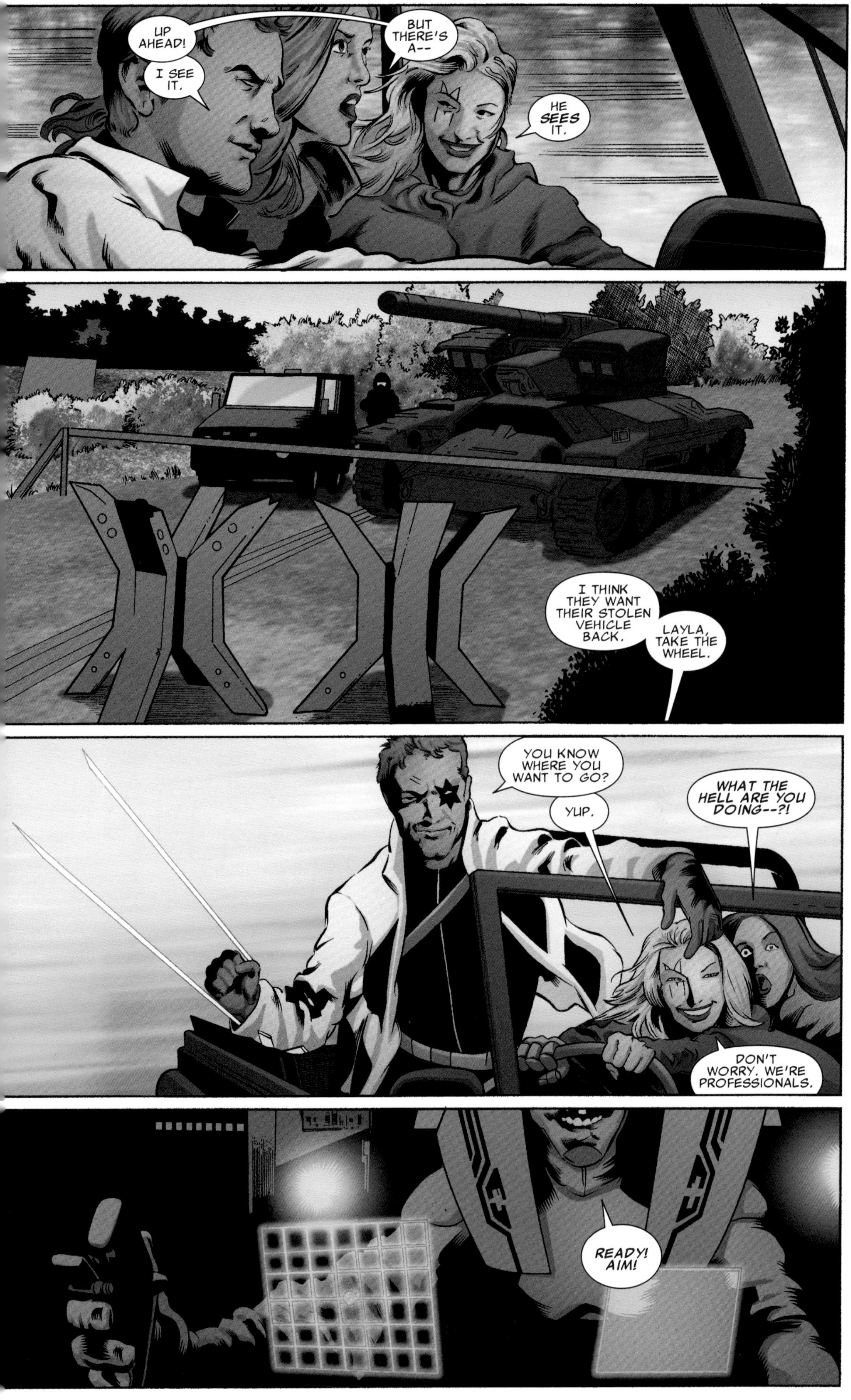
UP AHEAD!
BUT THERE'S A--
I SEE IT.
HE SEES IT.
I THINK THEY WANT THEIR STOLEN VEHICLE BACK.
LAYLA, TAKE THE WHEEL.
YOU KNOW WHERE YOU WANT TO GO?
YUP.
WHAT THE HELL ARE YOU DOING--?!
DON'T WORRY. WE'RE PROFESSIONALS.
READY! AIM!

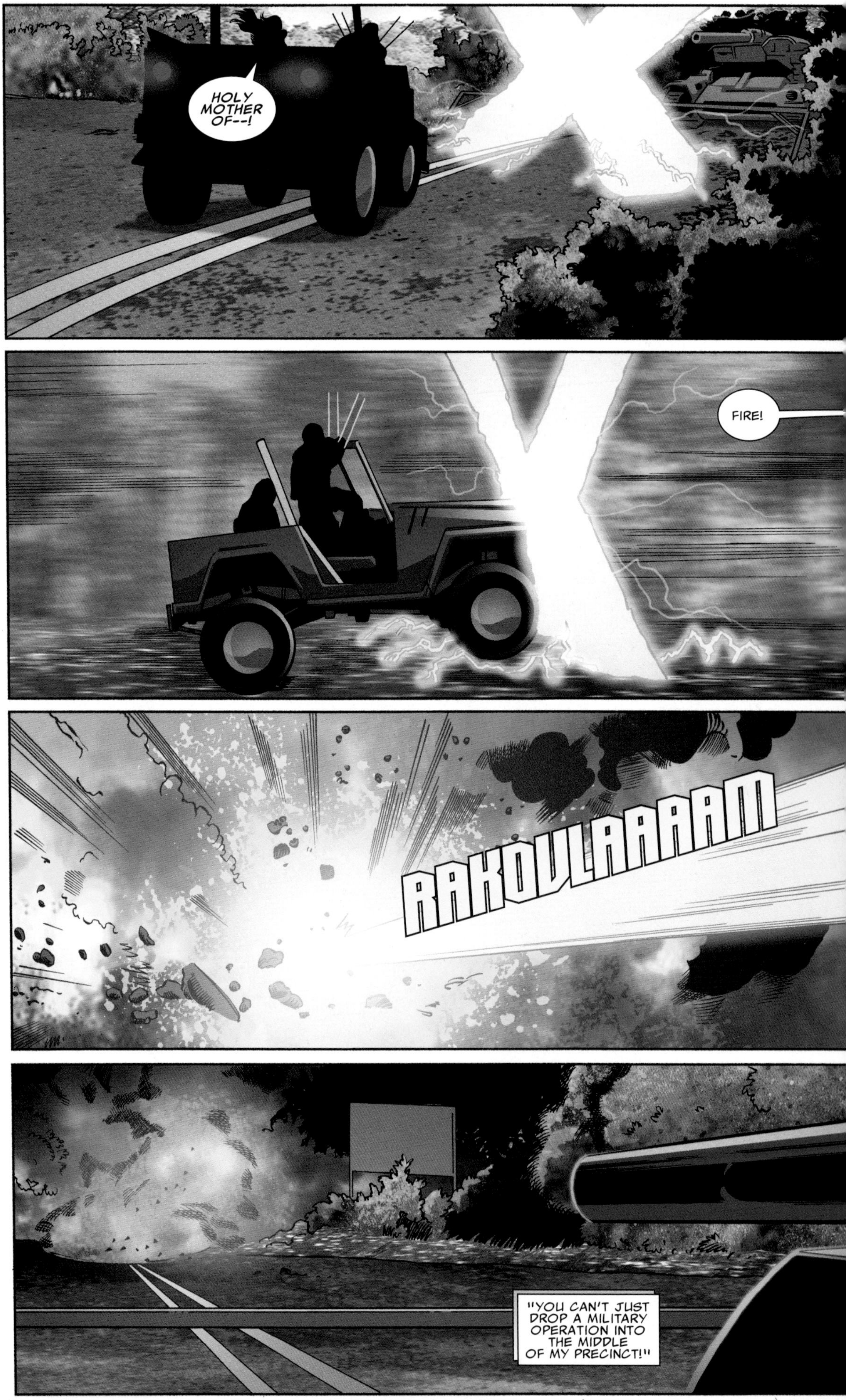
HOLY MOTHER OF--!
FIRE!
RAKOOLAAAAM
"YOU CAN'T JUST DROP A MILITARY OPERATION INTO THE MIDDLE OF MY PRECINCT!"

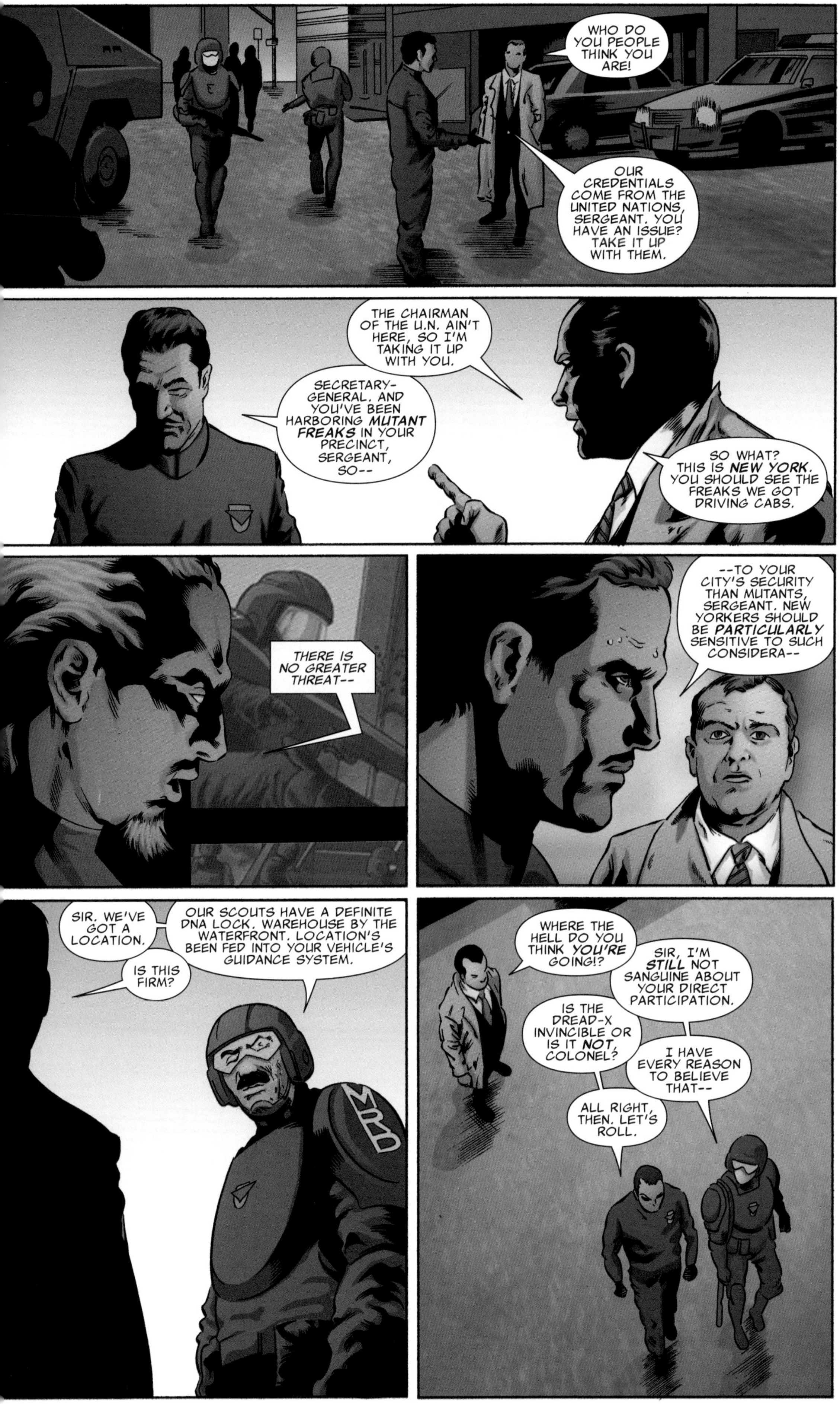
WHO DO YOU PEOPLE THINK YOU ARE!
OUR CREDENTIALS COME FROM THE UNITED NATIONS, SERGEANT. YOU HAVE AN ISSUE? TAKE IT UP WITH THEM.
THE CHAIRMAN OF THE U.N. AIN'T HERE, SO I'M TAKING IT UP WITH YOU.
SECRETARY-GENERAL. AND YOU'VE BEEN HARBORING MUTANT FREAKS IN YOUR PRECINCT, SERGEANT, SO--
SO WHAT? THIS IS NEW YORK. YOU SHOULD SEE THE FREAKS WE GOT DRIVING CABS.
THERE IS NO GREATER THREAT--
--TO YOUR CITY'S SECURITY THAN MUTANTS, SERGEANT. NEW YORKERS SHOULD BE PARTICULARLY SENSITIVE TO SUCH CONSIDERA--
SIR. WE'VE GOT A LOCATION.
IS THIS FIRM?
OUR SCOUTS HAVE A DEFINITE DNA LOCK. WAREHOUSE BY THE WATERFRONT. LOCATION'S BEEN FED INTO YOUR VEHICLE'S GUIDANCE SYSTEM.
MRD
WHERE THE HELL DO YOU THINK YOU'RE GOING!?
SIR, I'M STILL NOT SANGUINE ABOUT YOUR DIRECT PARTICIPATION.
IS THE DREAD-X INVINCIBLE OR IS IT NOT, COLONEL?
I HAVE EVERY REASON TO BELIEVE THAT--
ALL RIGHT, THEN. LET'S ROLL.

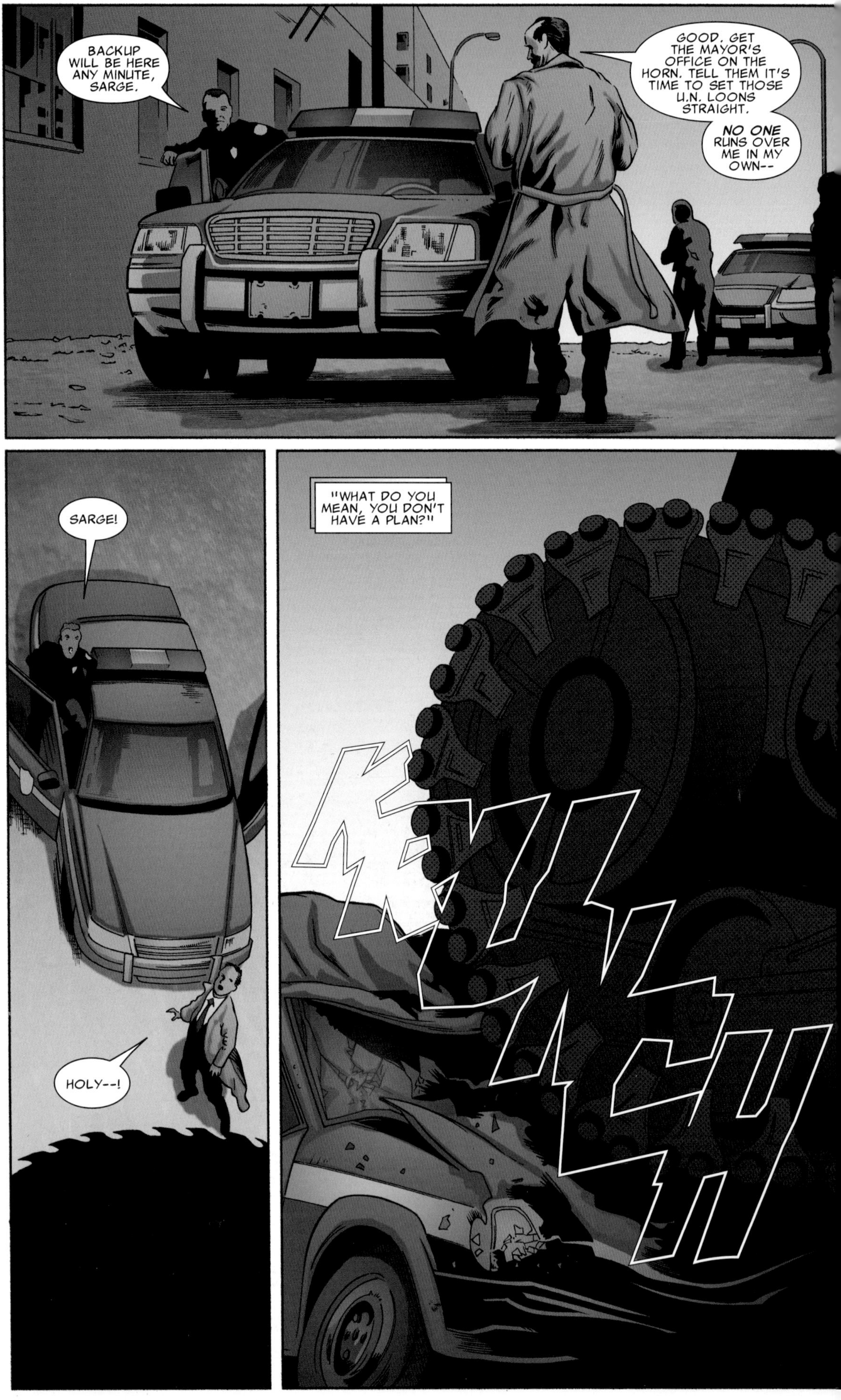
BACKUP WILL BE HERE ANY MINUTE, SARGE.
GOOD. GET THE MAYOR'S OFFICE ON THE HORN. TELL THEM IT'S TIME TO SET THOSE U.N. LOONS STRAIGHT.
NO ONE RUNS OVER ME IN MY OWN--
SARGE!
HOLY--!
"WHAT DO YOU MEAN, YOU DON'T HAVE A PLAN?"
KRUNCH

YOU CREATED THIS "SAFEHOUSE" AS A BACKUP SHOULD SOMETHING LIKE THIS OCCUR.

IF YOU ANTICIPATED THIS EVENTUALITY, MADROX, THEN YOU *MUST* HAVE PLANNED FOR WHAT HAPPENED NEXT.

YEAH, RICTOR, YOU'D *THINK* THAT, WOULDN'T YOU.

SO WE GOT NOTHING IS WHAT YOU'RE SAYING.

I DIDN'T THINK WE'D BE *DOWN* HALF THE TEAM!

BUT WHAT IF THE MRD TRACKS US HERE!

DON'T WORRY. QUALITY, *NOT* QUANTITY, IS WHAT'S IMPORTANT.

OH, SO SAYS *LUCK BOY.*

SO SAY I, YES.

WELL, WHY DON'T YOU TURN THAT LUCK OF YOURS TO GETTING US SOME *REINFORCEMENTS?*

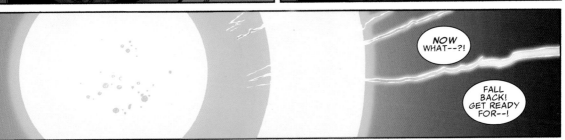

NOW WHAT--?!

FALL BACK! GET READY FOR--!

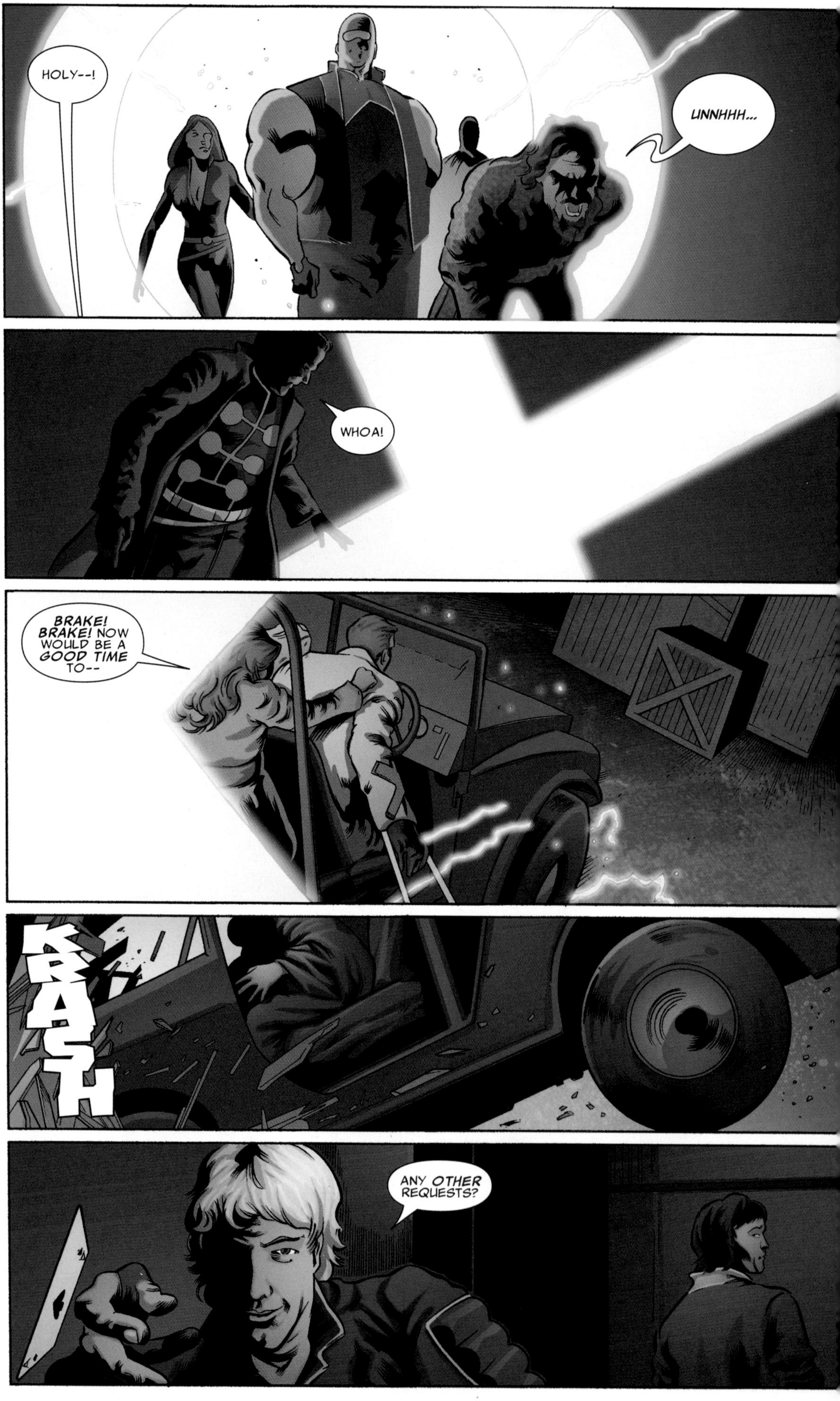
HOLY--!
UNNHHH...
WHOA!
BRAKE! BRAKE! NOW WOULD BE A GOOD TIME TO--
KRASH
ANY OTHER REQUESTS?

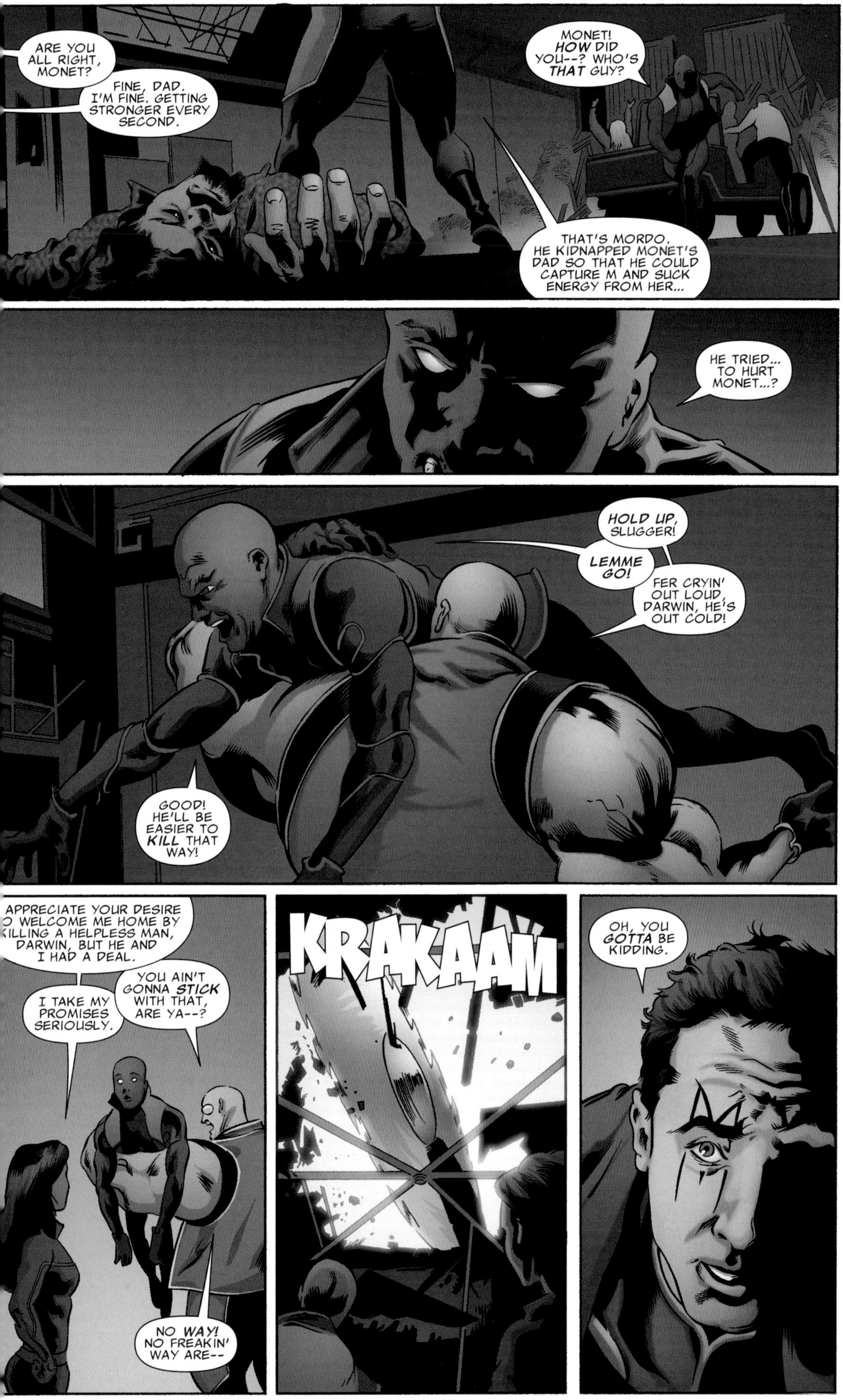
ARE YOU ALL RIGHT, MONET?
FINE, DAD. I'M FINE. GETTING STRONGER EVERY SECOND.
MONET! HOW DID YOU--? WHO'S THAT GUY?
THAT'S MORDO. HE KIDNAPPED MONET'S DAD SO THAT HE COULD CAPTURE M AND SUCK ENERGY FROM HER...
HE TRIED... TO HURT MONET...?
HOLD UP, SLUGGER!
LEMME GO!
FER CRYIN' OUT LOUD, DARWIN, HE'S OUT COLD!
GOOD! HE'LL BE EASIER TO KILL THAT WAY!
APPRECIATE YOUR DESIRE O WELCOME ME HOME BY ILLING A HELPLESS MAN, DARWIN, BUT HE AND I HAD A DEAL.
I TAKE MY PROMISES SERIOUSLY.
YOU AIN'T GONNA STICK WITH THAT, ARE YA--?
NO WAY! NO FREAKIN' WAY ARE--
KRAKAAM
OH, YOU GOTTA BE KIDDING.

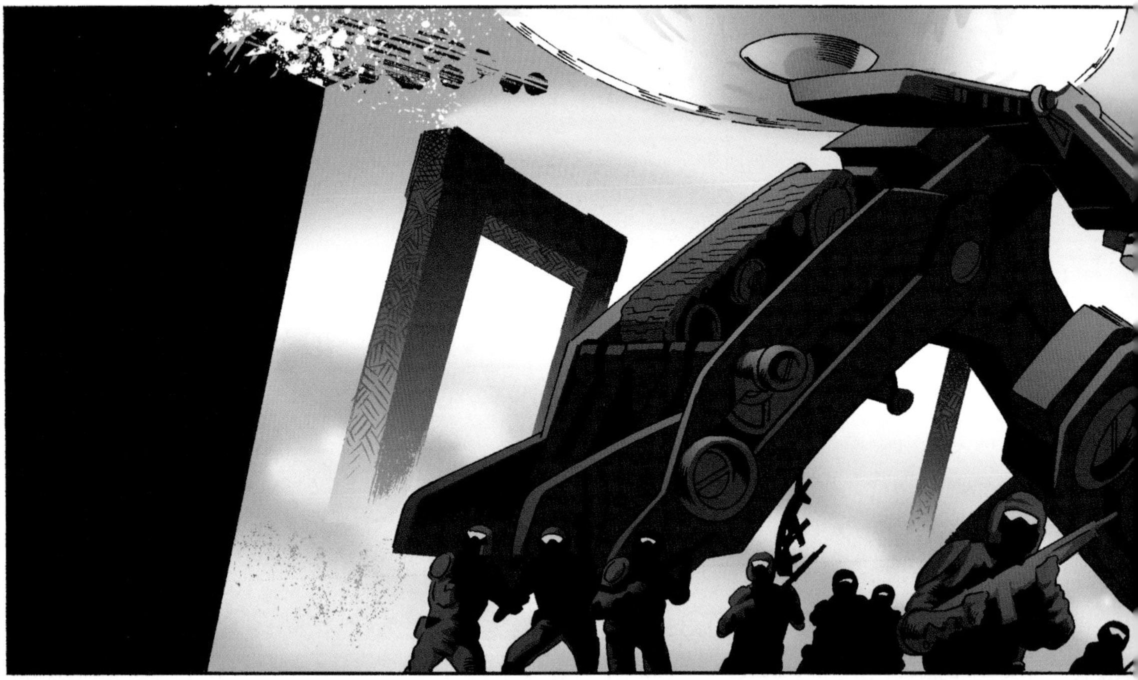

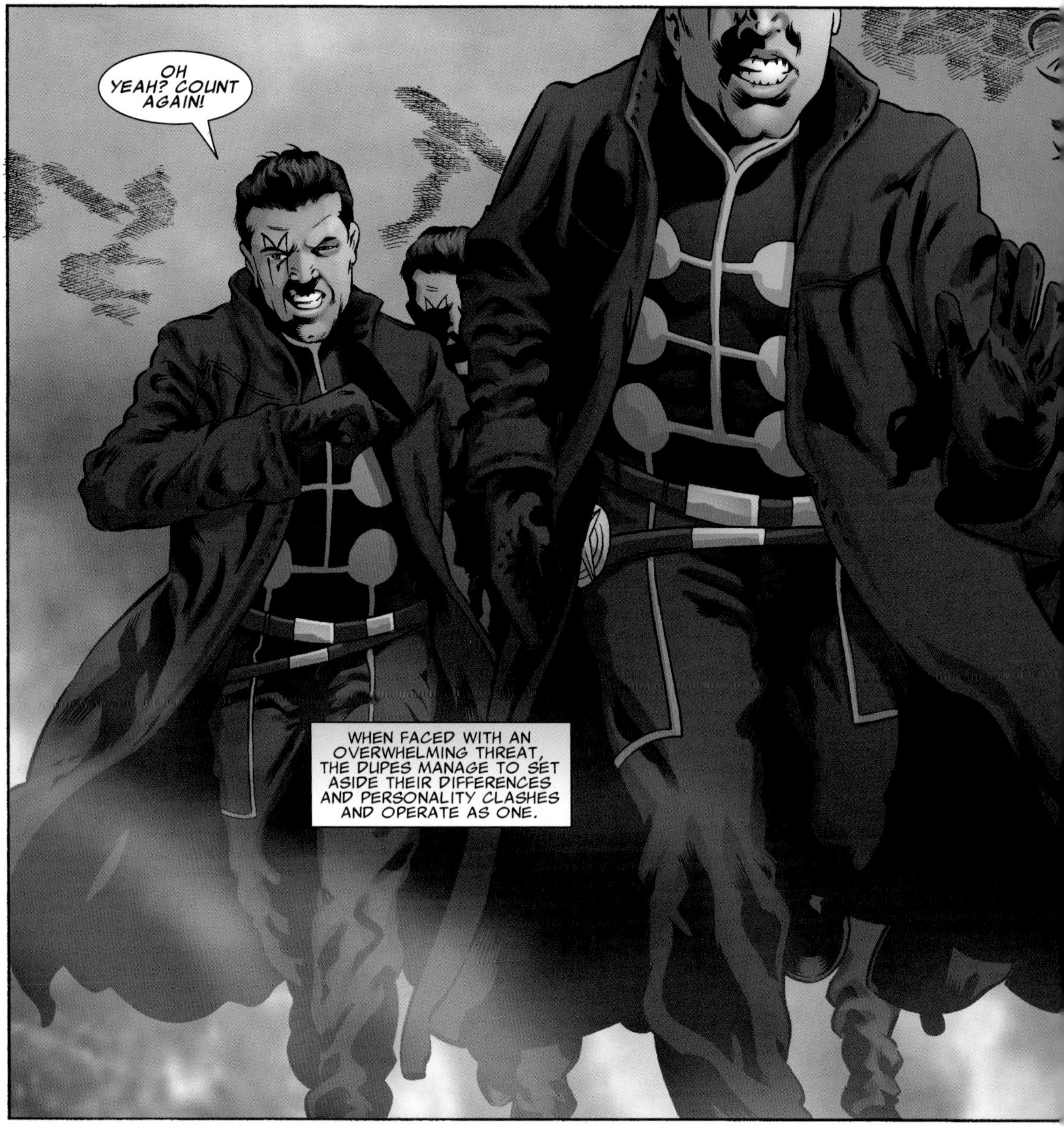
OH YEAH? COUNT AGAIN!
WHEN FACED WITH AN OVERWHELMING THREAT, THE DUPES MANAGE TO SET ASIDE THEIR DIFFERENCES AND PERSONALITY CLASHES AND OPERATE AS ONE.

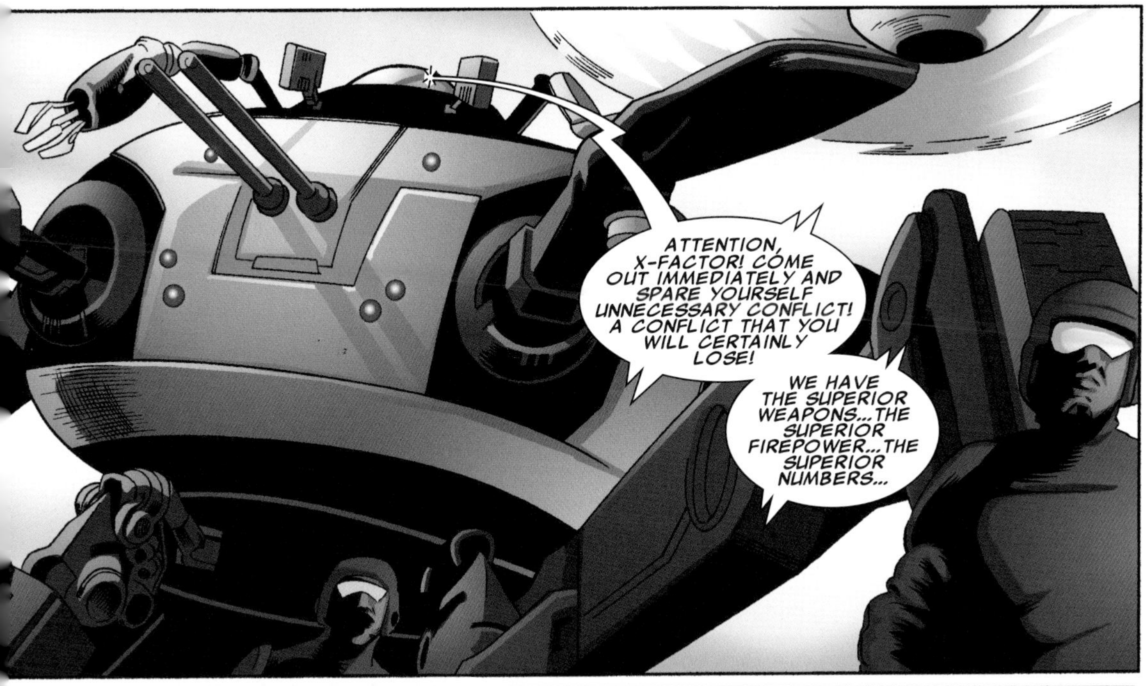
ATTENTION, X-FACTOR! COME OUT IMMEDIATELY AND SPARE YOURSELF UNNECESSARY CONFLICT! A CONFLICT THAT YOU WILL CERTAINLY LOSE!
WE HAVE THE SUPERIOR WEAPONS...THE SUPERIOR FIREPOWER...THE SUPERIOR NUMBERS...

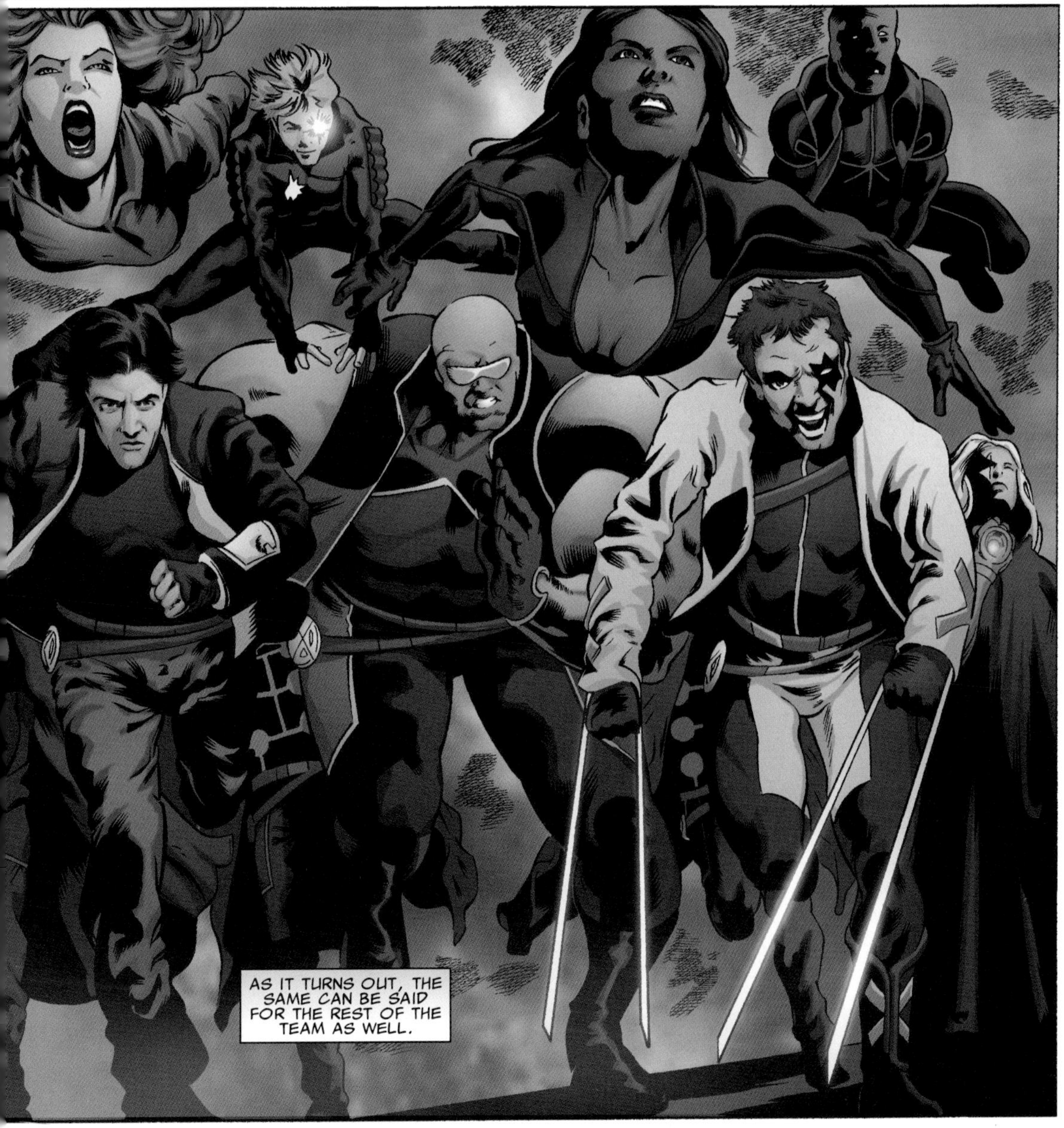
AS IT TURNS OUT, THE SAME CAN BE SAID FOR THE REST OF THE TEAM AS WELL.

SKREEEEEE

THERE'S *TERRY*, CREATING A WALL OF SOUND TO ACT AS A BUFFER...

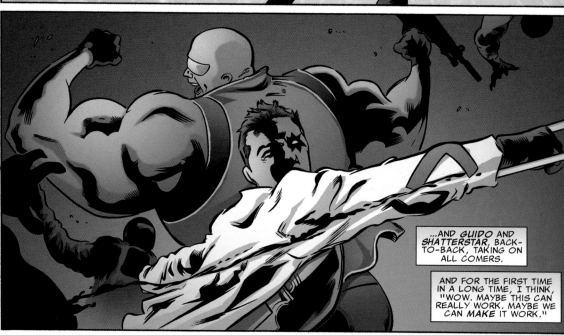

...AND *GUIDO* AND *SHATTERSTAR*, BACK-TO-BACK, TAKING ON ALL COMERS.

AND FOR THE FIRST TIME IN A LONG TIME, I THINK, "WOW. MAYBE THIS CAN REALLY WORK. MAYBE WE CAN *MAKE* IT WORK."

AND THEN I FEEL MY DUPES DYING BY THE DOZEN, GUNNED DOWN BY THAT GIANT WALKING TANK, AND IT'S LIKE A THOUSAND NEEDLES BEING JAMMED INTO MY MIND...

...AND SUDDENLY NOTHING SEEMS LIKE IT'LL WORK, EVER AGAIN.

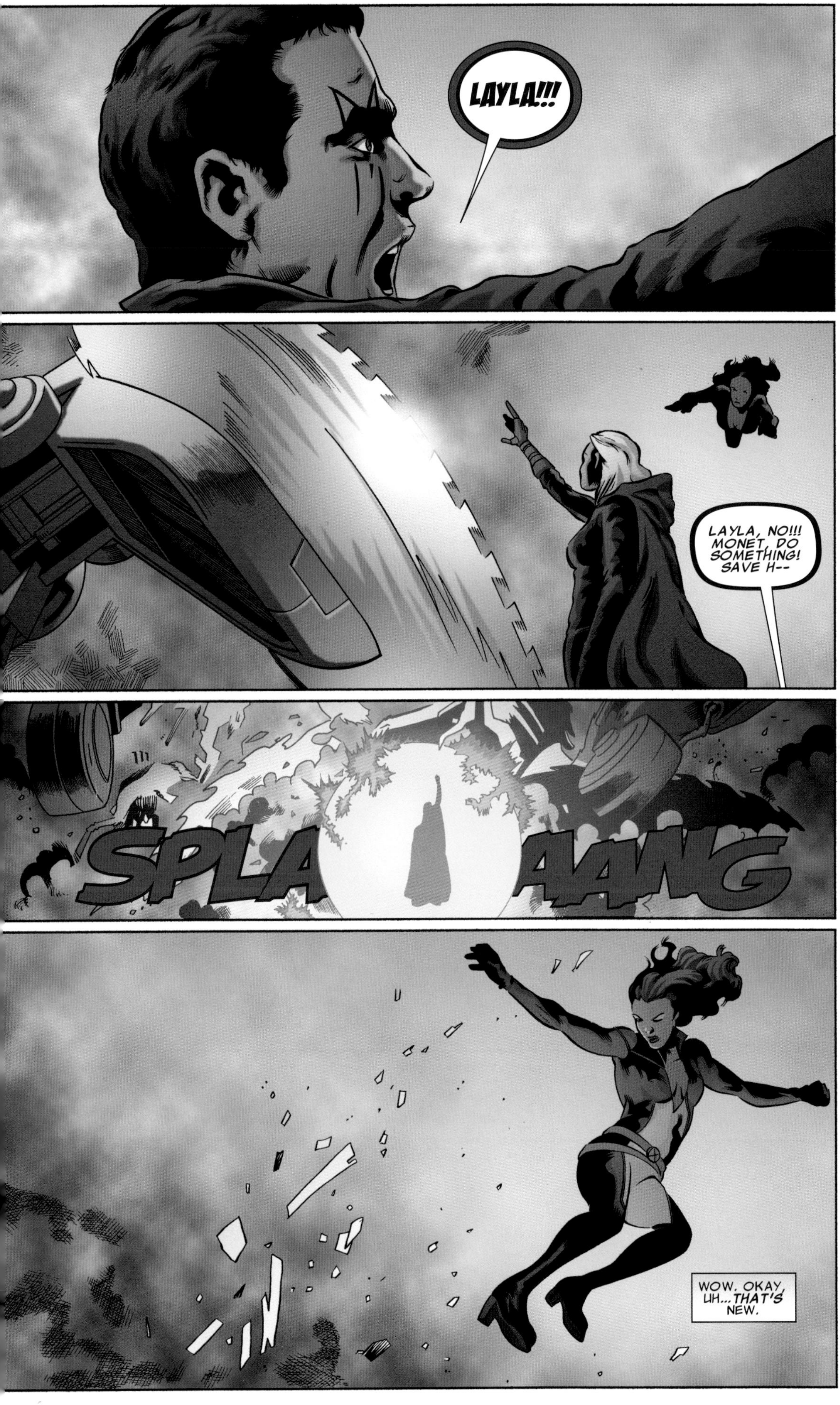
LAYLA!!!
LAYLA, NO!!! MONET, DO SOMETHING! SAVE H--
SPLAAANG
WOW. OKAY, UH...THAT'S NEW.

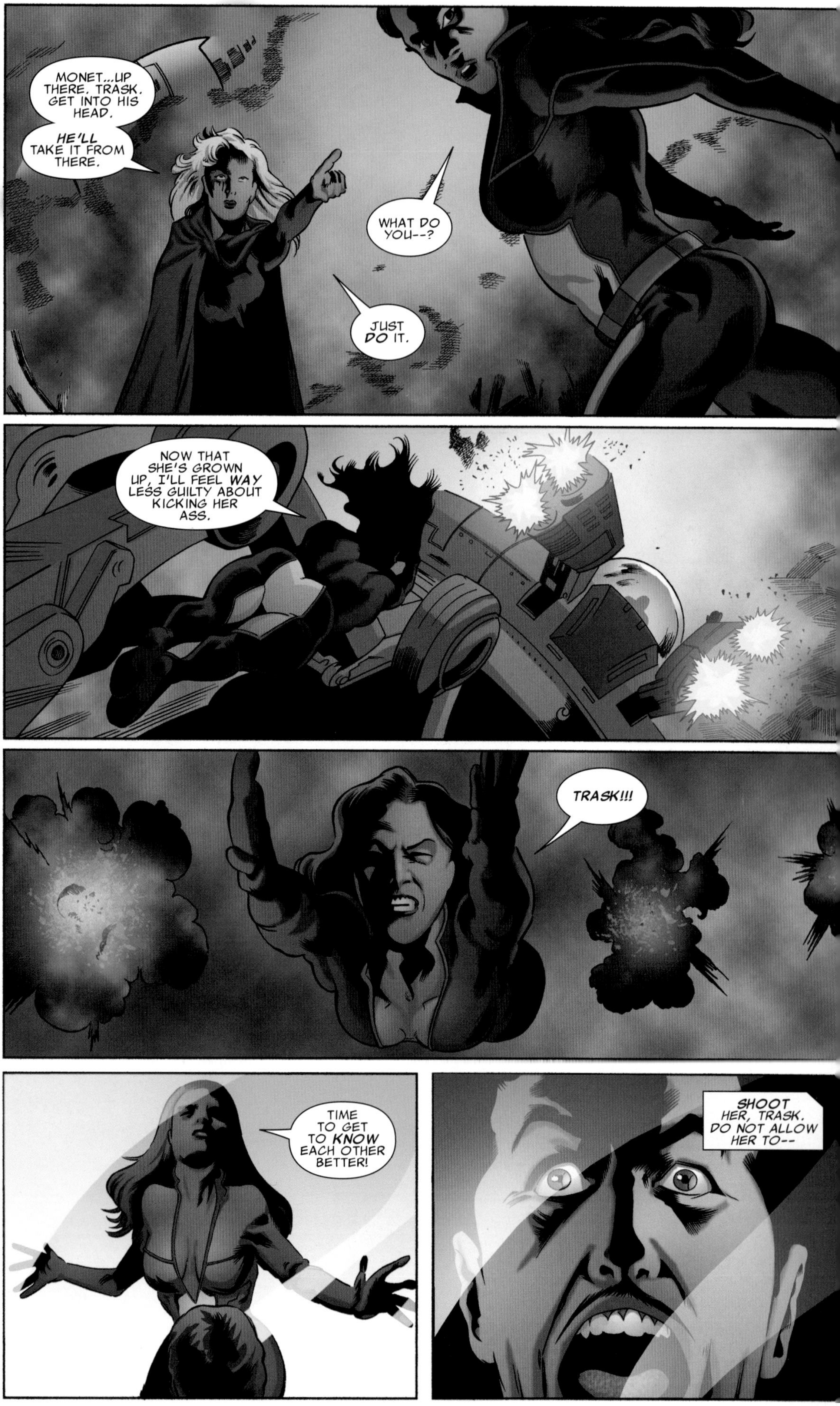
MONET...UP THERE. TRASK. GET INTO HIS HEAD.
HE'LL TAKE IT FROM THERE.
WHAT DO YOU--?
JUST DO IT.
NOW THAT SHE'S GROWN UP, I'LL FEEL WAY LESS GUILTY ABOUT KICKING HER ASS.
TRASK!!!
TIME TO GET TO KNOW EACH OTHER BETTER!
SHOOT HER, TRASK. DO NOT ALLOW HER TO--

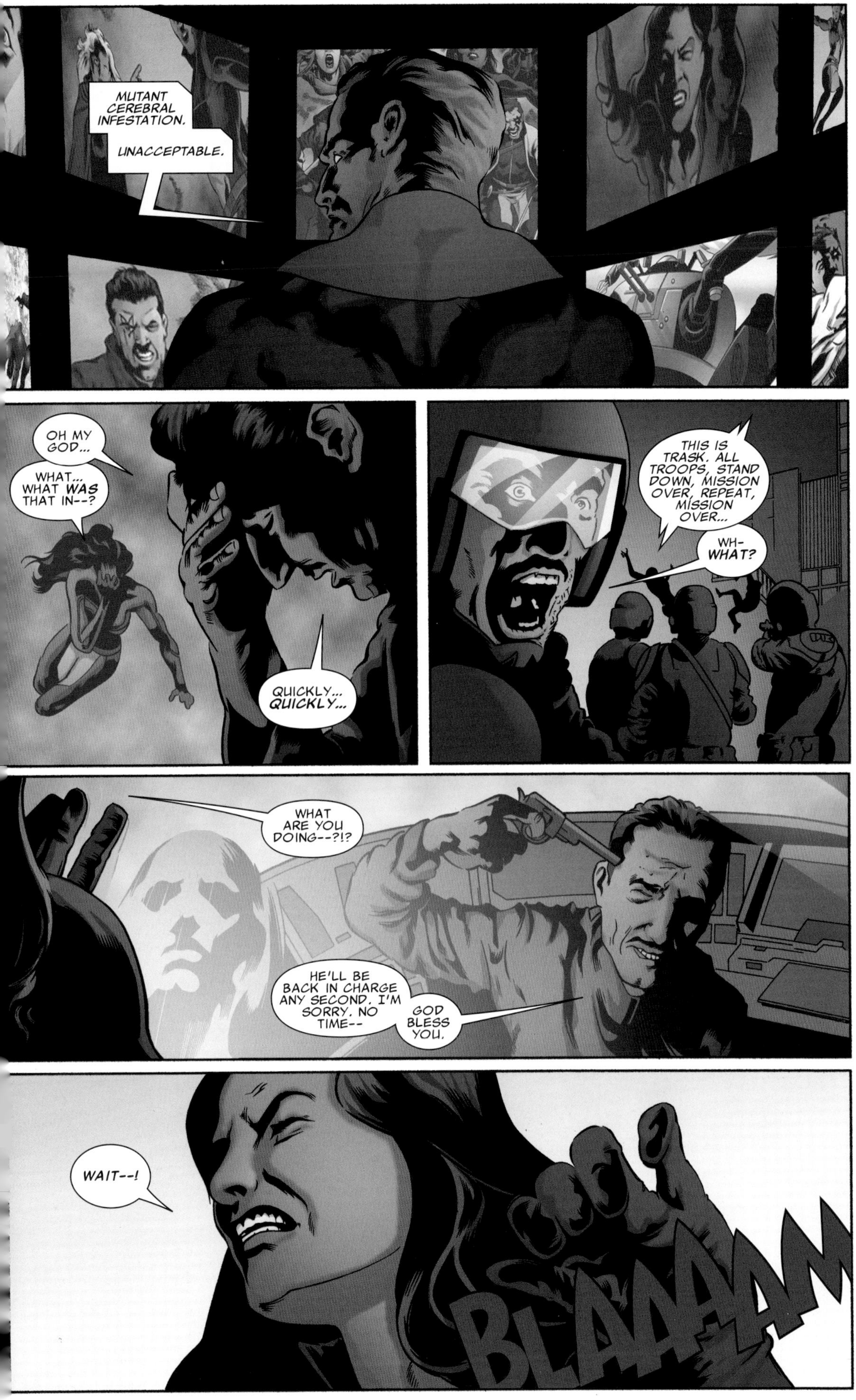
MUTANT CEREBRAL INFESTATION.
UNACCEPTABLE.
OH MY GOD...
WHAT... WHAT WAS THAT IN--?
QUICKLY... QUICKLY...
THIS IS TRASK. ALL TROOPS, STAND DOWN, MISSION OVER, REPEAT, MISSION OVER...
WH- WHAT?
WHAT ARE YOU DOING--?!?
HE'LL BE BACK IN CHARGE ANY SECOND. I'M SORRY. NO TIME--
GOD BLESS YOU.
WAIT--!
BLAAAAM

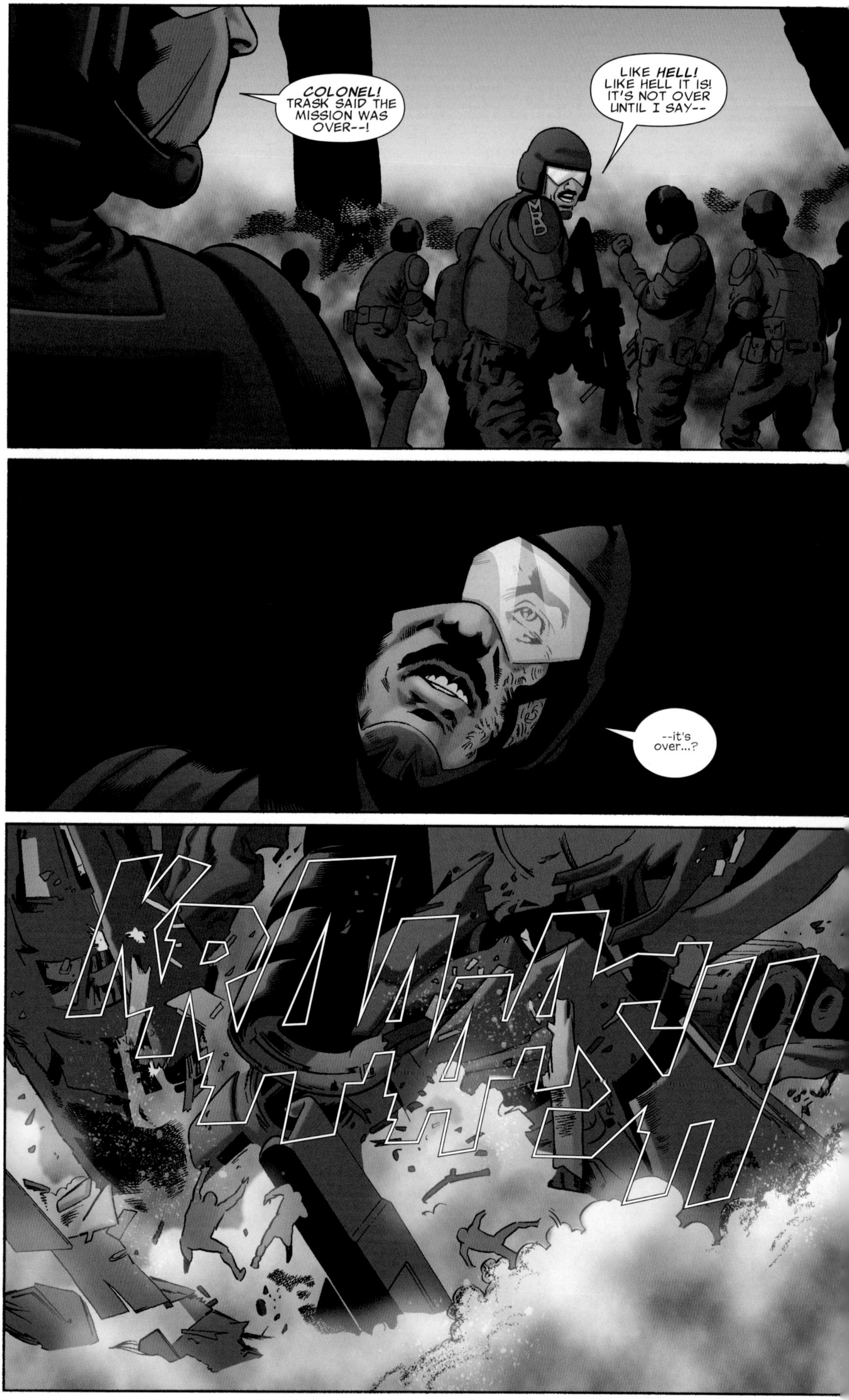
COLONEL! TRASK SAID THE MISSION WAS OVER--!
LIKE HELL! LIKE HELL IT IS! IT'S NOT OVER UNTIL I SAY--
--it's over...?

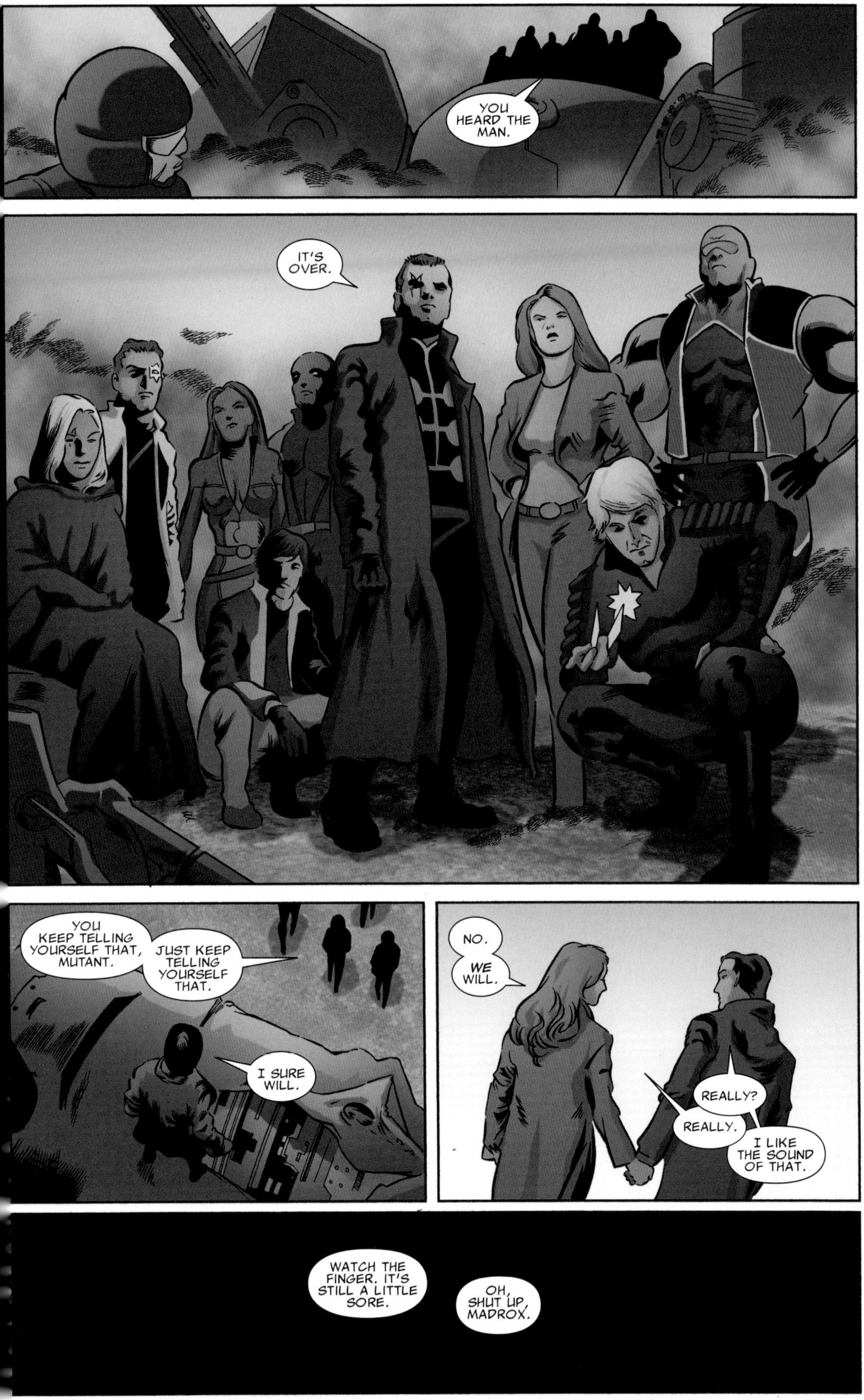
YOU HEARD THE MAN.
IT'S OVER.
YOU KEEP TELLING YOURSELF THAT, MUTANT.
JUST KEEP TELLING YOURSELF THAT.
I SURE WILL.
NO.
WE WILL.
REALLY?
REALLY.
I LIKE THE SOUND OF THAT.
WATCH THE FINGER. IT'S STILL A LITTLE SORE.
OH, SHUT UP, MADROX.

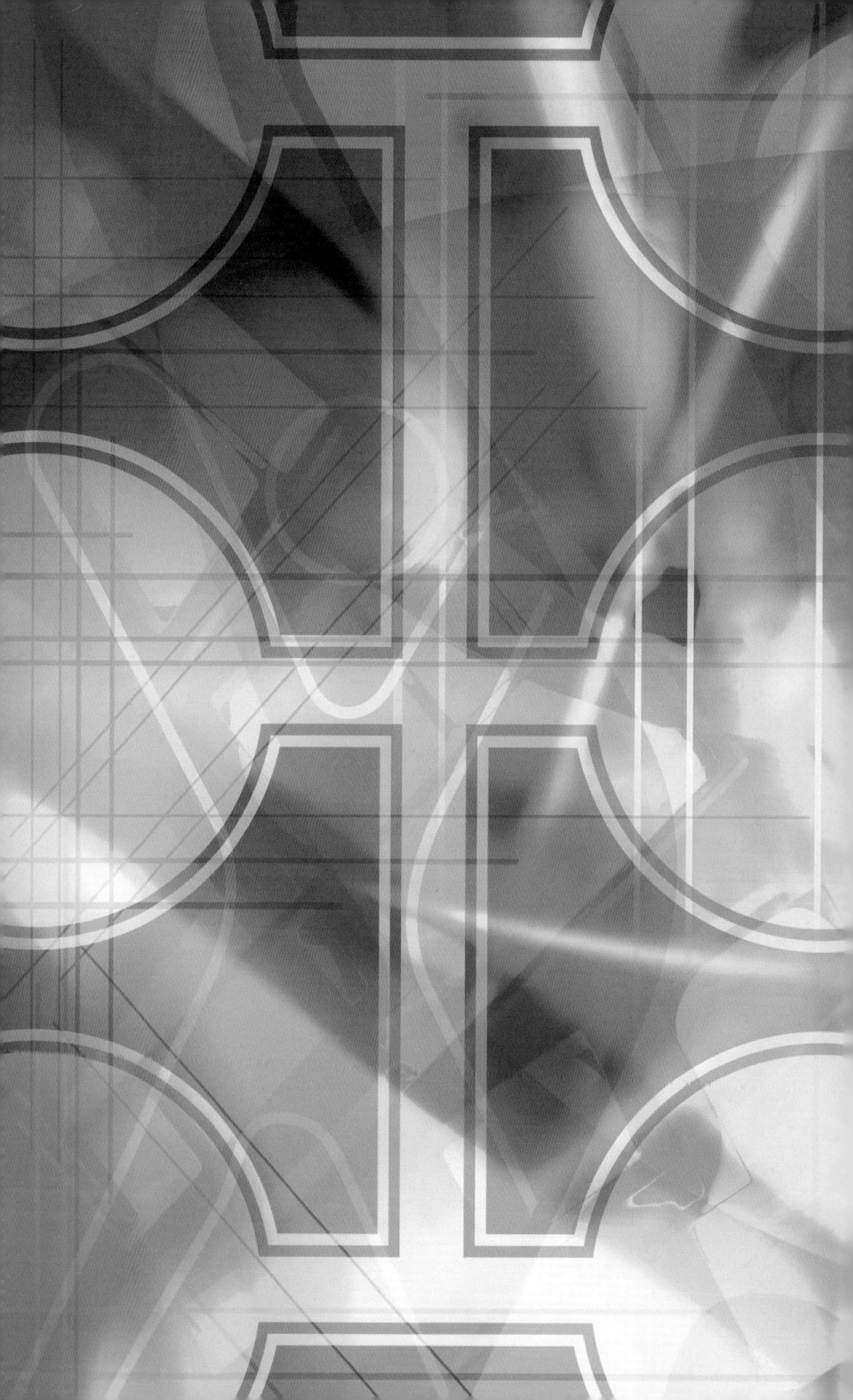

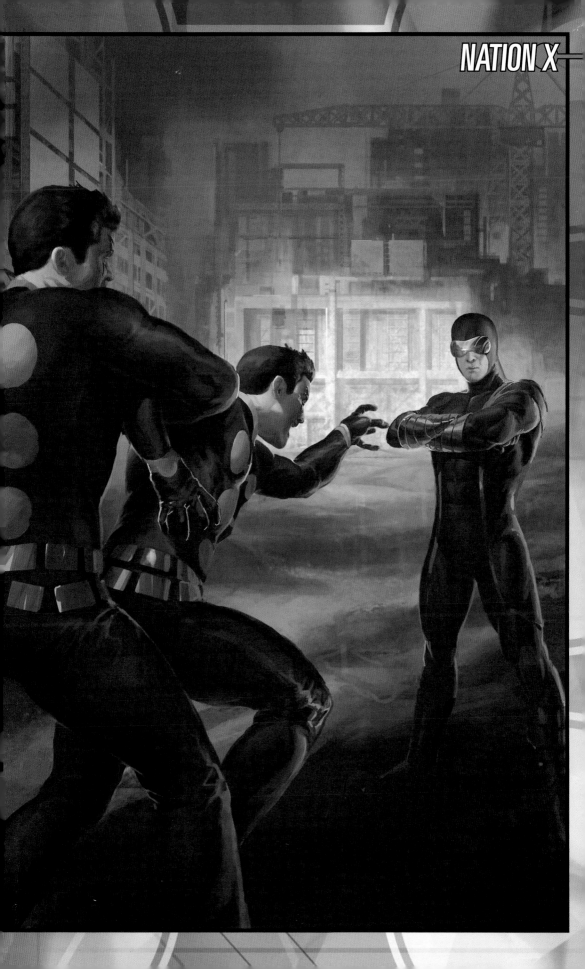

A tale of two islands:

One is called Utopia, floating off the coast of San Francisco, serving as the home to most of the remnants of the once populous species known as Homo Superior, a.k.a., mutants.

The other is called Manhattan, floating off the Hudson, serving as the home to ten million humans...and one small group of mutants calling themselves X-Factor, a detective agency specializing in the needs of the super hero and paranormal community.

One of them is about to visit the other.

The 22nd of April, in the year of their lord nineteen hundred and forty-three.

It will not last much longer now. The Warsaw ghetto will be cleaned out soon. In a way, a blessing, I suppose. Thousands here have already died of malnourishment and stinking poverty.

Then again, it is not as if the fate that awaits them is any more generous.

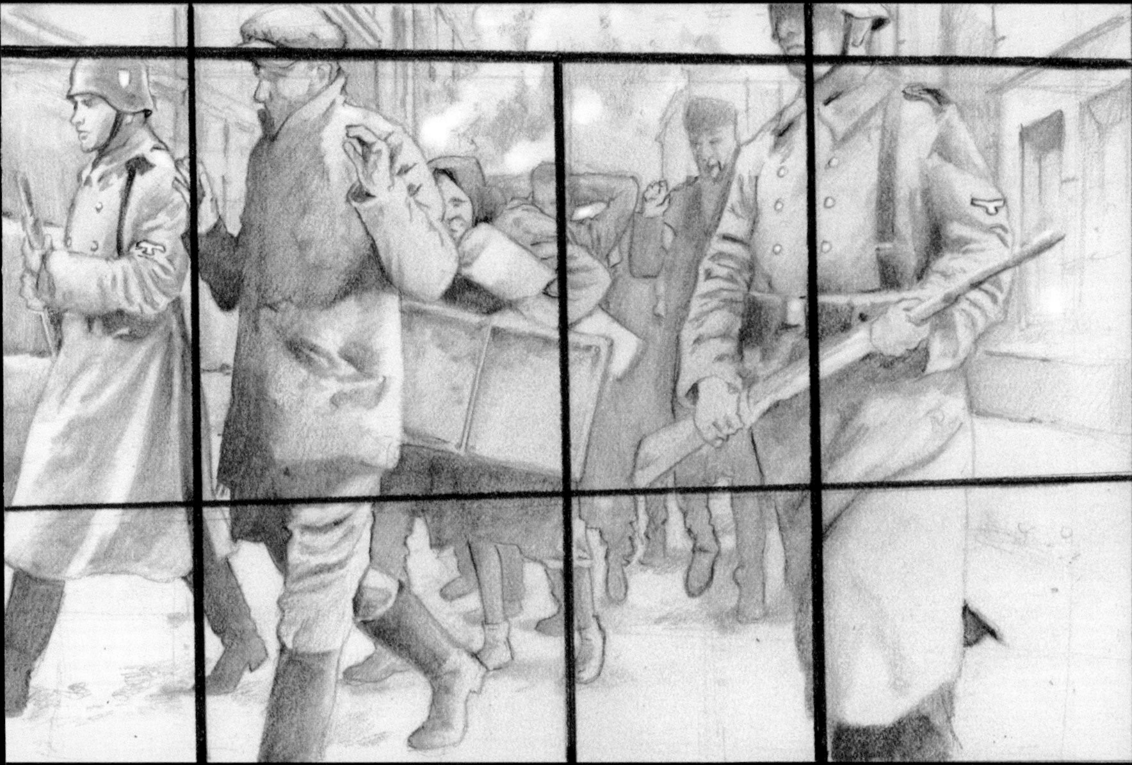

This war will not endure. It cannot. It will break under the weight of its own self-righteousness and excessive goals.

But how many will die before the final bullet flies?

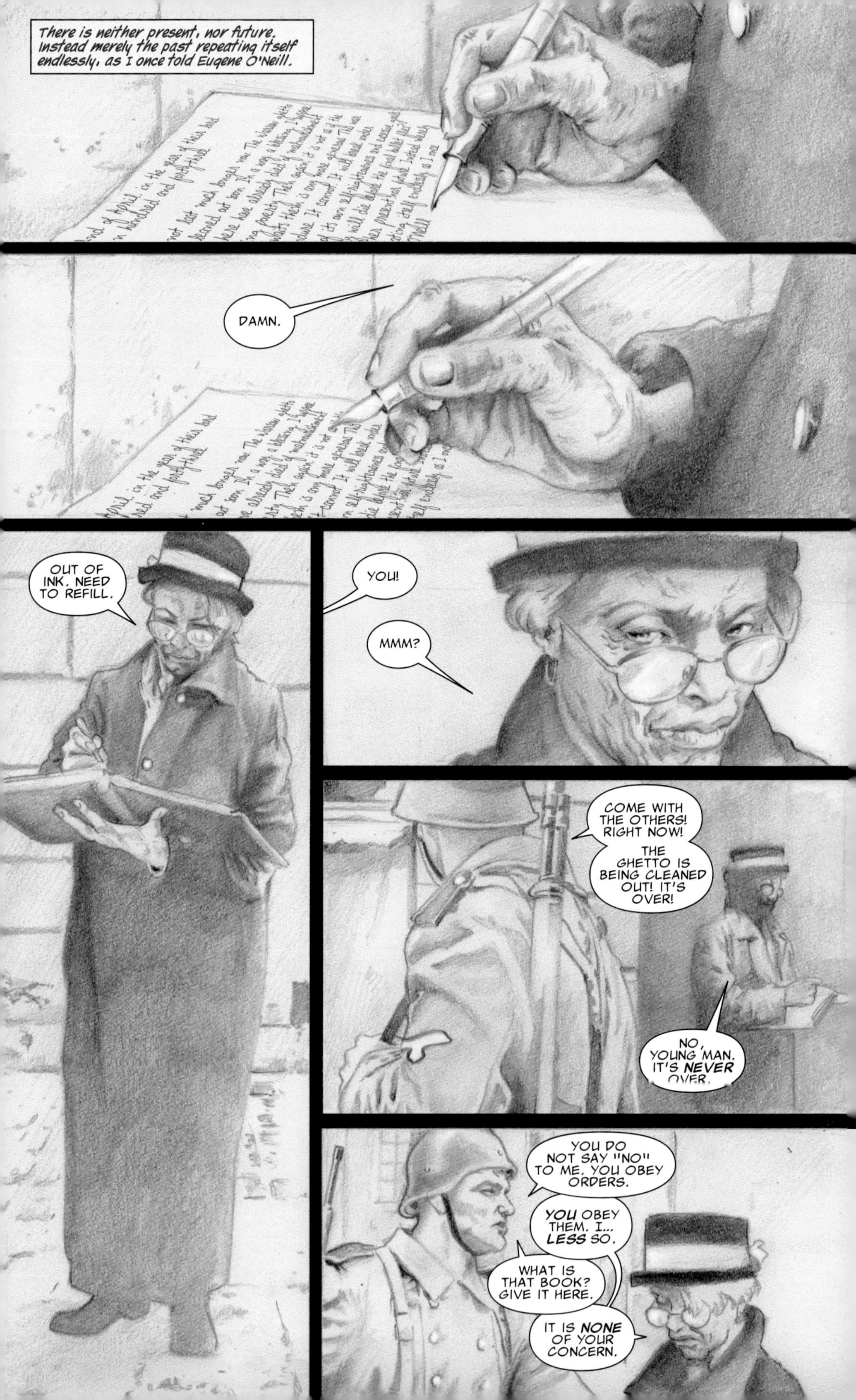
There is neither present, nor future. Instead merely the past repeating itself endlessly, as I once told Eugene O'Neill.
DAMN.
OUT OF INK. NEED TO REFILL.
YOU!
MMM?
COME WITH THE OTHERS! RIGHT NOW!
THE GHETTO IS BEING CLEANED OUT! IT'S OVER!
NO, YOUNG MAN. IT'S NEVER OVER.
YOU DO NOT SAY "NO" TO ME. YOU OBEY ORDERS.
YOU OBEY THEM. I... LESS SO.
WHAT IS THAT BOOK? GIVE IT HERE.
IT IS NONE OF YOUR CONCERN.

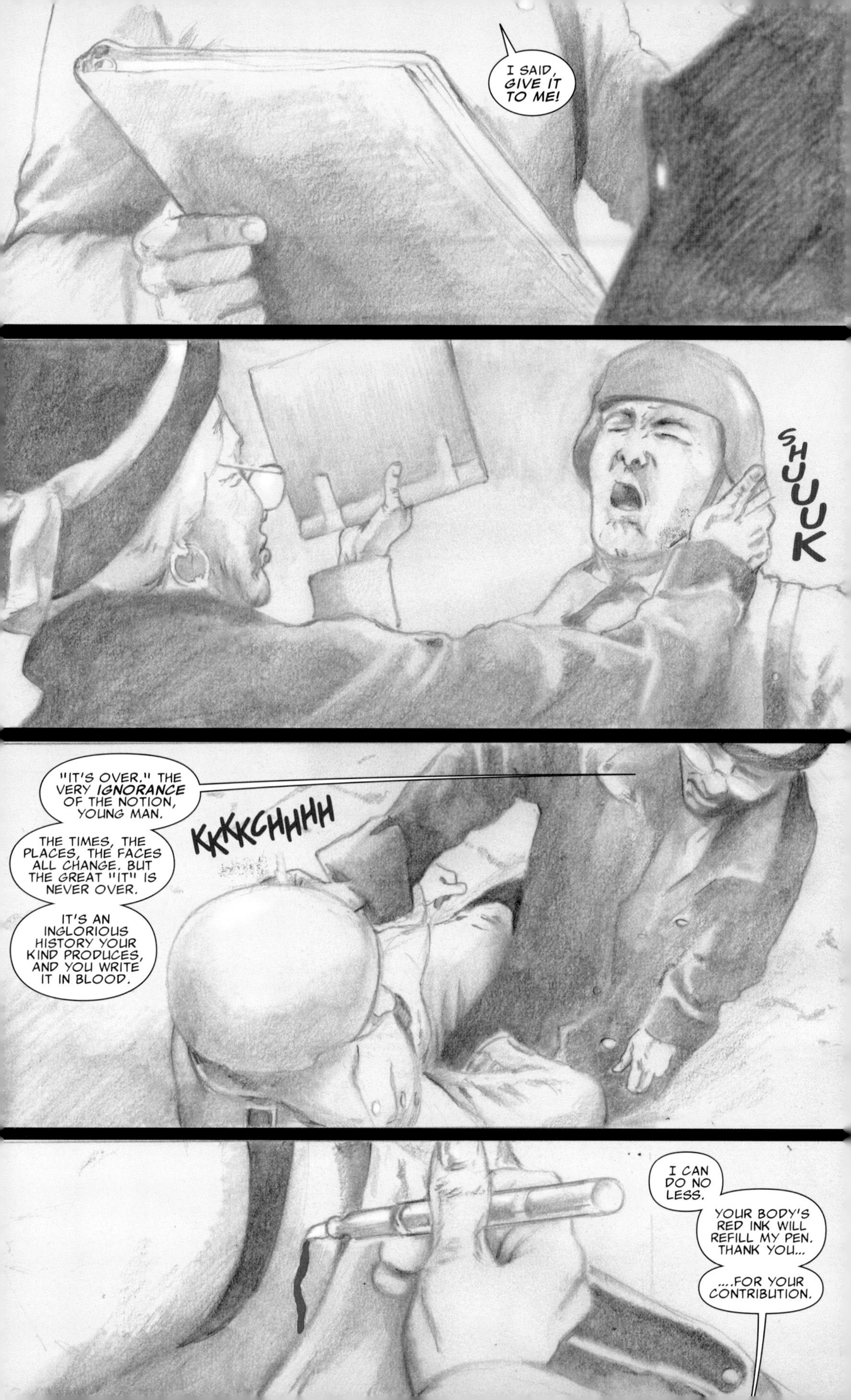
I SAID, GIVE IT TO ME!
SHUUUK
"IT'S OVER." THE VERY IGNORANCE OF THE NOTION, YOUNG MAN.
THE TIMES, THE PLACES, THE FACES ALL CHANGE. BUT THE GREAT "IT" IS NEVER OVER.
IT'S AN INGLORIOUS HISTORY YOUR KIND PRODUCES, AND YOU WRITE IT IN BLOOD.
KKKKCHHHH
I CAN DO NO LESS.
YOUR BODY'S RED INK WILL REFILL MY PEN. THANK YOU...
....FOR YOUR CONTRIBUTION.

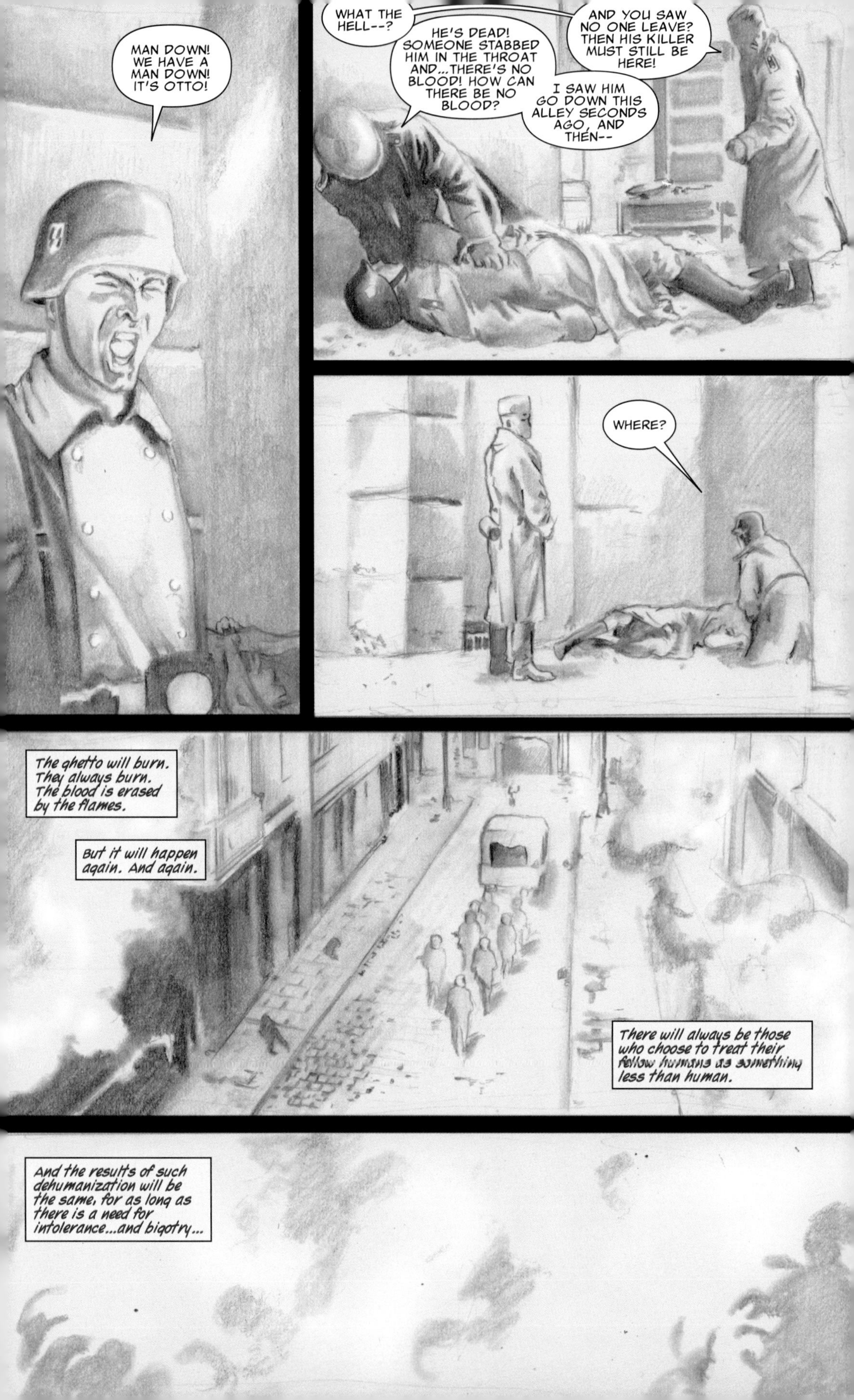
MAN DOWN! WE HAVE A MAN DOWN! IT'S OTTO!
WHAT THE HELL--?
HE'S DEAD! SOMEONE STABBED HIM IN THE THROAT AND...THERE'S NO BLOOD! HOW CAN THERE BE NO BLOOD?
AND YOU SAW NO ONE LEAVE? THEN HIS KILLER MUST STILL BE HERE!
I SAW HIM GO DOWN THIS ALLEY SECONDS AGO, AND THEN--
WHERE?
The ghetto will burn. They always burn. The blood is erased by the flames.
But it will happen again. And again.
There will always be those who choose to treat their fellow humans as something less than human.
And the results of such dehumanization will be the same, for as long as there is a need for intolerance...and bigotry...

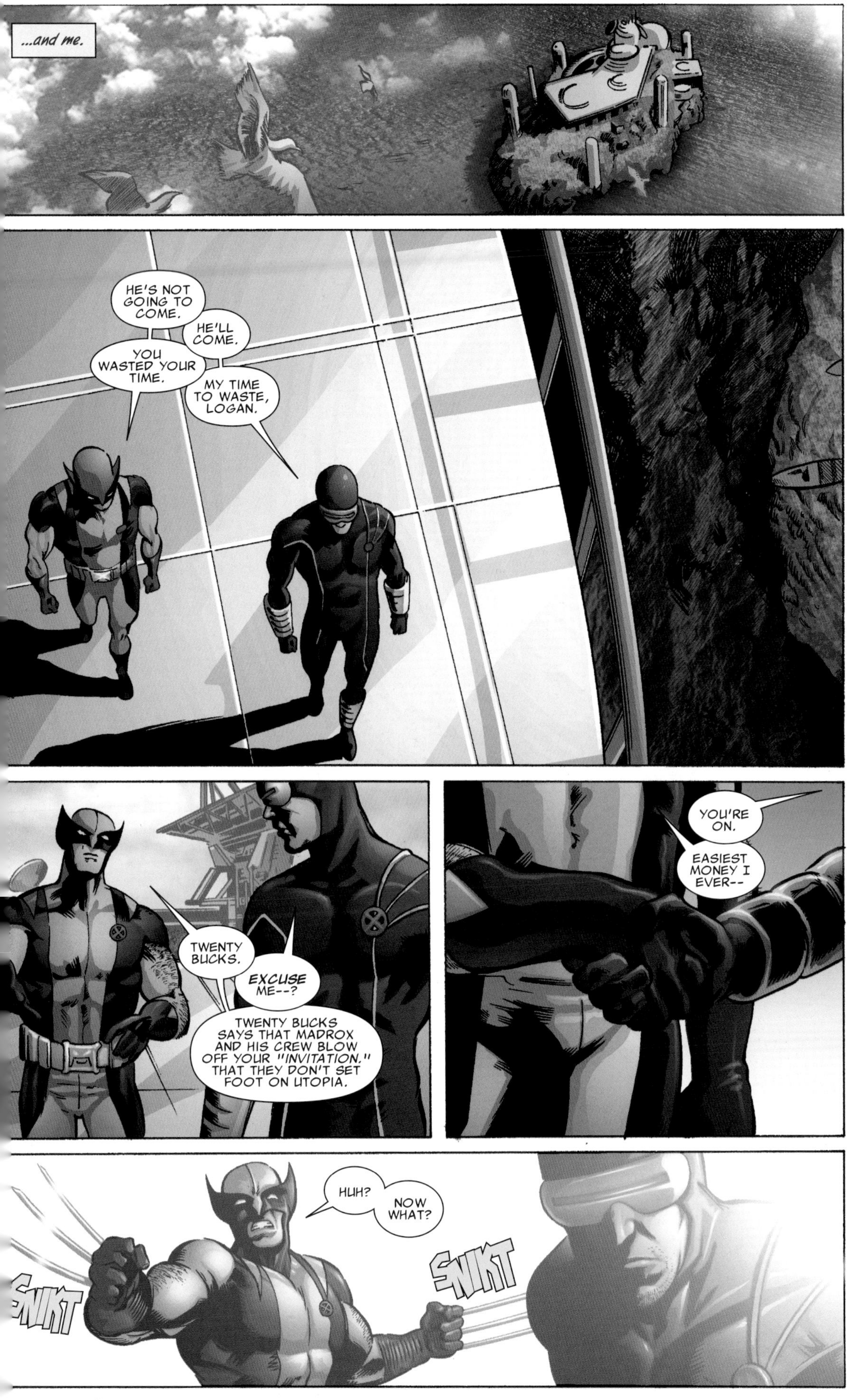
...and me.
HE'S NOT GOING TO COME.
HE'LL COME.
YOU WASTED YOUR TIME.
MY TIME TO WASTE, LOGAN.
TWENTY BUCKS.
EXCUSE ME--?
TWENTY BUCKS SAYS THAT MADROX AND HIS CREW BLOW OFF YOUR "INVITATION." THAT THEY DON'T SET FOOT ON UTOPIA.
YOU'RE ON.
EASIEST MONEY I EVER--
HUH?
NOW WHAT?
SNIKT
SNIKT

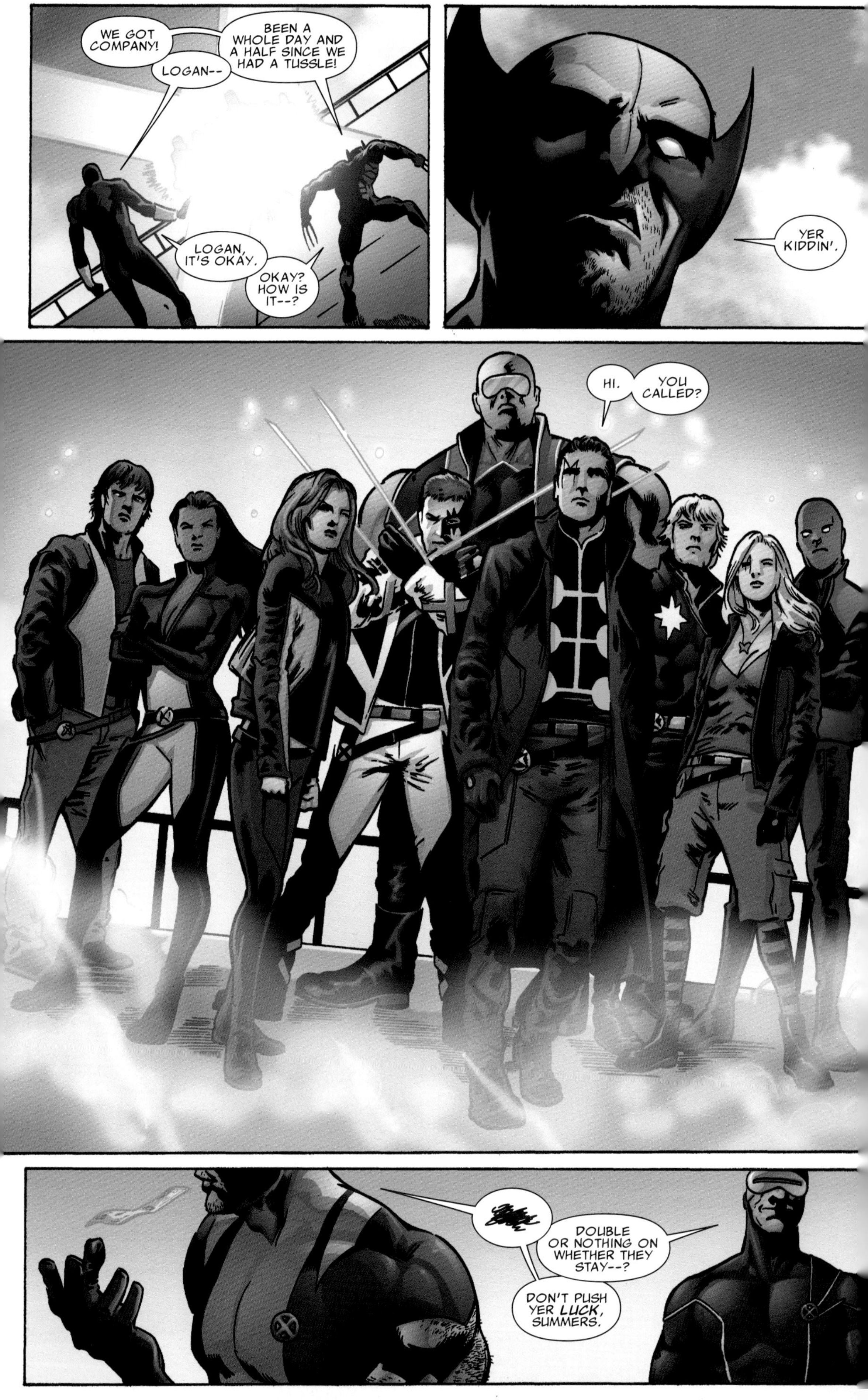
WE GOT COMPANY!
LOGAN--
BEEN A WHOLE DAY AND A HALF SINCE WE HAD A TUSSLE!
LOGAN, IT'S OKAY.
OKAY? HOW IS IT--?
YER KIDDIN'.
HI.
YOU CALLED?
DOUBLE OR NOTHING ON WHETHER THEY STAY--?
DON'T PUSH YER LUCK, SUMMERS.

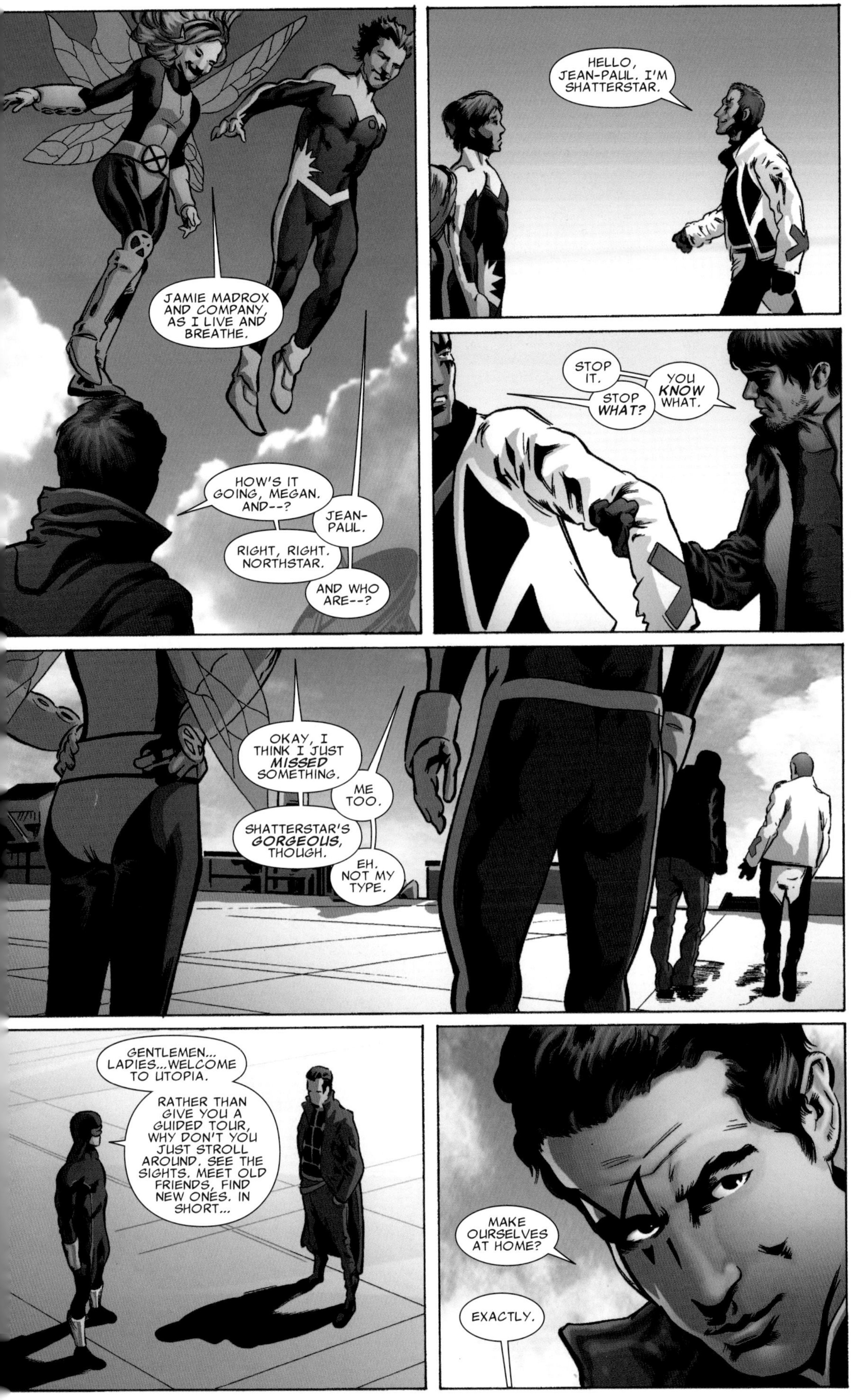
JAMIE MADROX AND COMPANY, AS I LIVE AND BREATHE.
HOW'S IT GOING, MEGAN. AND--?
JEAN-PAUL.
RIGHT, RIGHT. NORTHSTAR.
AND WHO ARE--?
HELLO, JEAN-PAUL. I'M SHATTERSTAR.
STOP IT.
STOP WHAT?
YOU KNOW WHAT.
OKAY, I THINK I JUST MISSED SOMETHING.
ME TOO.
SHATTERSTAR'S GORGEOUS, THOUGH.
EH. NOT MY TYPE.
GENTLEMEN... LADIES...WELCOME TO UTOPIA.
RATHER THAN GIVE YOU A GUIDED TOUR, WHY DON'T YOU JUST STROLL AROUND. SEE THE SIGHTS. MEET OLD FRIENDS, FIND NEW ONES. IN SHORT...
MAKE OURSELVES AT HOME?
EXACTLY.

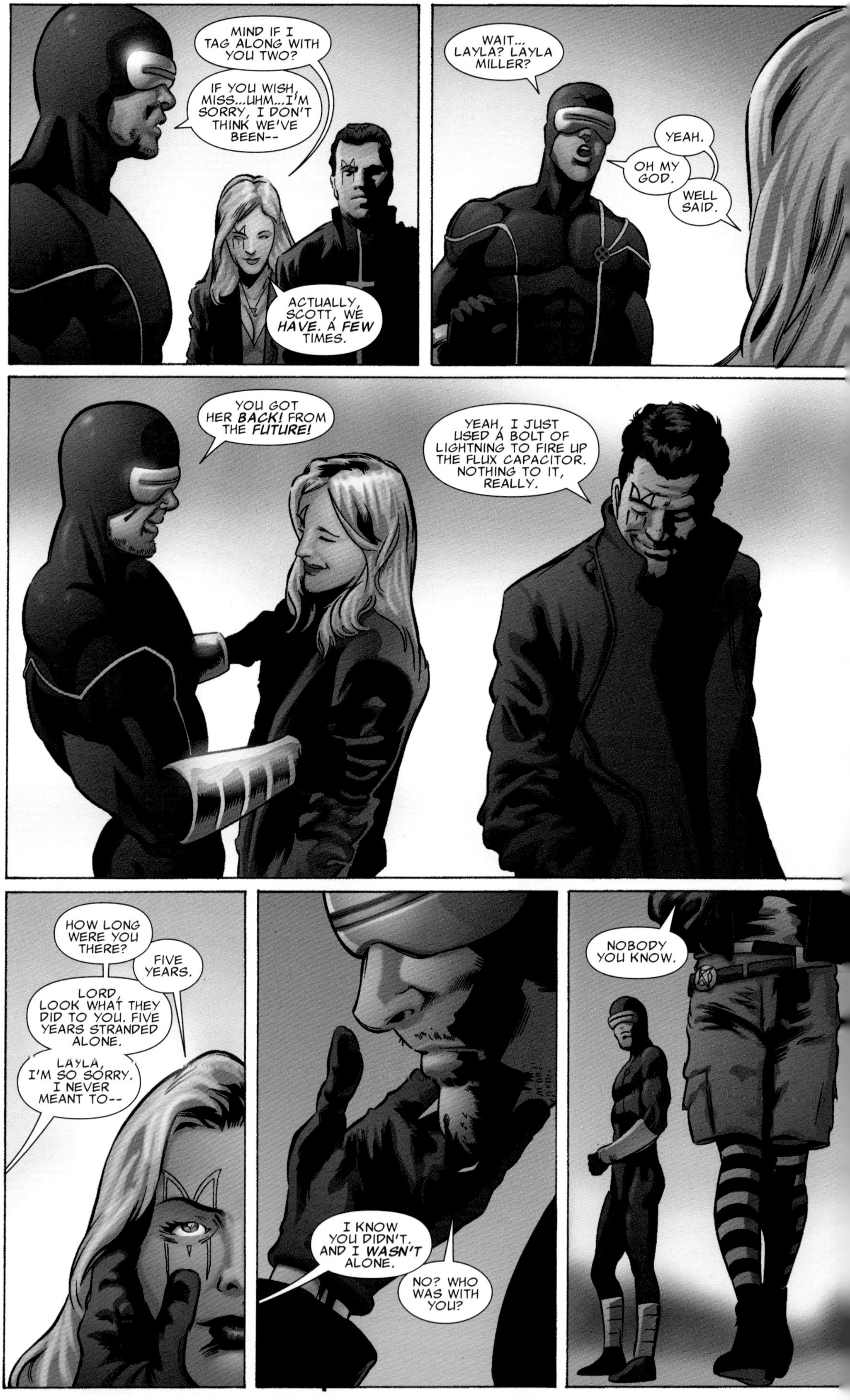
MIND IF I TAG ALONG WITH YOU TWO?
IF YOU WISH, MISS...UHM...I'M SORRY, I DON'T THINK WE'VE BEEN--
ACTUALLY, SCOTT, WE HAVE. A FEW TIMES.
WAIT... LAYLA? LAYLA MILLER?
YEAH.
OH MY GOD.
WELL SAID.
YOU GOT HER BACK! FROM THE FUTURE!
YEAH, I JUST USED A BOLT OF LIGHTNING TO FIRE UP THE FLUX CAPACITOR. NOTHING TO IT, REALLY.
HOW LONG WERE YOU THERE?
FIVE YEARS.
LORD, LOOK WHAT THEY DID TO YOU. FIVE YEARS STRANDED ALONE.
LAYLA, I'M SO SORRY. I NEVER MEANT TO--
I KNOW YOU DIDN'T. AND I WASN'T ALONE.
NO? WHO WAS WITH YOU?
NOBODY YOU KNOW.

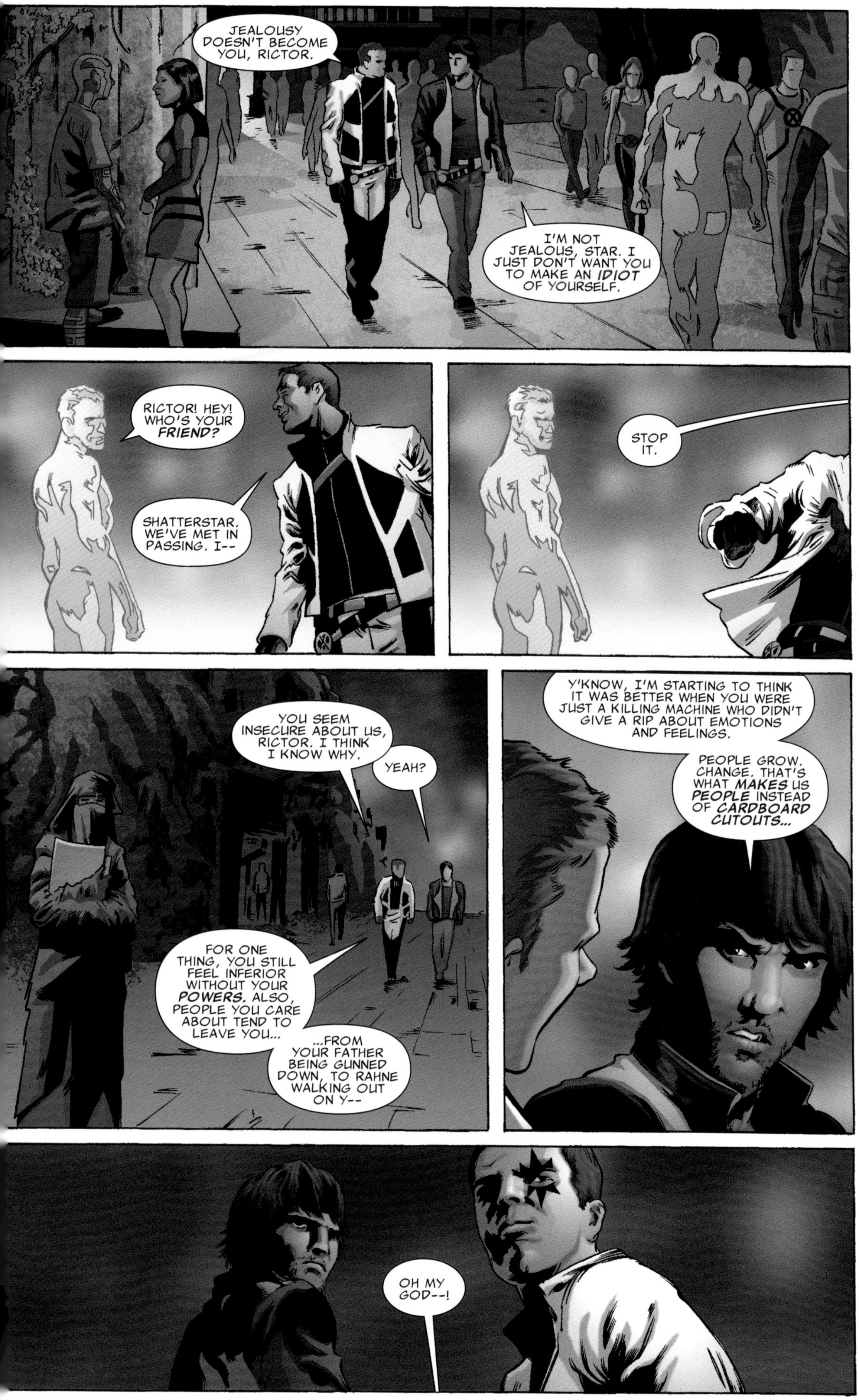

JEALOUSY DOESN'T BECOME YOU, RICTOR.
I'M NOT JEALOUS, STAR. I JUST DON'T WANT YOU TO MAKE AN IDIOT OF YOURSELF.
RICTOR! HEY! WHO'S YOUR FRIEND?
SHATTERSTAR. WE'VE MET IN PASSING. I--
STOP IT.
YOU SEEM INSECURE ABOUT US, RICTOR. I THINK I KNOW WHY.
YEAH?
FOR ONE THING, YOU STILL FEEL INFERIOR WITHOUT YOUR POWERS. ALSO, PEOPLE YOU CARE ABOUT TEND TO LEAVE YOU...
...FROM YOUR FATHER BEING GUNNED DOWN, TO RAHNE WALKING OUT ON Y--
Y'KNOW, I'M STARTING TO THINK IT WAS BETTER WHEN YOU WERE JUST A KILLING MACHINE WHO DIDN'T GIVE A RIP ABOUT EMOTIONS AND FEELINGS.
PEOPLE GROW. CHANGE. THAT'S WHAT MAKES US PEOPLE INSTEAD OF CARDBOARD CUTOUTS...
OH MY GOD--!

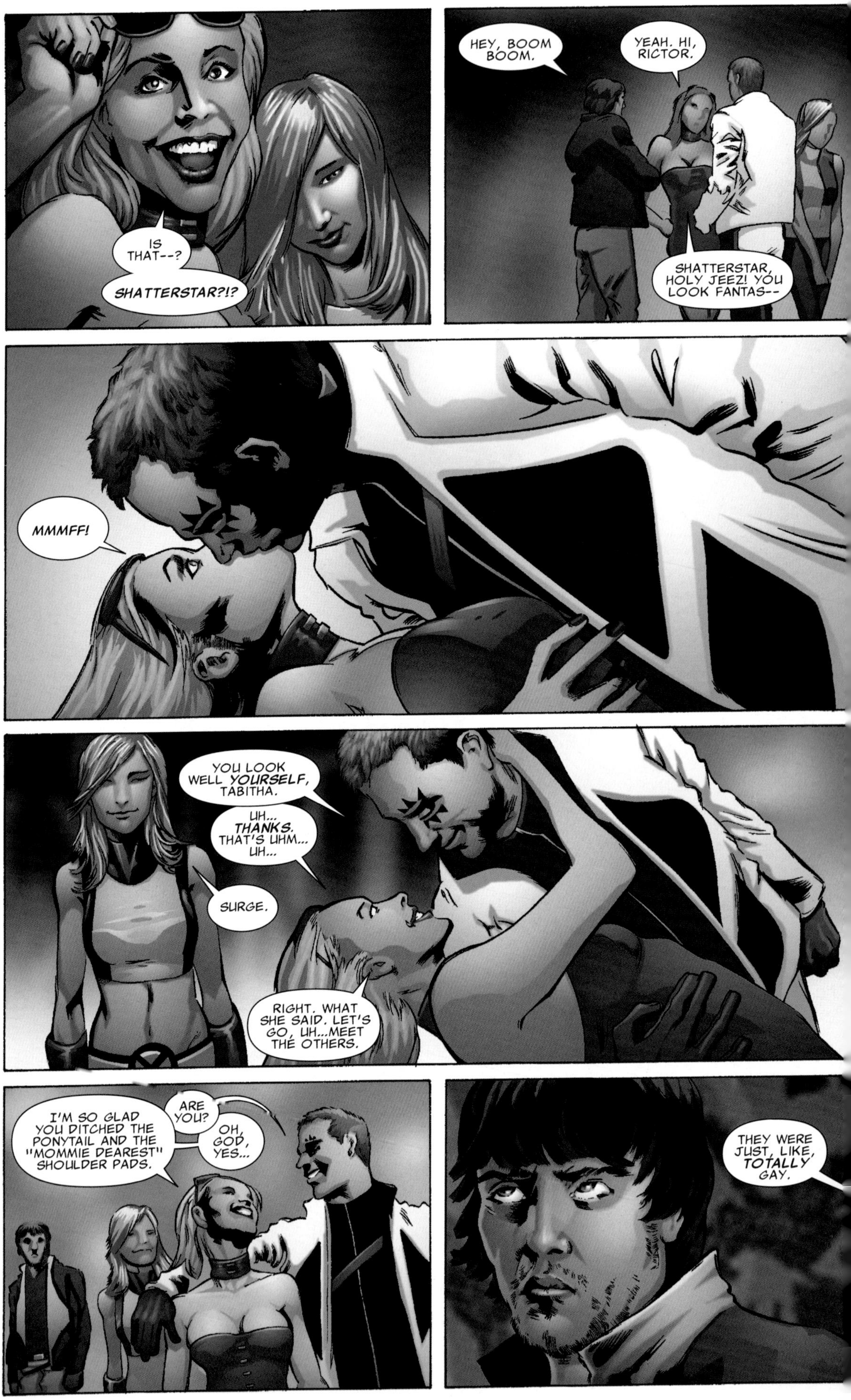
IS THAT--?
SHATTERSTAR?!?
HEY, BOOM BOOM.
YEAH. HI, RICTOR.
SHATTERSTAR, HOLY JEEZ! YOU LOOK FANTAS--
MMMFF!
YOU LOOK WELL YOURSELF, TABITHA.
UH... THANKS. THAT'S UHM... UH...
SURGE.
RIGHT. WHAT SHE SAID. LET'S GO, UH...MEET THE OTHERS.
I'M SO GLAD YOU DITCHED THE PONYTAIL AND THE "MOMMIE DEAREST" SHOULDER PADS.
ARE YOU?
OH, GOD, YES...
THEY WERE JUST, LIKE, TOTALLY GAY.

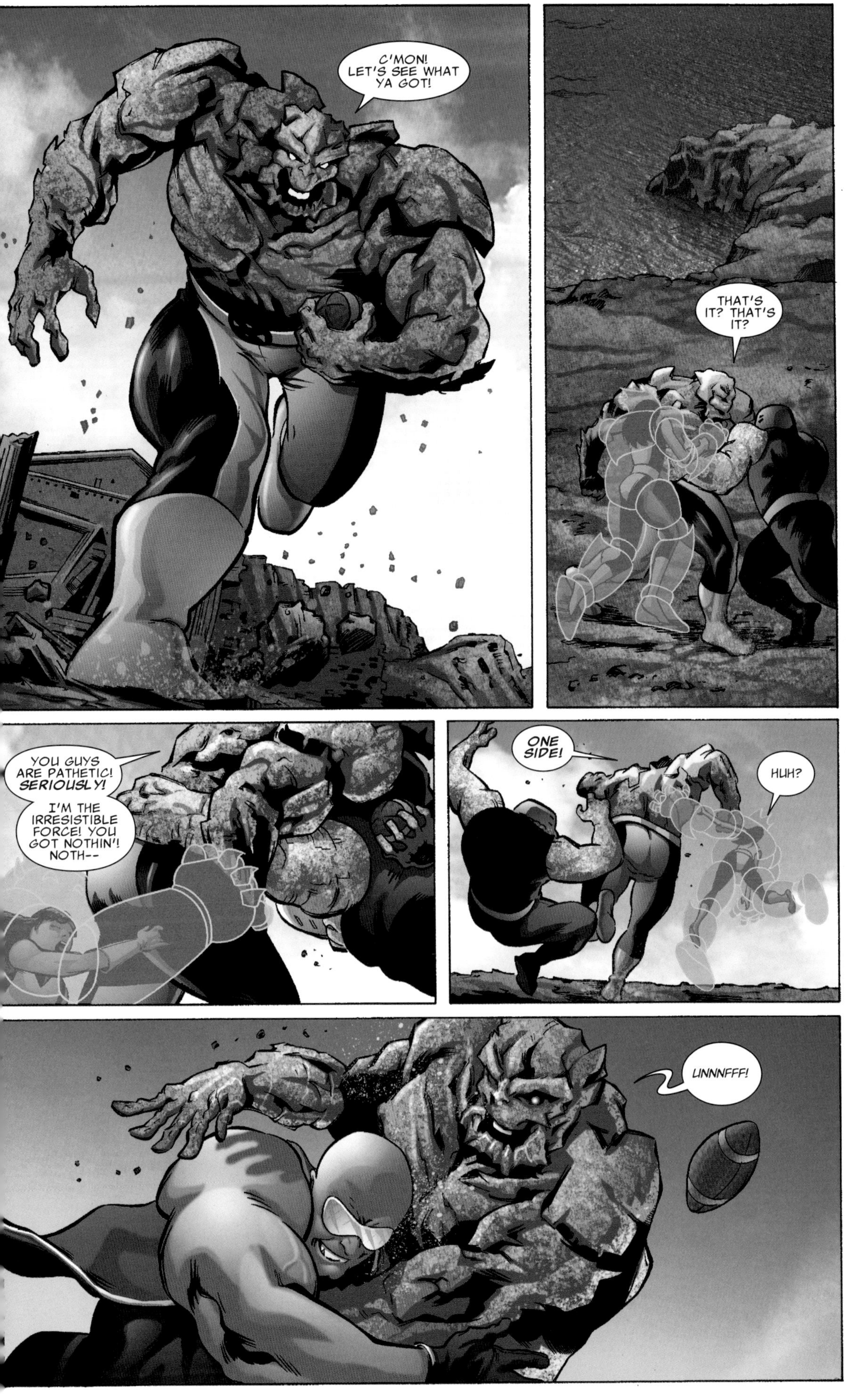

C'MON! LET'S SEE WHAT YA GOT!
THAT'S IT? THAT'S IT?
YOU GUYS ARE PATHETIC! SERIOUSLY!
I'M THE IRRESISTIBLE FORCE! YOU GOT NOTHIN'! NOTH--
ONE SIDE!
HUH?
UNNNFFF!

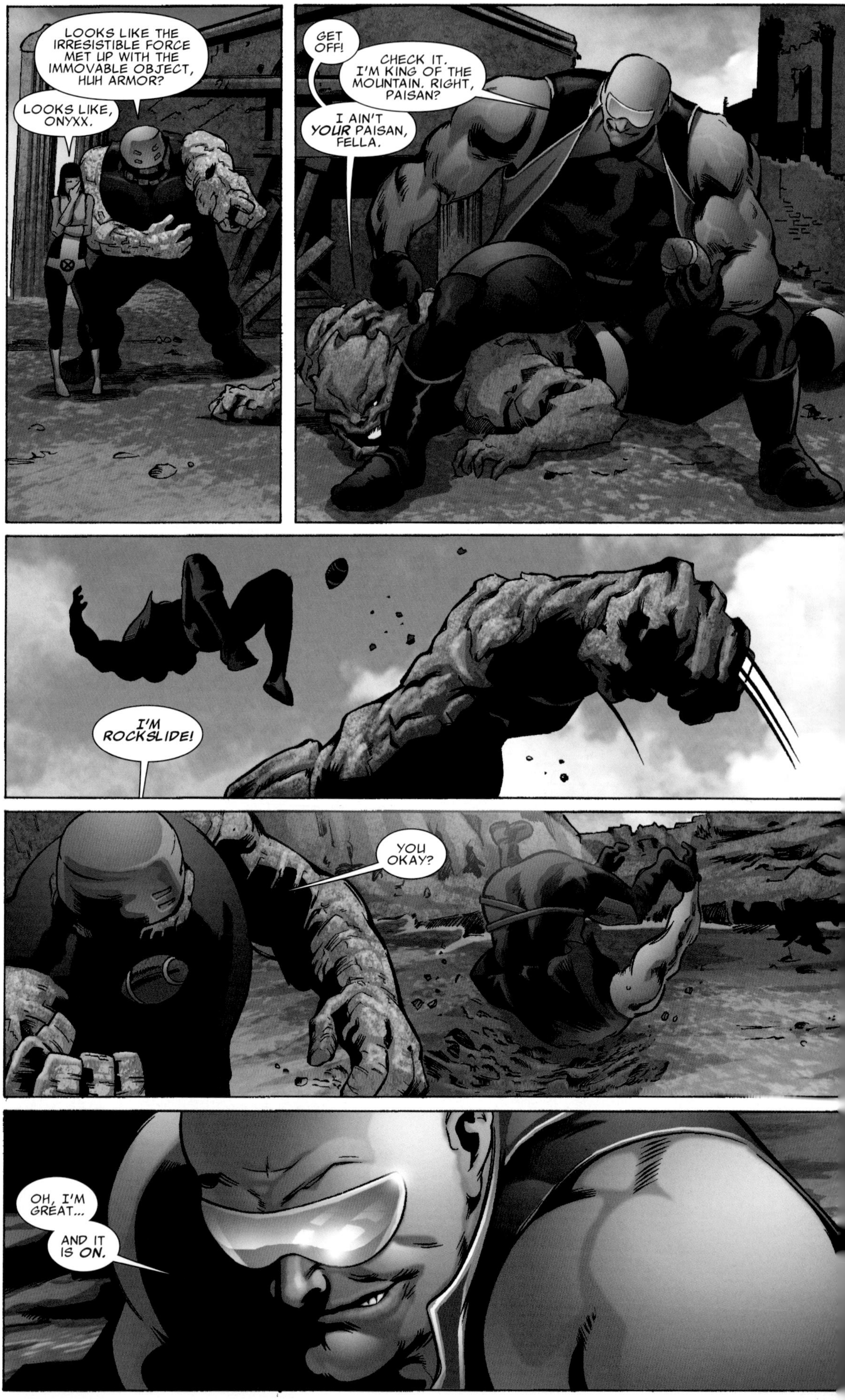
LOOKS LIKE THE IRRESISTIBLE FORCE MET UP WITH THE IMMOVABLE OBJECT, HUH ARMOR?
LOOKS LIKE, ONYXX.
GET OFF!
CHECK IT. I'M KING OF THE MOUNTAIN. RIGHT, PAISAN?
I AIN'T YOUR PAISAN, FELLA.
I'M ROCKSLIDE!
YOU OKAY?
OH, I'M GREAT...
AND IT IS ON.

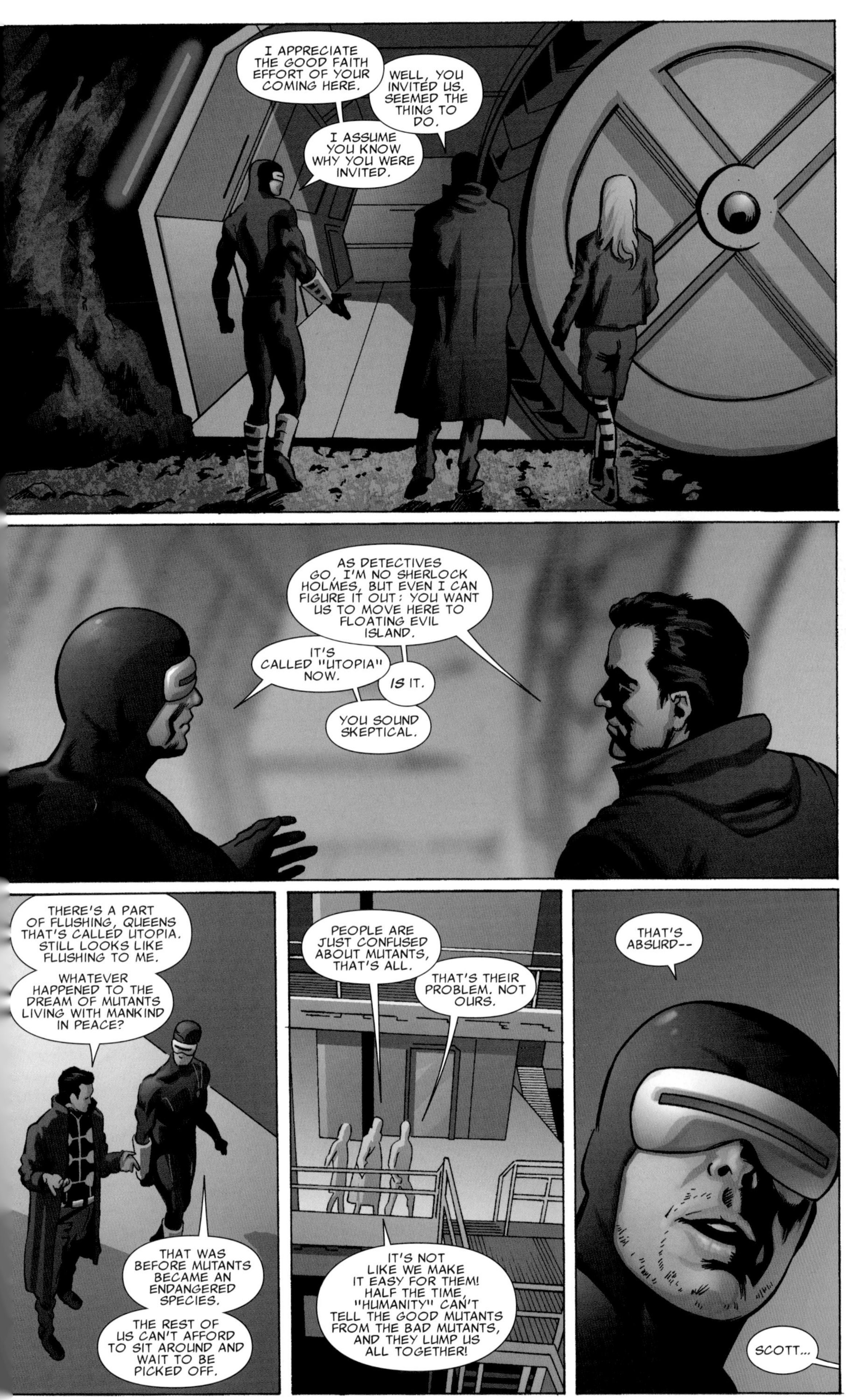
I APPRECIATE THE GOOD FAITH EFFORT OF YOUR COMING HERE.
WELL, YOU INVITED US. SEEMED THE THING TO DO.
I ASSUME YOU KNOW WHY YOU WERE INVITED.
AS DETECTIVES GO, I'M NO SHERLOCK HOLMES, BUT EVEN I CAN FIGURE IT OUT: YOU WANT US TO MOVE HERE TO FLOATING EVIL ISLAND.
IT'S CALLED "UTOPIA" NOW.
IS IT.
YOU SOUND SKEPTICAL.
THERE'S A PART OF FLUSHING, QUEENS THAT'S CALLED UTOPIA. STILL LOOKS LIKE FLUSHING TO ME.
WHATEVER HAPPENED TO THE DREAM OF MUTANTS LIVING WITH MANKIND IN PEACE?
THAT WAS BEFORE MUTANTS BECAME AN ENDANGERED SPECIES.
THE REST OF US CAN'T AFFORD TO SIT AROUND AND WAIT TO BE PICKED OFF.
PEOPLE ARE JUST CONFUSED ABOUT MUTANTS, THAT'S ALL.
THAT'S THEIR PROBLEM. NOT OURS.
IT'S NOT LIKE WE MAKE IT EASY FOR THEM! HALF THE TIME, "HUMANITY" CAN'T TELL THE GOOD MUTANTS FROM THE BAD MUTANTS, AND THEY LUMP US ALL TOGETHER!
THAT'S ABSURD--
SCOTT...

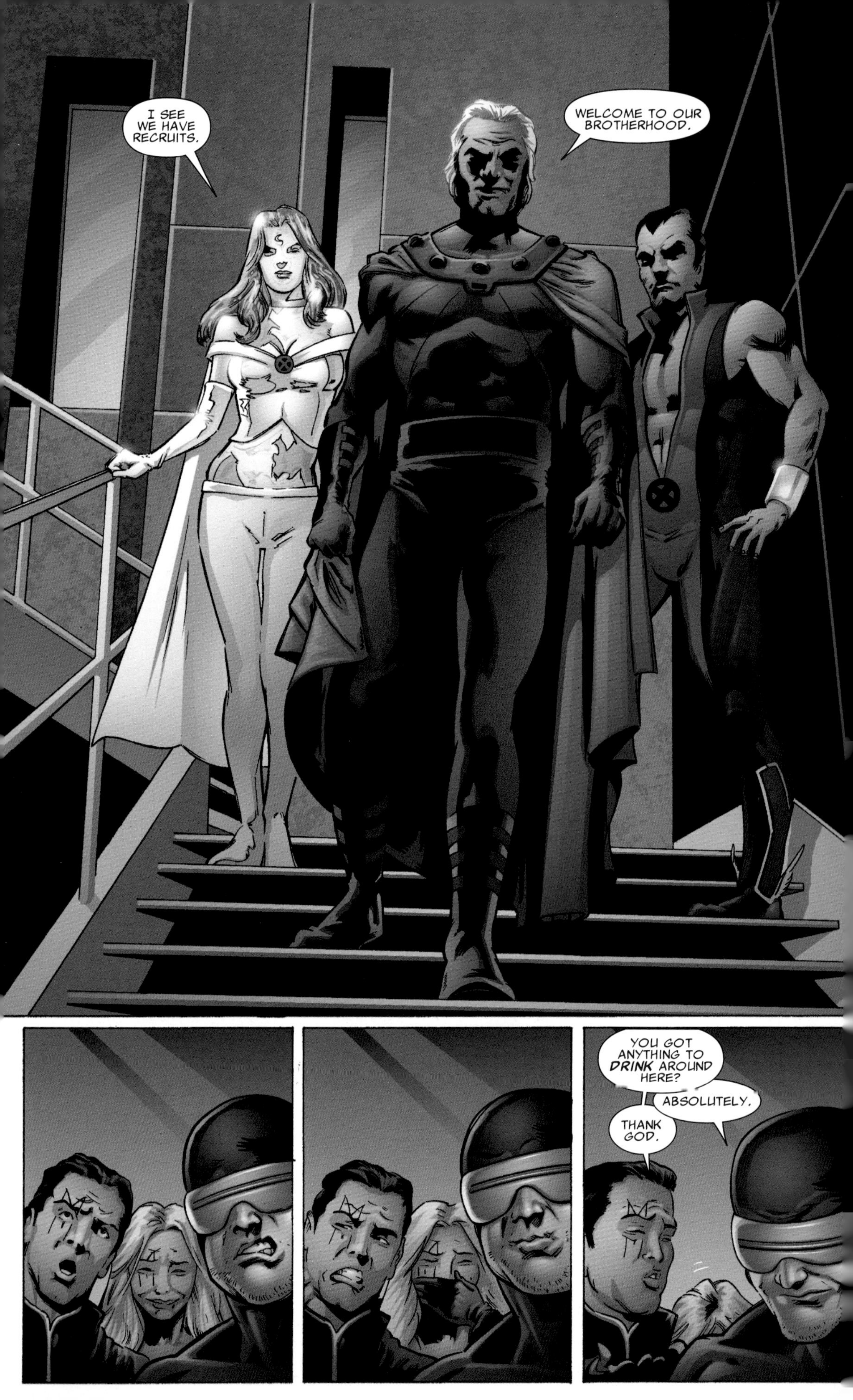
I SEE WE HAVE RECRUITS.
WELCOME TO OUR BROTHERHOOD.
YOU GOT ANYTHING TO DRINK AROUND HERE?
ABSOLUTELY.
THANK GOD.

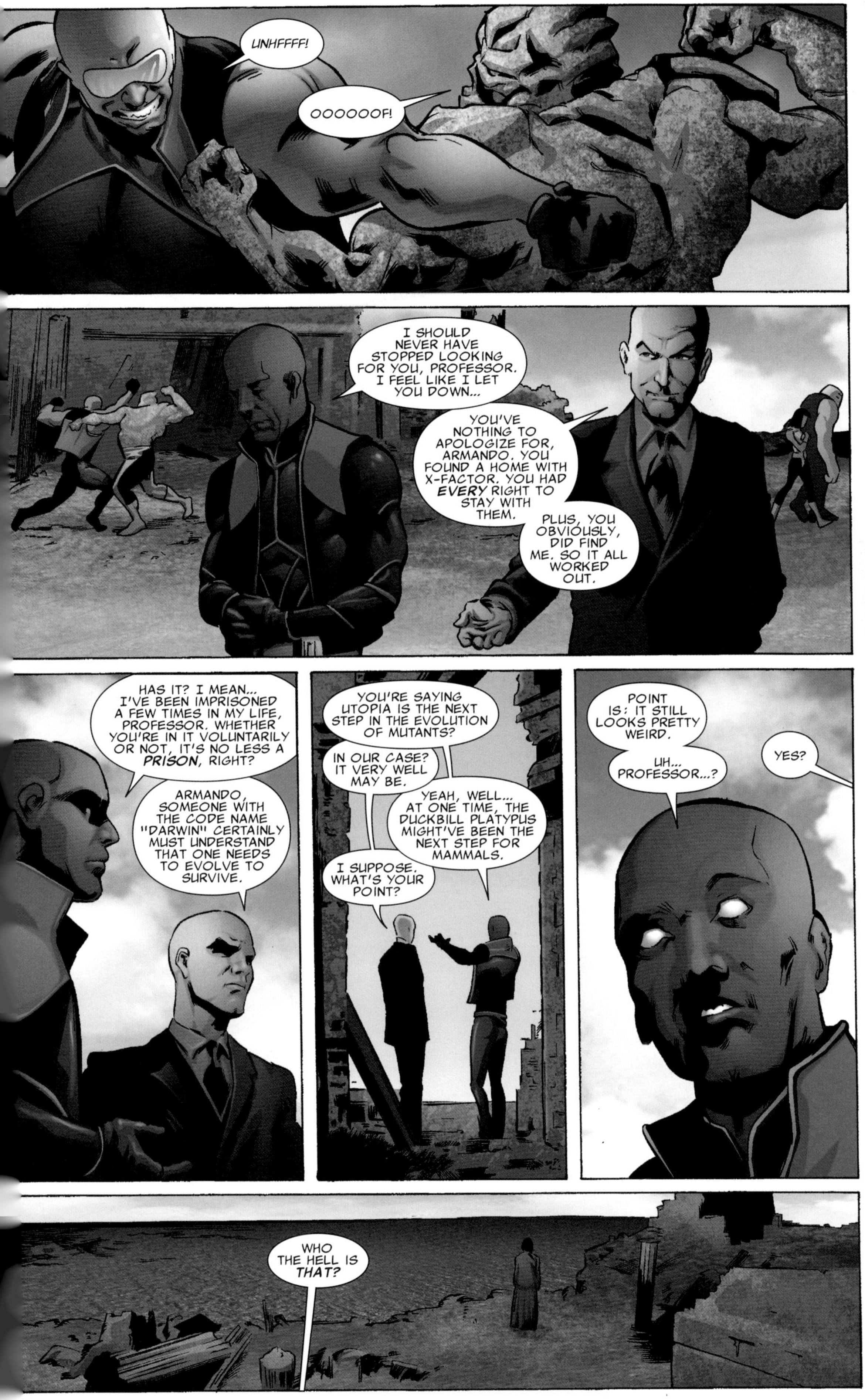
UNHFFFF!
OOOOOOF!
I SHOULD NEVER HAVE STOPPED LOOKING FOR YOU, PROFESSOR. I FEEL LIKE I LET YOU DOWN...
YOU'VE NOTHING TO APOLOGIZE FOR, ARMANDO. YOU FOUND A HOME WITH X-FACTOR. YOU HAD *EVERY* RIGHT TO STAY WITH THEM.
PLUS, YOU OBVIOUSLY, DID FIND ME. SO IT ALL WORKED OUT.
HAS IT? I MEAN... I'VE BEEN IMPRISONED A FEW TIMES IN MY LIFE, PROFESSOR. WHETHER YOU'RE IN IT VOLUNTARILY OR NOT, IT'S NO LESS A *PRISON*, RIGHT?
ARMANDO, SOMEONE WITH THE CODE NAME "DARWIN" CERTAINLY MUST UNDERSTAND THAT ONE NEEDS TO EVOLVE TO SURVIVE.
YOU'RE SAYING UTOPIA IS THE NEXT STEP IN THE EVOLUTION OF MUTANTS?
IN OUR CASE? IT VERY WELL MAY BE.
YEAH, WELL... AT ONE TIME, THE DUCKBILL PLATYPUS MIGHT'VE BEEN THE NEXT STEP FOR MAMMALS.
I SUPPOSE. WHAT'S YOUR POINT?
POINT IS: IT STILL LOOKS PRETTY WEIRD.
UH... PROFESSOR...?
YES?
WHO THE HELL IS *THAT?*

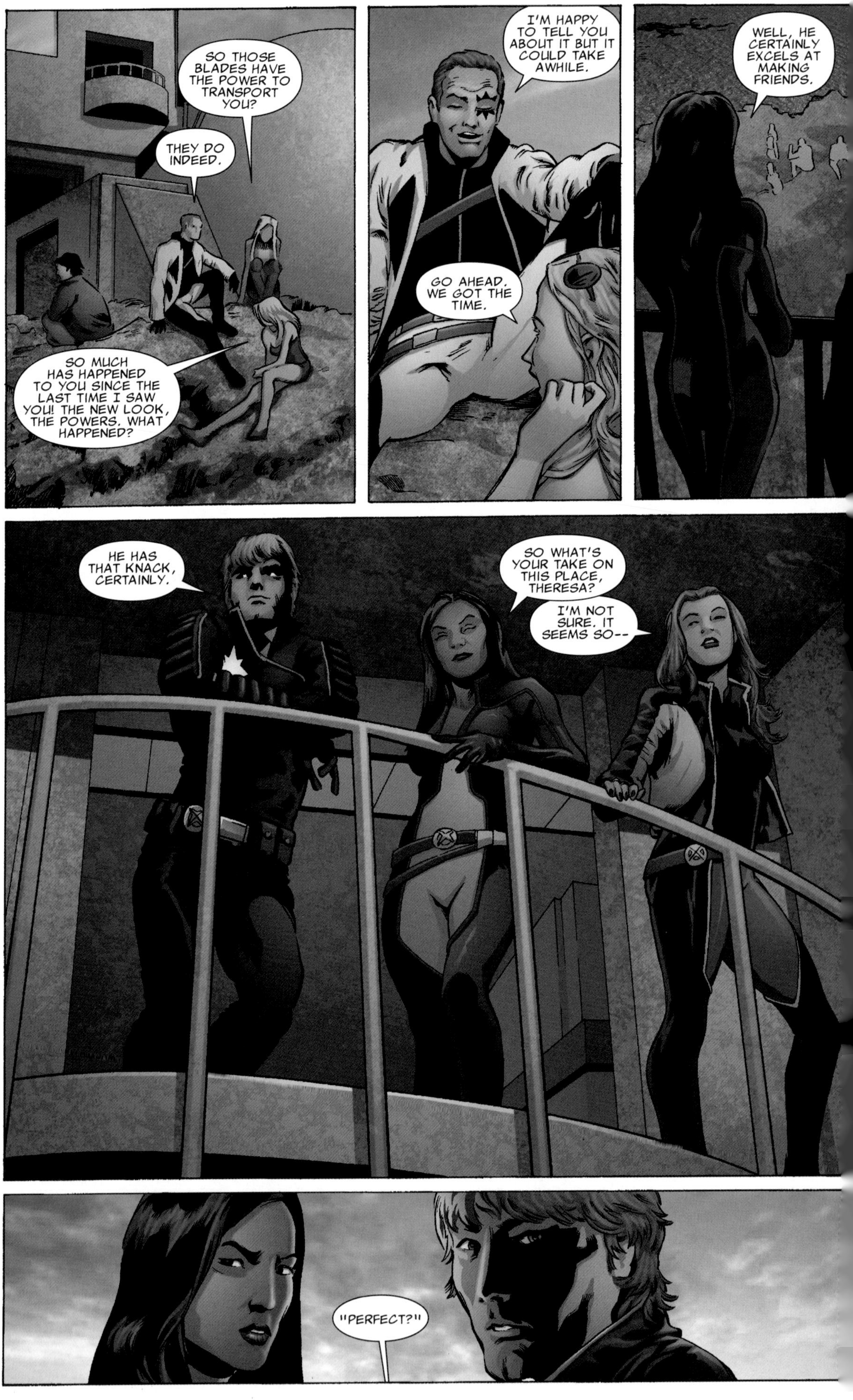
SO THOSE BLADES HAVE THE POWER TO TRANSPORT YOU?
THEY DO INDEED.
SO MUCH HAS HAPPENED TO YOU SINCE THE LAST TIME I SAW YOU! THE NEW LOOK, THE POWERS. WHAT HAPPENED?
I'M HAPPY TO TELL YOU ABOUT IT BUT IT COULD TAKE AWHILE.
GO AHEAD. WE GOT THE TIME.
WELL, HE CERTAINLY EXCELS AT MAKING FRIENDS.
HE HAS THAT KNACK, CERTAINLY.
SO WHAT'S YOUR TAKE ON THIS PLACE, THERESA?
I'M NOT SURE. IT SEEMS SO--
"PERFECT?"

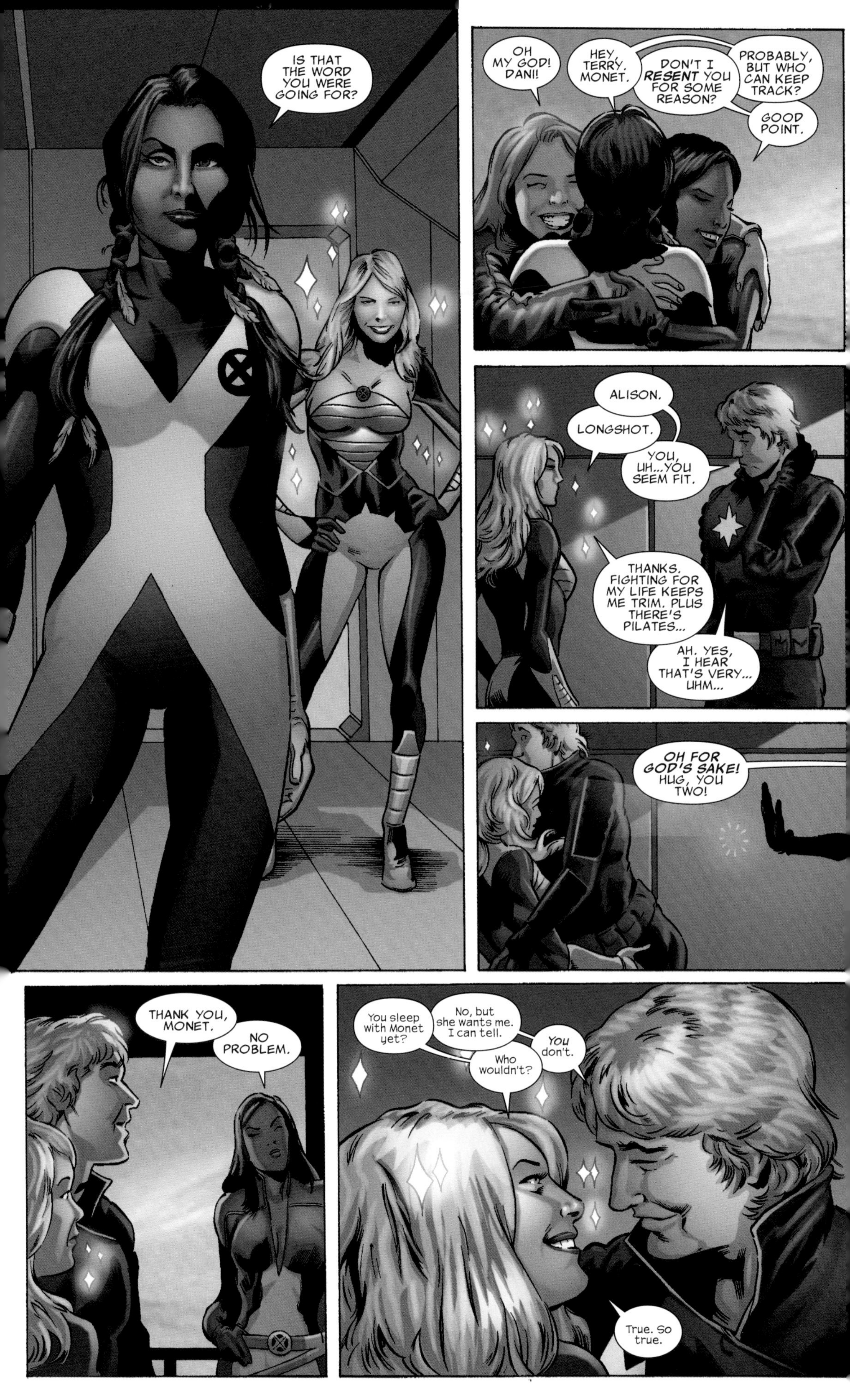
IS THAT THE WORD YOU WERE GOING FOR?
OH MY GOD! DANI!
HEY, TERRY. MONET.
DON'T I **RESENT** YOU FOR SOME REASON?
PROBABLY, BUT WHO CAN KEEP TRACK?
GOOD POINT.
ALISON.
LONGSHOT.
YOU, UH...YOU SEEM FIT.
THANKS. FIGHTING FOR MY LIFE KEEPS ME TRIM. PLUS THERE'S PILATES...
AH. YES, I HEAR THAT'S VERY... UHM...
OH FOR GOD'S SAKE! HUG, YOU TWO!
THANK YOU, MONET.
NO PROBLEM.
You sleep with Monet yet?
No, but she wants me. I can tell.
Who wouldn't?
You don't.
True. So true.

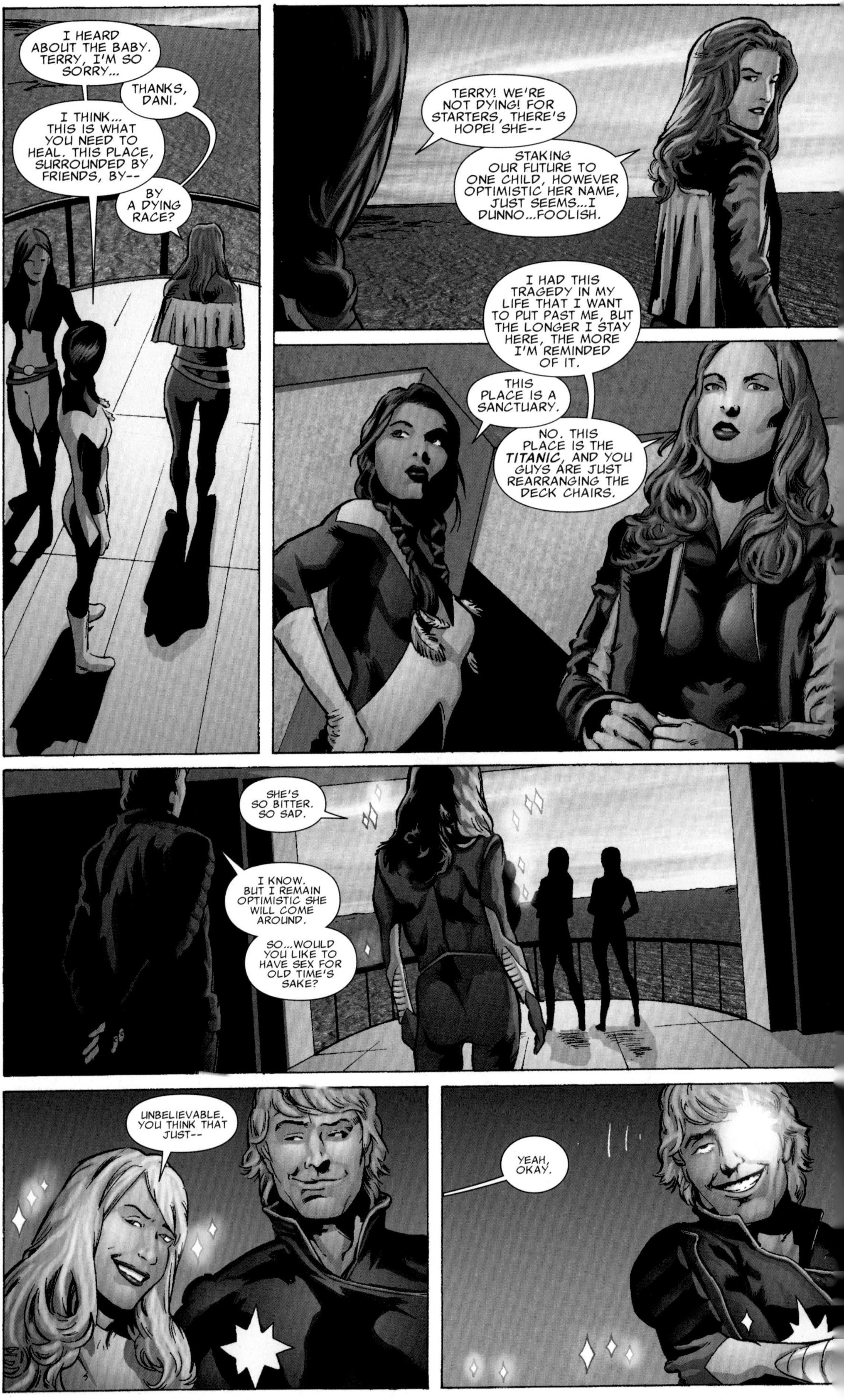
I HEARD ABOUT THE BABY. TERRY, I'M SO SORRY...
THANKS, DANI.
I THINK... THIS IS WHAT YOU NEED TO HEAL. THIS PLACE, SURROUNDED BY FRIENDS, BY--
BY A DYING RACE?
TERRY! WE'RE NOT DYING! FOR STARTERS, THERE'S HOPE! SHE--
STAKING OUR FUTURE TO ONE CHILD, HOWEVER OPTIMISTIC HER NAME, JUST SEEMS...I DUNNO...FOOLISH.
I HAD THIS TRAGEDY IN MY LIFE THAT I WANT TO PUT PAST ME, BUT THE LONGER I STAY HERE, THE MORE I'M REMINDED OF IT.
THIS PLACE IS A SANCTUARY.
NO. THIS PLACE IS THE TITANIC, AND YOU GUYS ARE JUST REARRANGING THE DECK CHAIRS.
SHE'S SO BITTER. SO SAD.
I KNOW. BUT I REMAIN OPTIMISTIC SHE WILL COME AROUND.
SO...WOULD YOU LIKE TO HAVE SEX FOR OLD TIME'S SAKE?
UNBELIEVABLE. YOU THINK THAT JUST--
YEAH, OKAY.

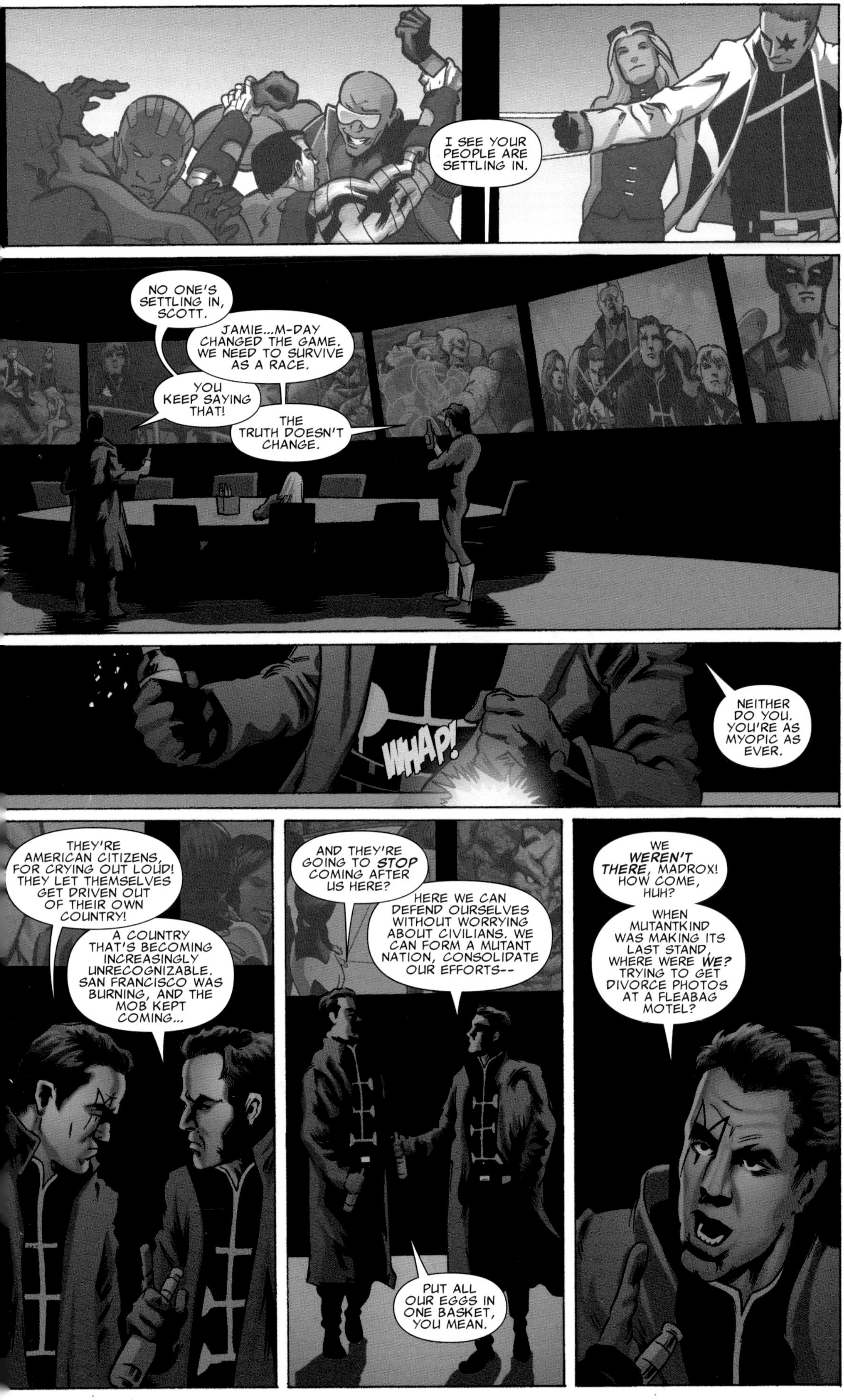
I SEE YOUR PEOPLE ARE SETTLING IN.
NO ONE'S SETTLING IN, SCOTT.
JAMIE...M-DAY CHANGED THE GAME. WE NEED TO SURVIVE AS A RACE.
YOU KEEP SAYING THAT!
THE TRUTH DOESN'T CHANGE.
WHAP!
NEITHER DO YOU. YOU'RE AS MYOPIC AS EVER.
THEY'RE AMERICAN CITIZENS, FOR CRYING OUT LOUD! THEY LET THEMSELVES GET DRIVEN OUT OF THEIR OWN COUNTRY!
A COUNTRY THAT'S BECOMING INCREASINGLY UNRECOGNIZABLE. SAN FRANCISCO WAS BURNING, AND THE MOB KEPT COMING...
AND THEY'RE GOING TO STOP COMING AFTER US HERE?
HERE WE CAN DEFEND OURSELVES WITHOUT WORRYING ABOUT CIVILIANS. WE CAN FORM A MUTANT NATION, CONSOLIDATE OUR EFFORTS--
PUT ALL OUR EGGS IN ONE BASKET, YOU MEAN.
WE WEREN'T THERE, MADROX! HOW COME, HUH?
WHEN MUTANTKIND WAS MAKING ITS LAST STAND, WHERE WERE WE? TRYING TO GET DIVORCE PHOTOS AT A FLEABAG MOTEL?

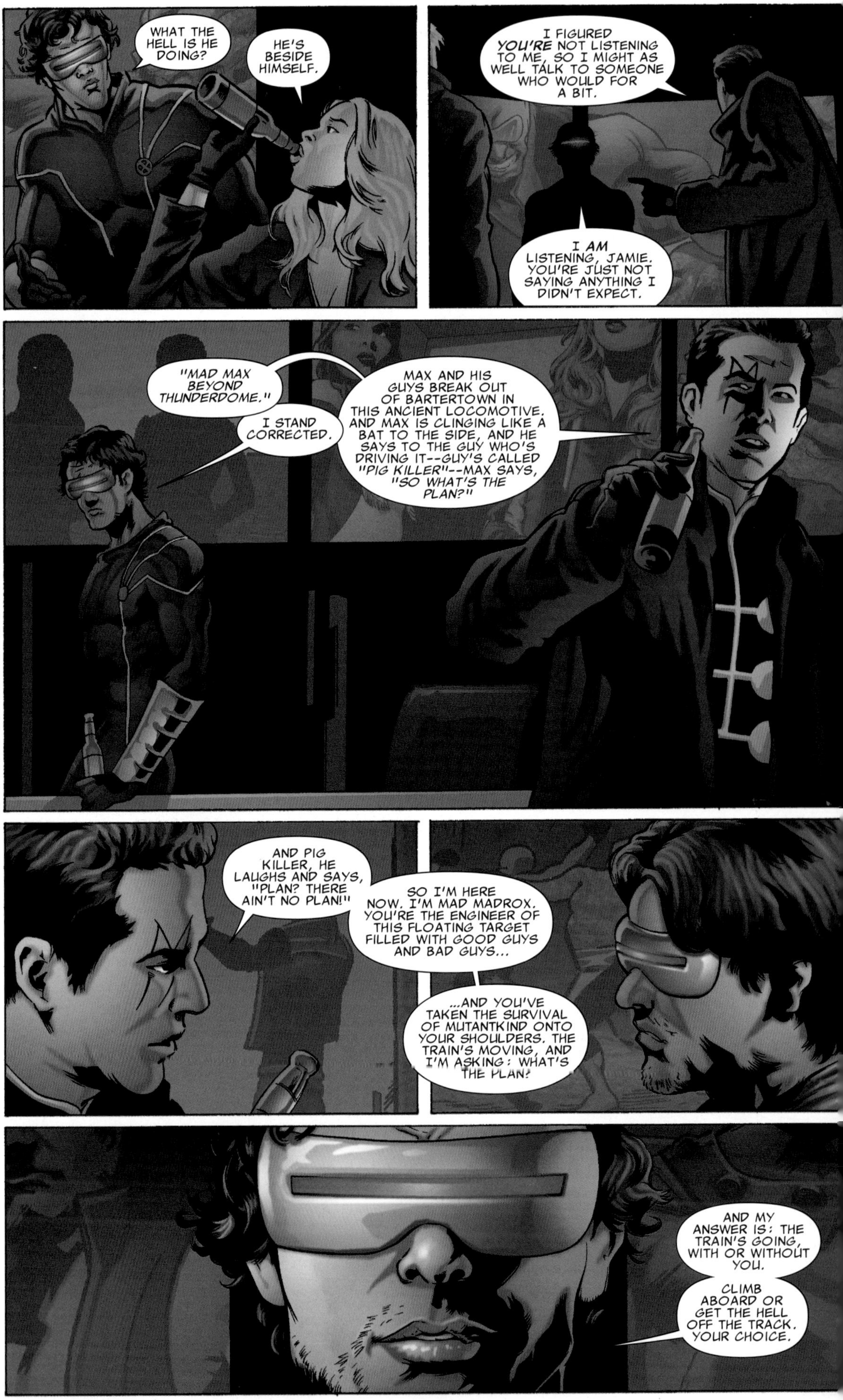
WHAT THE HELL IS HE DOING?
HE'S BESIDE HIMSELF.
I FIGURED YOU'RE NOT LISTENING TO ME, SO I MIGHT AS WELL TALK TO SOMEONE WHO WOULD FOR A BIT.
I AM LISTENING, JAMIE. YOU'RE JUST NOT SAYING ANYTHING I DIDN'T EXPECT.
MAX AND HIS GUYS BREAK OUT OF BARTERTOWN IN THIS ANCIENT LOCOMOTIVE. AND MAX IS CLINGING LIKE A BAT TO THE SIDE, AND HE SAYS TO THE GUY WHO'S DRIVING IT--GUY'S CALLED "PIG KILLER"--MAX SAYS, "SO WHAT'S THE PLAN?"
"MAD MAX BEYOND THUNDERDOME."
I STAND CORRECTED.
AND PIG KILLER, HE LAUGHS AND SAYS, "PLAN? THERE AIN'T NO PLAN!"
SO I'M HERE NOW. I'M MAD MADROX. YOU'RE THE ENGINEER OF THIS FLOATING TARGET FILLED WITH GOOD GUYS AND BAD GUYS...
...AND YOU'VE TAKEN THE SURVIVAL OF MUTANTKIND ONTO YOUR SHOULDERS. THE TRAIN'S MOVING, AND I'M ASKING: WHAT'S THE PLAN?
AND MY ANSWER IS: THE TRAIN'S GOING, WITH OR WITHOUT YOU.
CLIMB ABOARD OR GET THE HELL OFF THE TRACK. YOUR CHOICE.

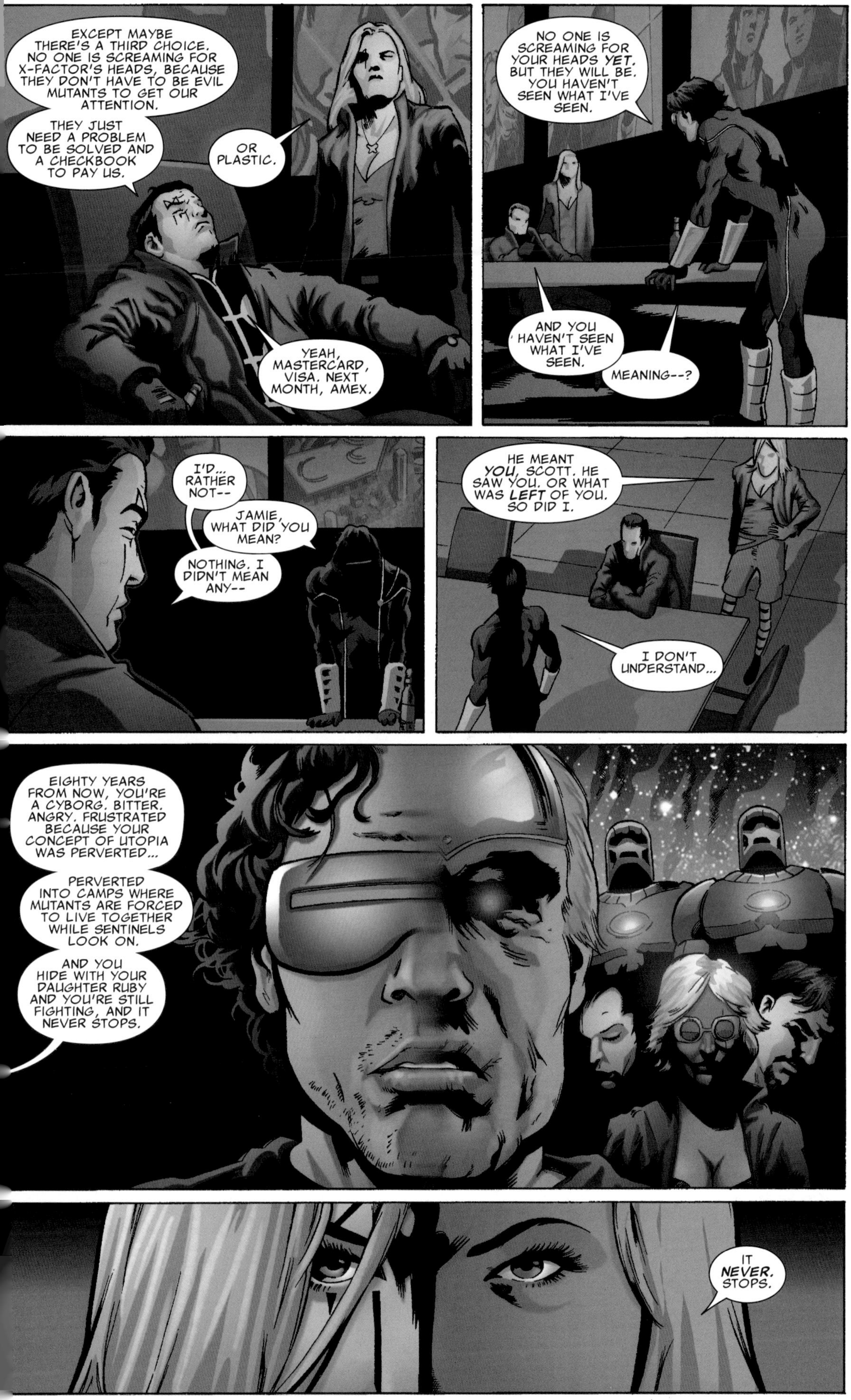
EXCEPT MAYBE THERE'S A THIRD CHOICE. NO ONE IS SCREAMING FOR X-FACTOR'S HEADS, BECAUSE THEY DON'T HAVE TO BE EVIL MUTANTS TO GET OUR ATTENTION.
THEY JUST NEED A PROBLEM TO BE SOLVED AND A CHECKBOOK TO PAY US.
OR PLASTIC.
YEAH, MASTERCARD, VISA. NEXT MONTH, AMEX.
NO ONE IS SCREAMING FOR YOUR HEADS YET. BUT THEY WILL BE. YOU HAVEN'T SEEN WHAT I'VE SEEN.
AND YOU HAVEN'T SEEN WHAT I'VE SEEN.
MEANING--?
I'D... RATHER NOT--
JAMIE, WHAT DID YOU MEAN?
NOTHING. I DIDN'T MEAN ANY--
HE MEANT YOU, SCOTT. HE SAW YOU. OR WHAT WAS LEFT OF YOU. SO DID I.
I DON'T UNDERSTAND...
EIGHTY YEARS FROM NOW, YOU'RE A CYBORG. BITTER. ANGRY. FRUSTRATED BECAUSE YOUR CONCEPT OF UTOPIA WAS PERVERTED...
PERVERTED INTO CAMPS WHERE MUTANTS ARE FORCED TO LIVE TOGETHER WHILE SENTINELS LOOK ON.
AND YOU HIDE WITH YOUR DAUGHTER RUBY AND YOU'RE STILL FIGHTING, AND IT NEVER STOPS.
IT NEVER. STOPS.

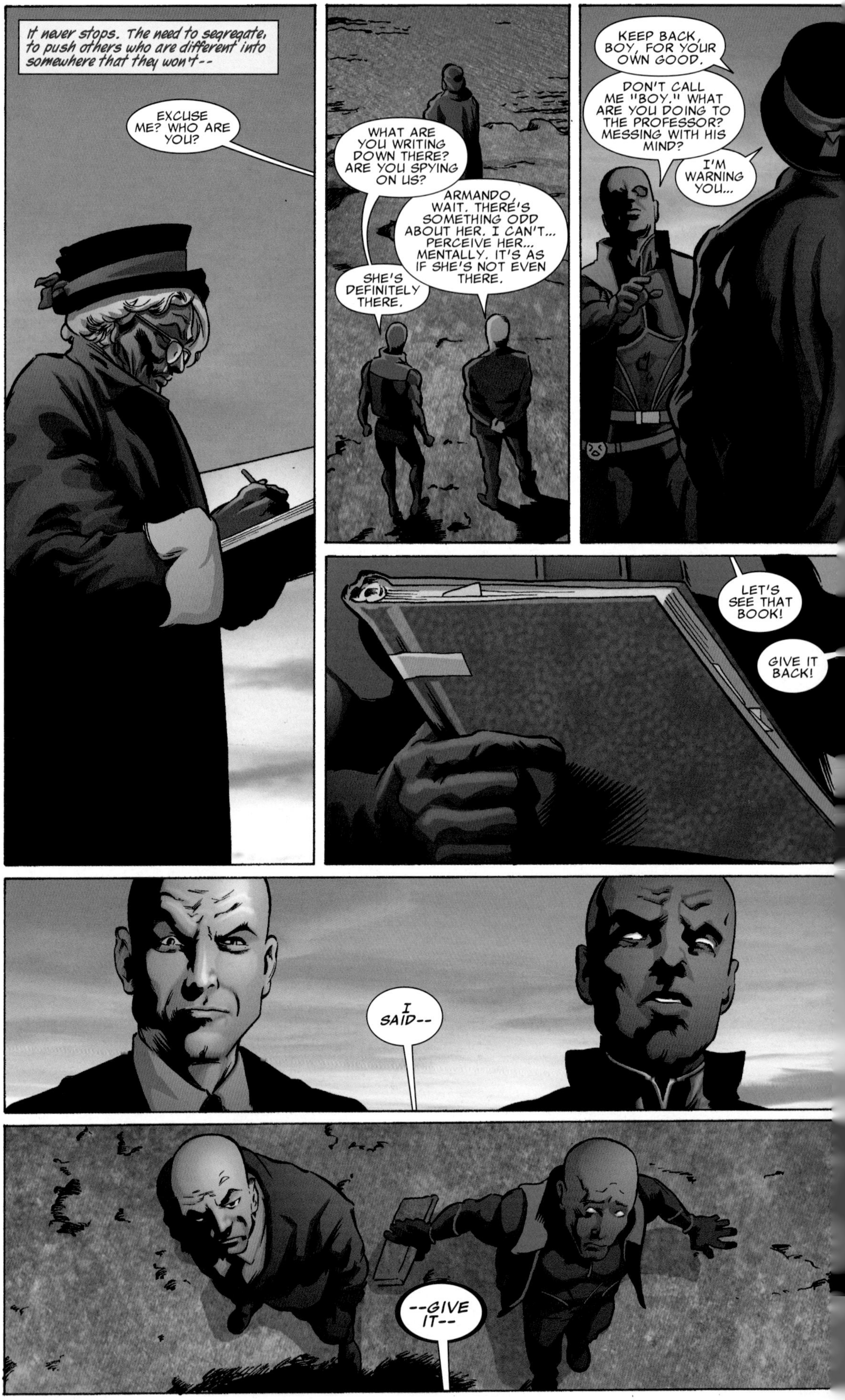
It never stops. The need to segregate, to push others who are different into somewhere that they won't--
EXCUSE ME? WHO ARE YOU?
WHAT ARE YOU WRITING DOWN THERE? ARE YOU SPYING ON US?
ARMANDO, WAIT. THERE'S SOMETHING ODD ABOUT HER. I CAN'T... PERCEIVE HER... MENTALLY. IT'S AS IF SHE'S NOT EVEN THERE.
SHE'S DEFINITELY THERE.
KEEP BACK, BOY, FOR YOUR OWN GOOD.
DON'T CALL ME "BOY." WHAT ARE YOU DOING TO THE PROFESSOR? MESSING WITH HIS MIND?
I'M WARNING YOU...
LET'S SEE THAT BOOK!
GIVE IT BACK!
I SAID--
--GIVE IT--

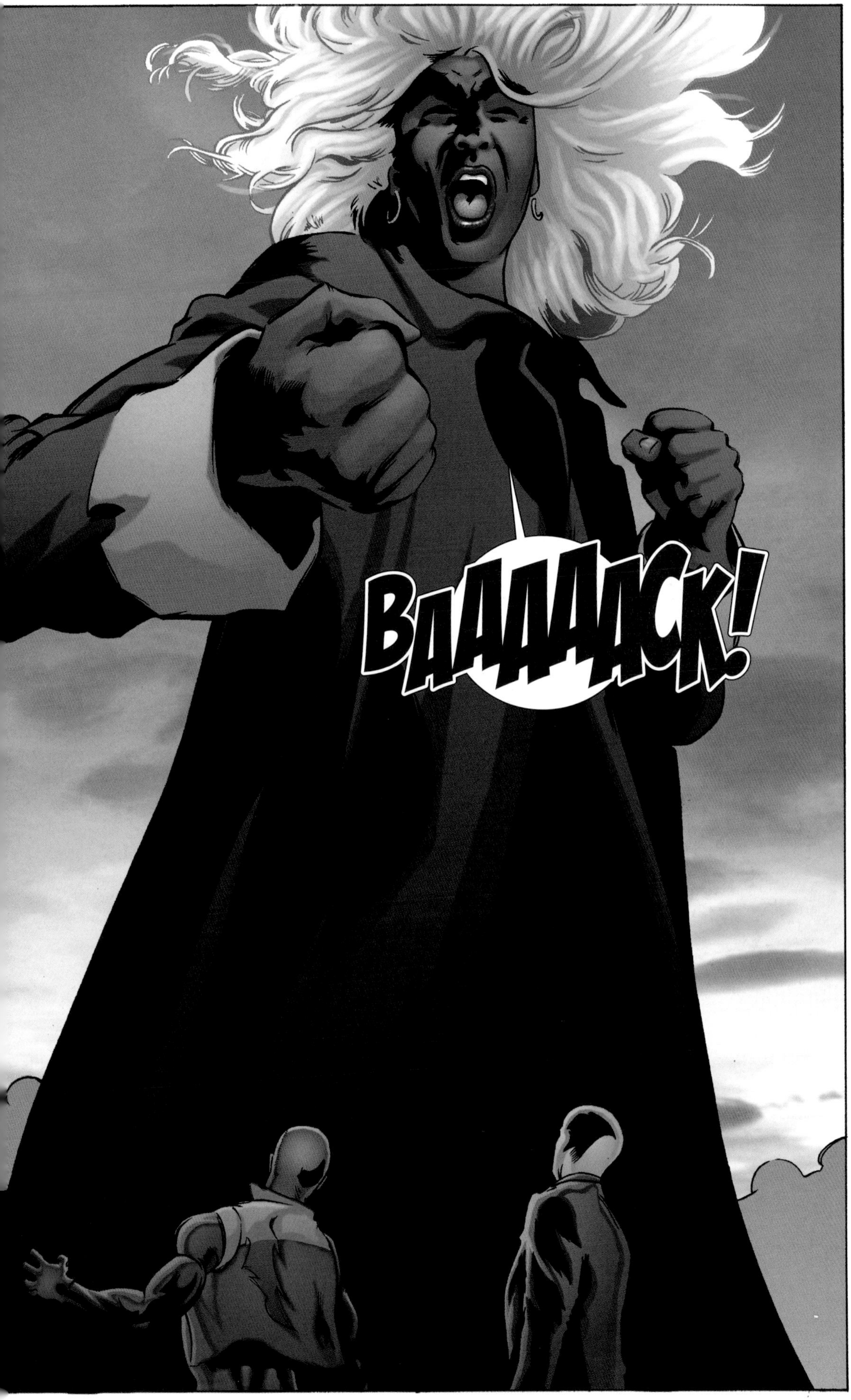
BAAAAACK!

I HAVE A DAUGHTER NAMED RUBY? DOES SHE HAVE MY EYES?

SCOTT, HOW CAN YOU--?

FAITH, JAMIE.

FAITH THAT THIS TIME, THIS PLACE, IS HAPPENING FOR A REASON OTHER THAN TO BE PERVERTED BY A FUTURE THAT MAY OR MAY NOT OCCUR.

♫ YA GOTTA HAVE FAITH-UH, FAITH-UH, FAITH, YA GOTTA HAVE-- ♫

YEAH, OKAY, *YOU'VE* OUTSTAYED YOUR WELCOME.

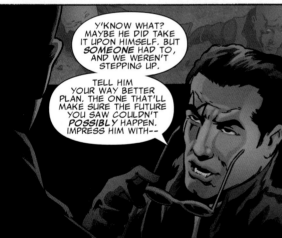

Y'KNOW WHAT? MAYBE HE DID TAKE IT UPON HIMSELF. BUT *SOMEONE* HAD TO, AND WE WEREN'T STEPPING UP.

TELL HIM YOUR WAY BETTER PLAN. THE ONE THAT'LL MAKE SURE THE FUTURE YOU SAW COULDN'T *POSSIBLY* HAPPEN. IMPRESS HIM WITH--

SORRY ABOUT THAT. THEY GET A LITTLE OUTTA CONTROL SOMETIMES.

HE WAS MAKING SENSE TO *ME.*

UHM... GUYS...

BIG PROBLEM.

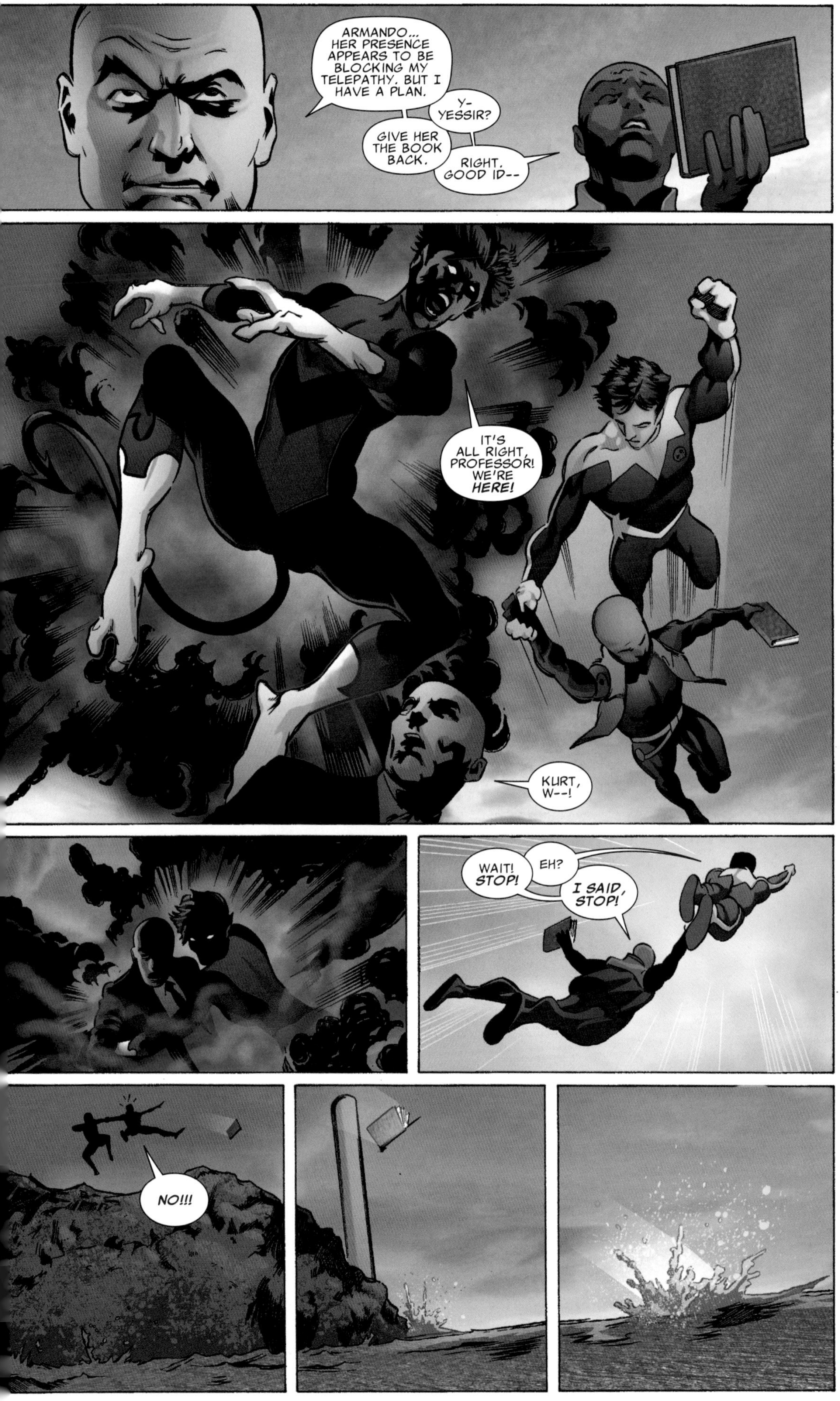
ARMANDO... HER PRESENCE APPEARS TO BE BLOCKING MY TELEPATHY. BUT I HAVE A PLAN.
Y-YESSIR?
GIVE HER THE BOOK BACK.
RIGHT. GOOD ID--
IT'S ALL RIGHT, PROFESSOR! WE'RE HERE!
KURT, W--!
WAIT! STOP!
EH?
I SAID, STOP!
NO!!!

HOW DARE--

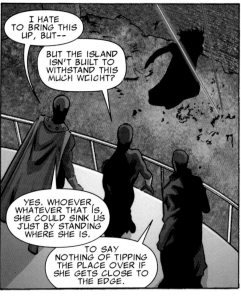

I HATE TO BRING THIS UP, BUT--

BUT THE ISLAND ISN'T BUILT TO WITHSTAND THIS MUCH WEIGHT?

YES. WHOEVER, WHATEVER THAT IS, SHE COULD SINK US JUST BY STANDING WHERE SHE IS.

TO SAY NOTHING OF TIPPING THE PLACE OVER IF SHE GETS CLOSE TO THE EDGE.

LAYLA?

"WHERE THE HELL DID SHE GO?"

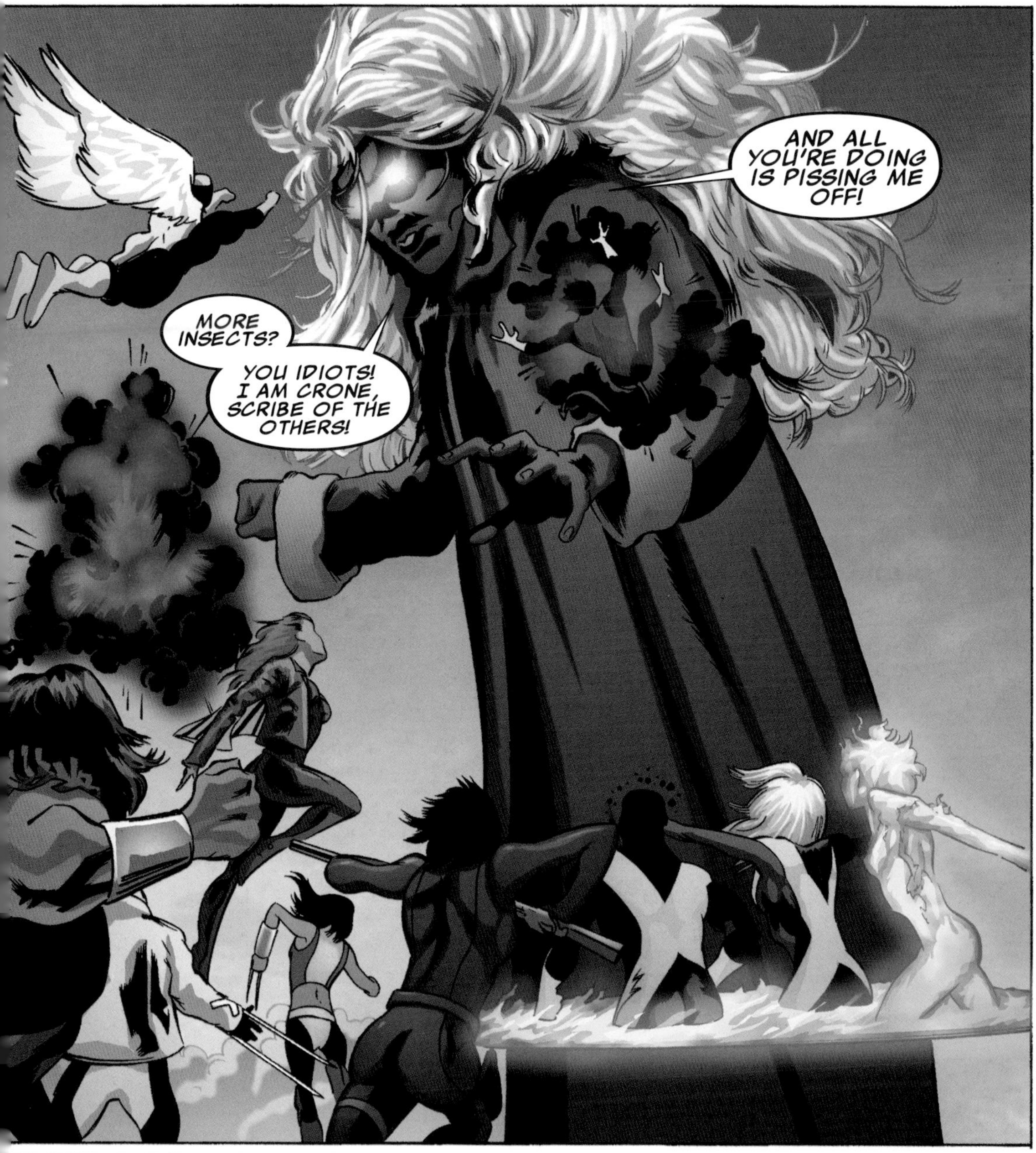
AND ALL YOU'RE DOING IS PISSING ME OFF!
MORE INSECTS?
YOU IDIOTS! I AM CRONE, SCRIBE OF THE OTHERS!

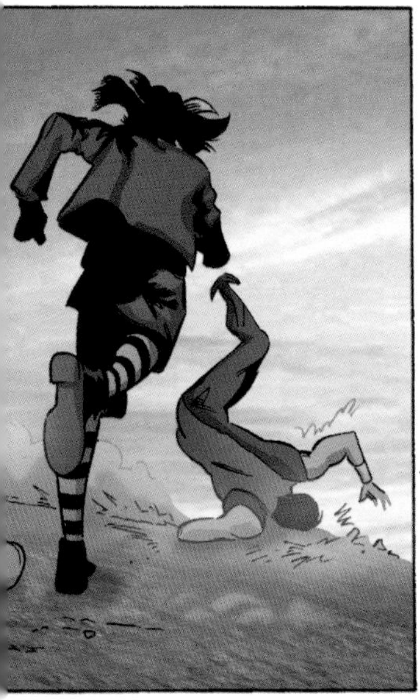

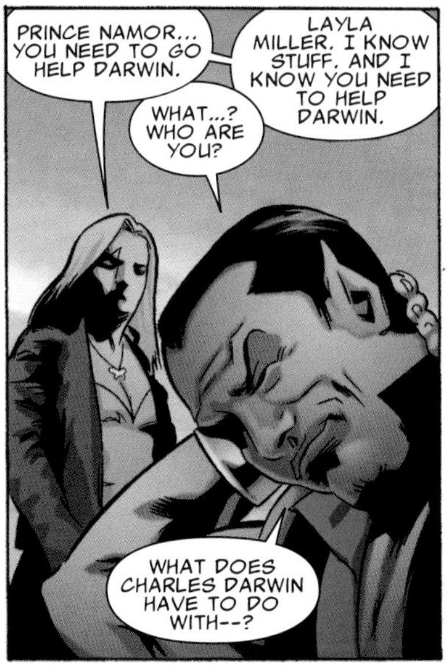
PRINCE NAMOR... YOU NEED TO GO HELP DARWIN.
LAYLA MILLER. I KNOW STUFF. AND I KNOW YOU NEED TO HELP DARWIN.
WHAT...? WHO ARE YOU?
WHAT DOES CHARLES DARWIN HAVE TO DO WITH--?

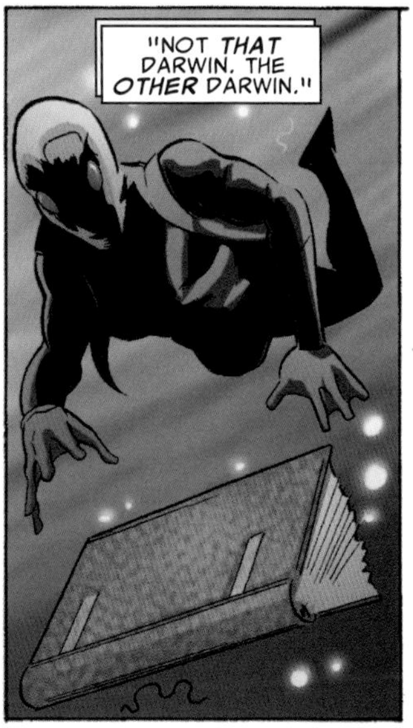
"NOT THAT DARWIN. THE OTHER DARWIN."

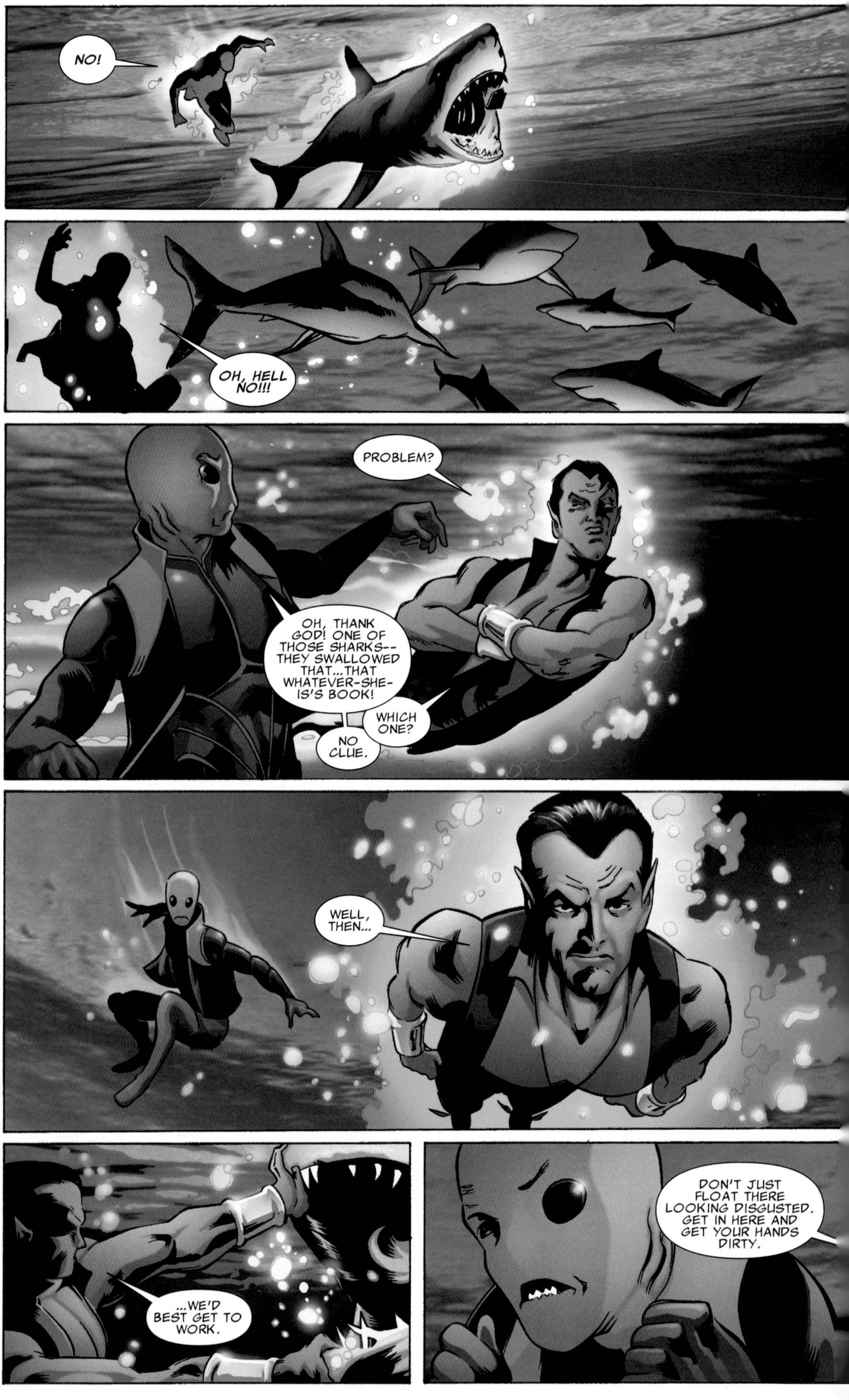
NO!
OH, HELL NO!!!
PROBLEM?
OH, THANK GOD! ONE OF THOSE SHARKS-- THEY SWALLOWED THAT...THAT WHATEVER-SHE-IS'S BOOK!
WHICH ONE?
NO CLUE.
WELL, THEN...
...WE'D BEST GET TO WORK.
DON'T JUST FLOAT THERE LOOKING DISGUSTED. GET IN HERE AND GET YOUR HANDS DIRTY.

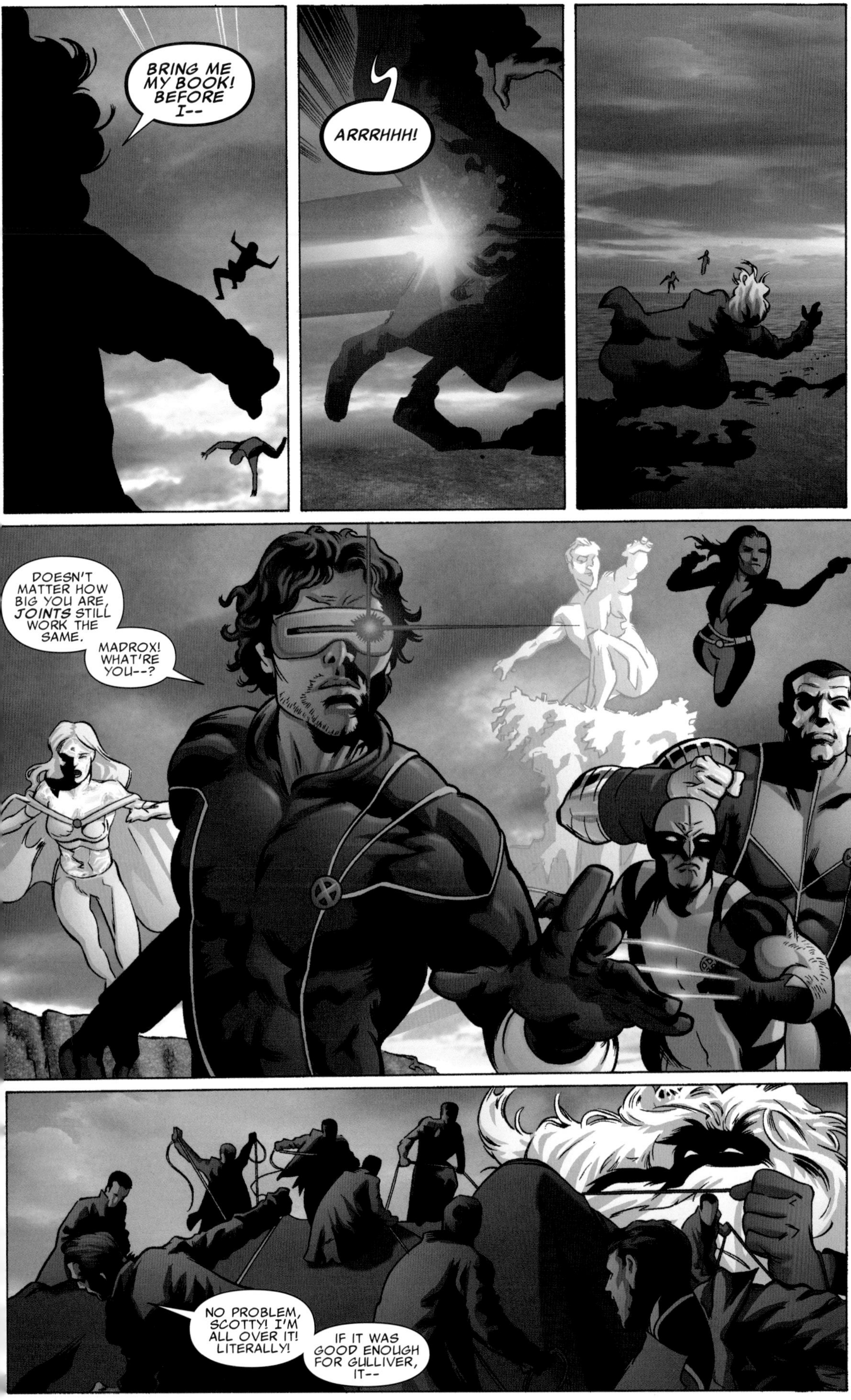
BRING ME MY BOOK! BEFORE I--
ARRRHHH!
DOESN'T MATTER HOW BIG YOU ARE, JOINTS STILL WORK THE SAME.
MADROX! WHAT'RE YOU--?
NO PROBLEM, SCOTTY! I'M ALL OVER IT! LITERALLY!
IF IT WAS GOOD ENOUGH FOR GULLIVER, IT--

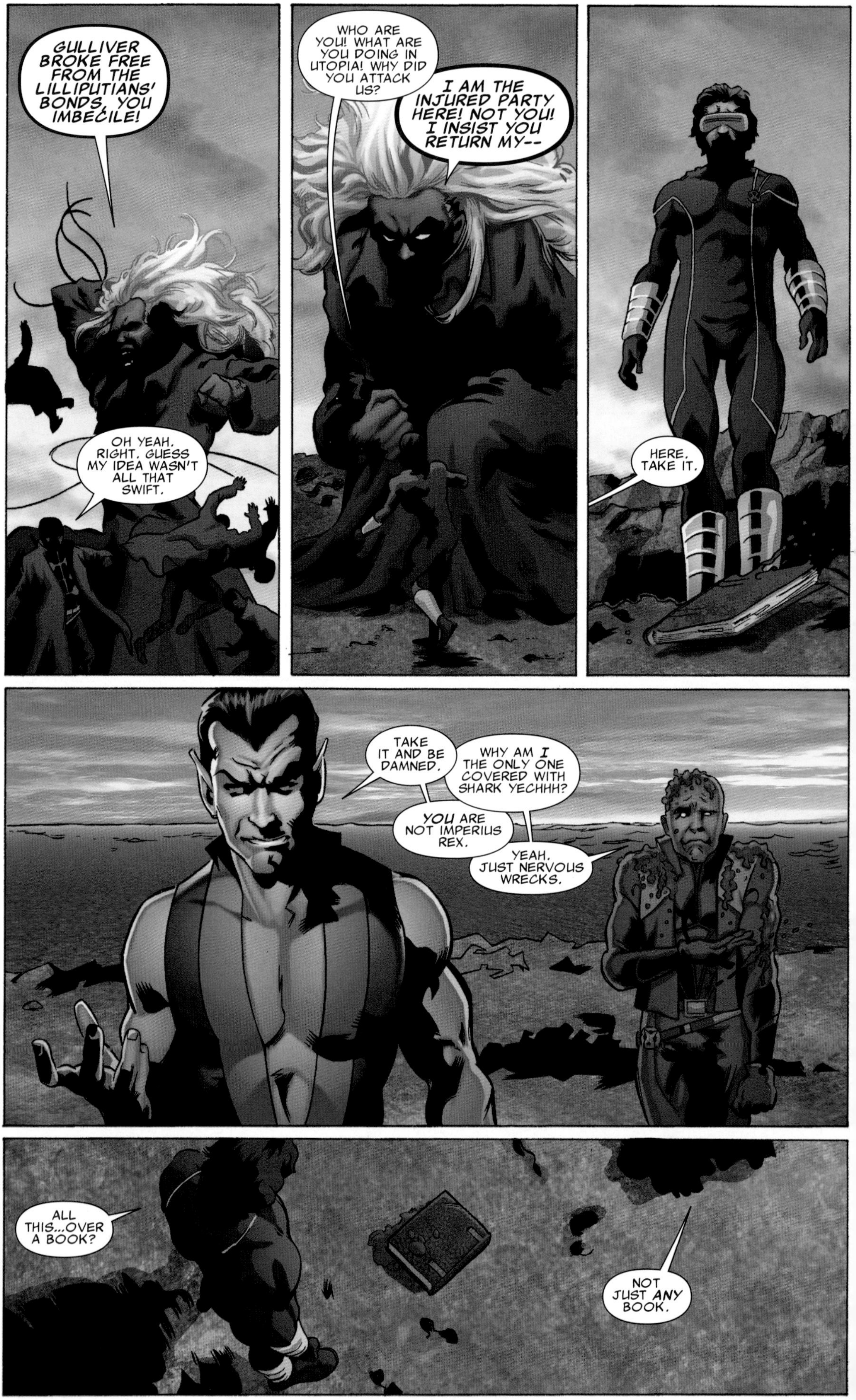
GULLIVER BROKE FREE FROM THE LILLIPUTIANS' BONDS, YOU IMBECILE!
OH YEAH. RIGHT. GUESS MY IDEA WASN'T ALL THAT SWIFT.
WHO ARE YOU! WHAT ARE YOU DOING IN UTOPIA! WHY DID YOU ATTACK US?
I AM THE INJURED PARTY HERE! NOT YOU! I INSIST YOU RETURN MY--
HERE. TAKE IT.
TAKE IT AND BE DAMNED.
YOU ARE NOT IMPERIUS REX.
WHY AM I THE ONLY ONE COVERED WITH SHARK YECHHH?
YEAH. JUST NERVOUS WRECKS.
ALL THIS...OVER A BOOK?
NOT JUST ANY BOOK.

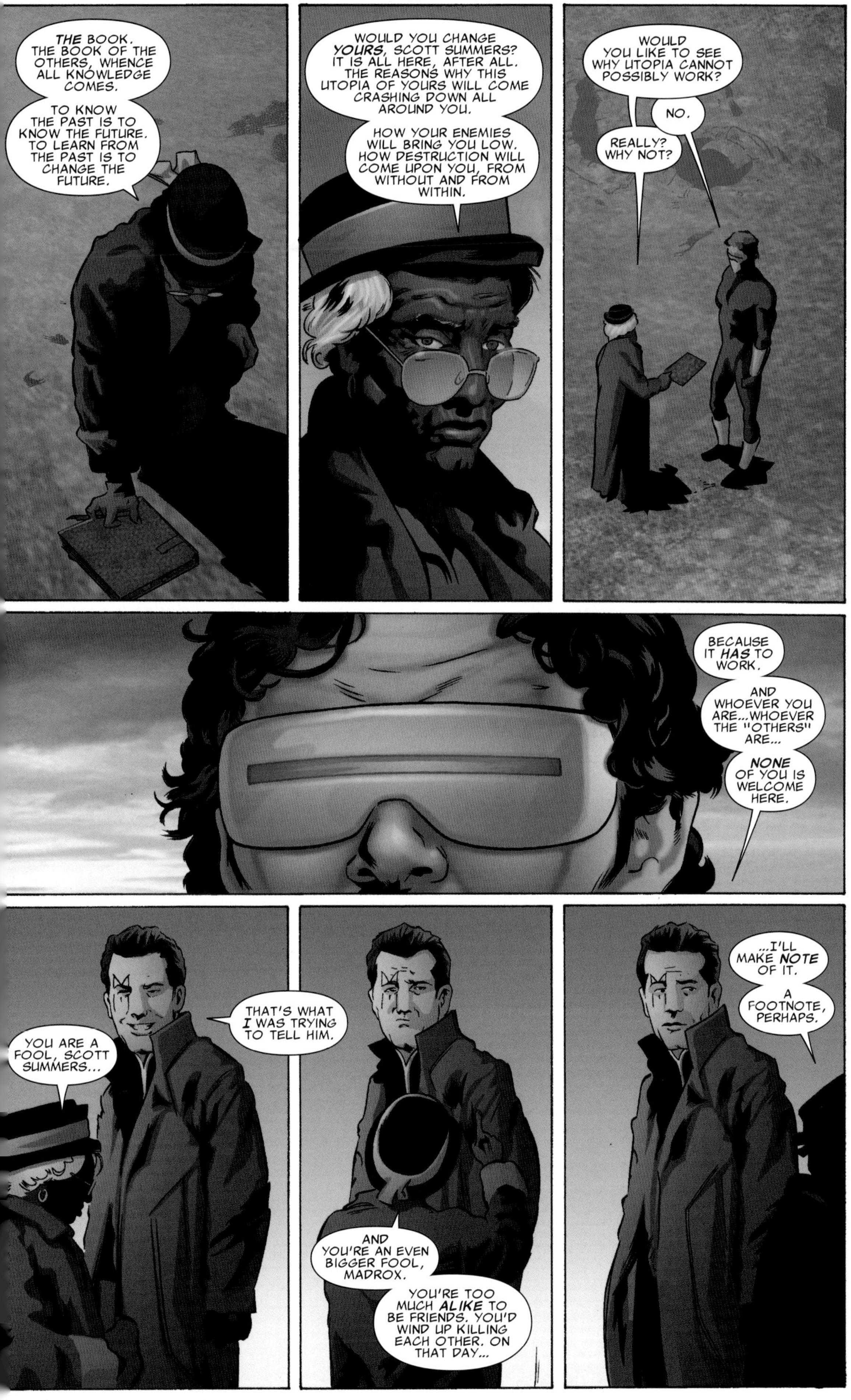
THE BOOK. THE BOOK OF THE OTHERS, WHENCE ALL KNOWLEDGE COMES.
TO KNOW THE PAST IS TO KNOW THE FUTURE. TO LEARN FROM THE PAST IS TO CHANGE THE FUTURE.
WOULD YOU CHANGE YOURS, SCOTT SUMMERS? IT IS ALL HERE, AFTER ALL. THE REASONS WHY THIS UTOPIA OF YOURS WILL COME CRASHING DOWN ALL AROUND YOU.
HOW YOUR ENEMIES WILL BRING YOU LOW. HOW DESTRUCTION WILL COME UPON YOU, FROM WITHOUT AND FROM WITHIN.
WOULD YOU LIKE TO SEE WHY UTOPIA CANNOT POSSIBLY WORK?
NO.
REALLY? WHY NOT?
BECAUSE IT HAS TO WORK.
AND WHOEVER YOU ARE...WHOEVER THE "OTHERS" ARE...
NONE OF YOU IS WELCOME HERE.
YOU ARE A FOOL, SCOTT SUMMERS...
THAT'S WHAT I WAS TRYING TO TELL HIM.
AND YOU'RE AN EVEN BIGGER FOOL, MADROX.
YOU'RE TOO MUCH ALIKE TO BE FRIENDS. YOU'D WIND UP KILLING EACH OTHER. ON THAT DAY...
...I'LL MAKE NOTE OF IT.
A FOOTNOTE, PERHAPS.

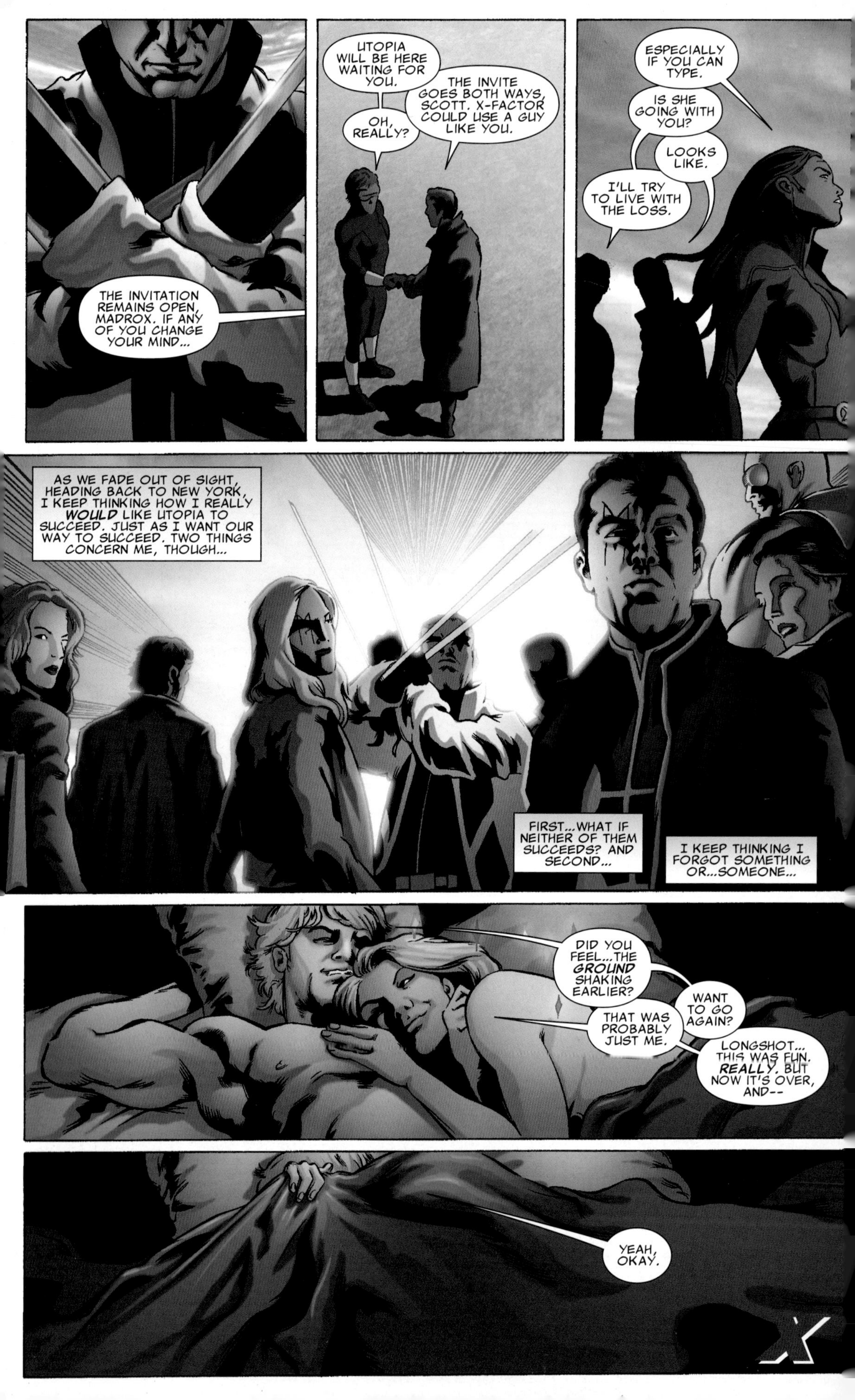
THE INVITATION REMAINS OPEN, MADROX. IF ANY OF YOU CHANGE YOUR MIND...
UTOPIA WILL BE HERE WAITING FOR YOU.
OH, REALLY?
THE INVITE GOES BOTH WAYS, SCOTT. X-FACTOR COULD USE A GUY LIKE YOU.
ESPECIALLY IF YOU CAN TYPE.
IS SHE GOING WITH YOU?
LOOKS LIKE.
I'LL TRY TO LIVE WITH THE LOSS.
AS WE FADE OUT OF SIGHT, HEADING BACK TO NEW YORK, I KEEP THINKING HOW I REALLY WOULD LIKE UTOPIA TO SUCCEED. JUST AS I WANT OUR WAY TO SUCCEED. TWO THINGS CONCERN ME, THOUGH...
FIRST...WHAT IF NEITHER OF THEM SUCCEEDS? AND SECOND...
I KEEP THINKING I FORGOT SOMETHING OR...SOMEONE...
DID YOU FEEL...THE GROUND SHAKING EARLIER?
THAT WAS PROBABLY JUST ME.
WANT TO GO AGAIN?
LONGSHOT... THIS WAS FUN. REALLY. BUT NOW IT'S OVER, AND--
YEAH, OKAY.

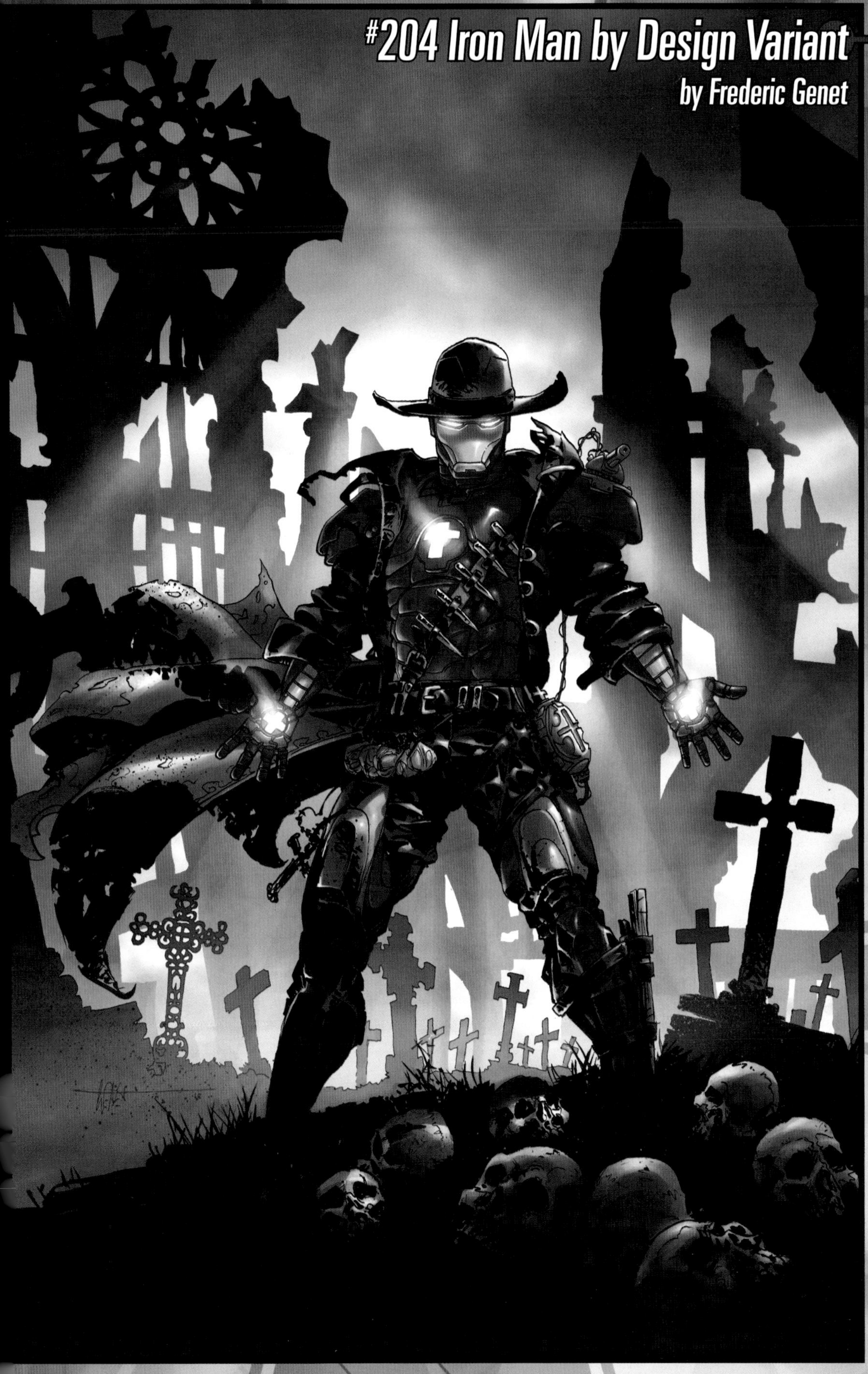

#204 Iron Man by Design Variant
by Frederic Genet

#205 Heroic Age Variant
by Nicolas Mitric & John Rauch

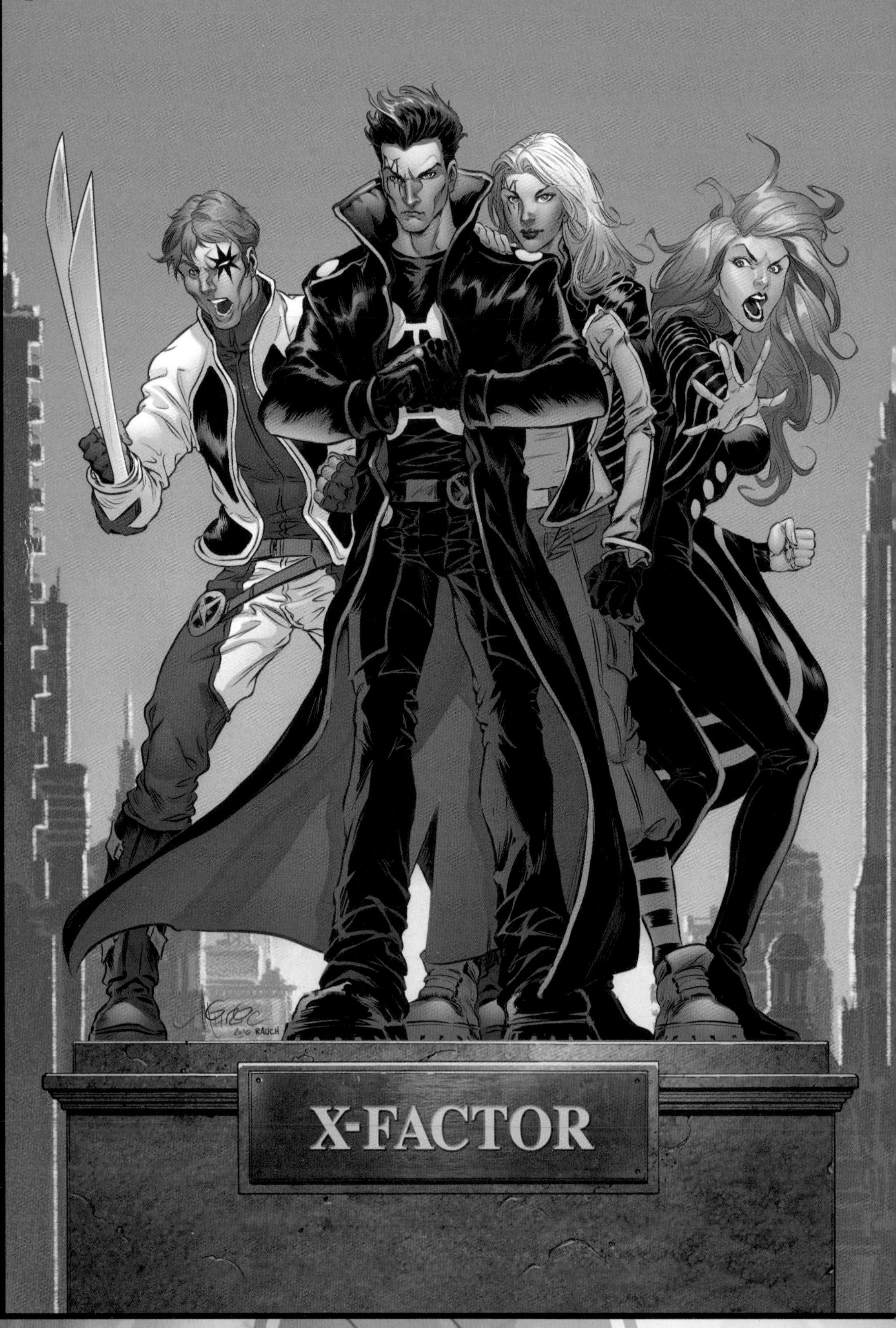
X-FACTOR